SAFE SCHOOL

Nonviolent School Intervention

Kevin Secours

Safe School
Copyright © 2023 by Kevin Secours

All rights reserved. No part of this publication may be reproduced, distributed, or transmitted in any form or by any means, including photocopying, recording, or other electronic or mechanical methods, without the prior written permission of the author, except in the case of brief quotations embodied in critical reviews and certain other non-commercial uses permitted by copyright law.

tellwell

Tellwell Talent
www.tellwell.ca

ISBN
978-0-2288-8742-3 (Paperback)
978-0-2288-9470-4 (eBook)

I dedicate this to my teachers whose examples and lessons shaped me and inspired me to become an educator.

TABLE OF CONTENTS

INTRODUCTION	xi
A HISTORY OF VIOLENCE	1
STANDING IN THE DOORWAY	4
HOW AM I SUPPOSED TO REMEMBER THIS?	5
PUTTING THE "SELF" IN SELF-DEFENSE	8
STORY FROM THE FIELD:	10
IT'S YOUR RESPONSIBILITY	11
DISTANCE IS YOUR GREATEST ALLY	13
EXERCISE #1:	14
EXERCISE #2:	15
PERSONAL SPACE	16
STORY FROM THE FIELD:	18
GOOD FENCES MAKE GOOD NEIGHBORS	19
EXERCISE #3:	22
STORY FROM THE FIELD:	24
AGGRESSION vs. ASSERTIVENESS	26
EXERCISE #4:	28
GESTURE	31
EXERCISE #5:	33
CHURNING	34
STORY FROM THE FIELD:	37
THE POWER AND DANGER OF TOUCH	39
STORY FROM THE FIELD:	41
STAND STRONG	43
EXERCISE #6:	44
EXERCISE #7:	45
STORY FROM THE FIELD:	46
THE QUIET EYE	47
EXERCISE #8:	51
STORY FROM THE FIELD:	53
EXERCISE #9:	55
EXERCISE #10:	57
EXERCISE #11:	57
EXERCISE #12:	58
STORY FROM THE FIELD:	59

TO LOOK OR NOT TO LOOK	61
STORY FROM THE FIELD:	63
HAVE A PLAN	66
THE POWER OF WORDS	70
STORY FROM THE FIELD:	73
DON'T QUALIFY. BE QUALIFIED	75
DON'T THINK OF A LARGE WHITE POLAR BEAR	77
EXERCISE #13:	81
EXERCISE #14:	82
STORY FROM THE FIELD:	83
TONE	84
EXERCISE #15:	85
STORY FROM THE FIELD:	87
PACE	90
EXERCISE #16:	91
THE POWER...OF PAUSES	93
STORY FROM THE FIELD:	94
TAKE A BREATHER	97
EXERCISE #17:	97
STORY FROM THE FIELD:	100
RESISTANCE ISN'T FUTILE	101
EXERCISE #18:	102
JUST BE AWARE	103
MIRRORING	105
EXERCISE #19:	106
AGGRESSION CUES:	107
EXERCISE #20:	109
PREDICTING AGGRESSION IN YOUR SCHOOL	111
EXERCISE #21:	114
THE OODA LOOP	115
STORY FROM THE FIELD:	117
DHARMA	119
EMPATHY	121
EXERCISE #22:	124
RECAP	125
THE AUDIENCE EFFECT:	126
STORY FROM THE FIELD:	129
ACTIVE SHOOTER	131
RUN:	133
EXERCISE #23:	139
HIDE:	139

- FIGHT BACK: 142
- THE TEACHER AS GUARDIAN 143
  - EXERCISE #24: 144
- SAFE GAMES FOR A SAFE SCHOOL 145
- ACUTE STRESS RESPONSE 149
  - IDENTIFY: 150
  - CONNECT: 150
  - OFFER: 151
  - VERIFY: 151
  - ESTABLISH: 151
  - REQUEST: 151
  - EXERCISE #25: 152
- POST-TRAUMATIC STRESS 153
  - STORY FROM THE FIELD: 155
- INTEGRATING SPECIAL NEEDS 156
  - STORY FROM THE FIELD: 158
- INHALING GRATITUDE 160
  - EXERCISE #26: 160
  - EXERCISE #27: 161
  - EXERCISE #28: 162
- BUILDING OUR CONFIDENCE 164
  - STORY FROM THE FIELD: 165
- PHYSICAL INTERVENTION 171
- FLANKING 173
  - EXERCISE #29: 174
- FILMING 176
- SHIELDING 178
  - EXERCISE #30: 179
- RAMPING 180
  - EXERCISE #31: 183
- THE HARNESS 184
  - EXERCISE #32: 186
  - EXERCISE #33: 189
- MEETINGS, COMMUNICATION & PRE-ESCALATION 191
- CREATING CHANGE 193
  - STORY FROM THE FIELD: 196
- TEACH THEM TO CARE 198
- IN 1-ON-1 CONFERENCES 200
- CONCLUSION 203
- BIBLIOGRAPHY 207
- ABOUT THE AUTHOR 215

ACKNOWLEDGMENTS

Special thanks to the many professionals featured throughout this book. Their experiences were hard-won in the face of profound dangers. I am a better man for knowing each of them. I hope their stories and mine will bring you new insight into your craft, new confidence and new hope to achieve a better tomorrow.

INTRODUCTION

*"Throughout your life advance daily, becoming more
skillful than yesterday and more skillful than today.
This is never-ending."*
-Yamamoto Tsunetomo, *Hagakure*-

We are all teachers. Each of us owns a unique life experience. With that comes the power to pass our fragile torch of understanding to the next generation. While gaining knowledge may be our first step towards personal wisdom, it is only through sharing that knowledge that we open our pathway to greater humanity. Some among us go a step further and choose education as our career: the teachers who are directly in the classrooms, the mentors and tutors who complement them, the administrators who lead the way, and the essential support staff that make it all possible. In doing this, every one of you from custodian to lunch monitor joins an honorable tradition of cultivating our youth that stretches back to the dawn of civilization itself. This is a legacy of survival, growth and, fundamentally of hope for a better future.

Throughout most of history, teaching was highly personalized: members of a tribe sharing essential survival skills, parents imparting to their children, and masters sharing secrets with their apprentices. The modern school, with its standardized curriculums, testing, and mandates may seem like a distant relative of these intimate traditions. Today, we rarely get to choose *who* we teach. Individual protégés have largely been replaced by large groups. We rarely have the autonomy to choose *what* we teach. Instead, we are challenged to use our creativity to make a given curriculum come alive. We carry an obligation to provide our students with the basic competency they'll need to operate in an ever-changing world. It's not surprising that many of the teachers I've met feel disconnected from their passion. The burden of deadlines, overcrowding, underfunding and underappreciation can tax even the most extreme enthusiasm and the intrinsic joy of teaching can easily get lost in the clutter. Now add the threat of physical violence and personal risk to this list of stressors and most institutions respond by saying *"don't get involved"* to which most teachers readily comply, saying *"no problem. I don't get paid enough for that anyway. That's not my job"*.

Abandoning hope, while understandable, is not the solution. Hope is our greatest ally. As educators, we are responsible for our students' welfare. The magnitude of that responsibility is immeasurable. As teachers, we control the climate of our classroom. Our mood can dictate the direction of every student's day. We can be an event our students dread or something they look forward to. We can be forgettable, or inspirational, imprinting not only our students' future but in effect, tattooing eternity itself. Teachers are legally and morally expected to care. **It is our duty**. This includes being a positive role model, being equitable and judicious, and protecting students from all reasonable and foreseeable risks of injury or harm.

In this book, we will explore this *duty of care* in the face of an increasingly litigious world. We will confront the challenge of violence in the school and battle the apathy and hopelessness it can often create in those who *must* care. What will be different is that I will not simply approach it based on my training and experience as a classroom teacher. I will also draw on my experience as a world-renowned self-defense and security expert.

One of the most common responses I get when I begin training teachers on non-violent intervention is: *"how is this going to make a difference in a real situation?"* How can the changes I suggest, which seem so simple and perhaps inconsequential, make any difference in an explosively violent encounter? To answer this, I will give you proof, beginning with my firsthand accounts of real-world danger and violence to show how these simple measures have made measurable, tested, reliable differences in some of the most dangerous and violent situations one can encounter. I will also call upon a vast array of personal friends and colleagues, from elite security experts, bodyguards, law enforcement, S.W.A.T., and special forces to have them share their own experiences and stories as well. I will show you that I am not somehow the exception. Rather, these same strategies have worked across a massive spectrum of situations to help keep a wide selection of professionals safe. These strategies have worked for them and they will work for you. I will also call upon other educators, to have them share their wisdom and personal tips for the management of violence and aggression in schools.

If you are reading this book, it's because you are looking for *more* answers, *more* ideas, and *more* strategies. It's because you still believe and hope that change and improvement are possible. Our true battle as classroom teachers far exceeds potentially violent students or parents. **Our true battle is with hopelessness itself.** In education, as with so many other organizations and professions, the prospect of making any real change can be so daunting that it may seem impossible. I share your frustration and your struggle. There are days I get worn down to despair just like everyone else. To this I can only say that consistently, the one thing I have learned in decades of teaching, learning, and studying under masters of their craft, is that change begins with the individual.

Colleen Wilcox said:

"Teaching is the greatest act of optimism"

It's a commitment to battle in the trenches of today for a better tomorrow. Often, that war is waged by an army of one. In this book, I will give you some of the tools, ammunition, and tactics you will need to succeed.

"Never doubt that a small group of thoughtful committed citizens can change the world: indeed, it's the only thing that ever has."
-Margaret Mead-

A HISTORY OF VIOLENCE

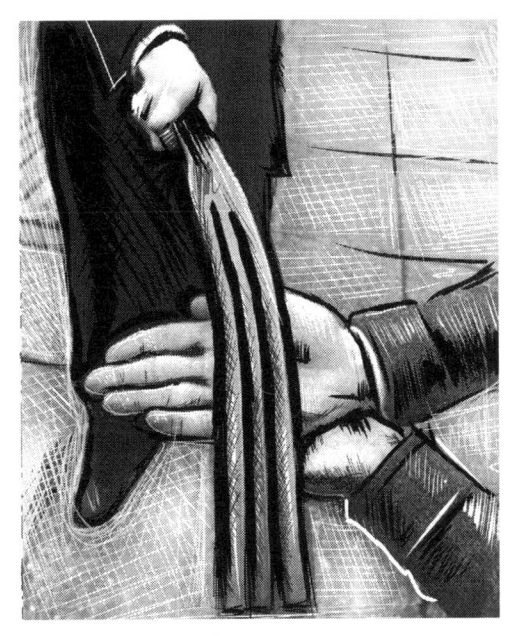

"The Strap"

When I was a boy, I went to a Catholic elementary school. Our principal had a wide leather strap hanging on the wall of his office. *"The Strap"* existed for the sole purpose of whipping our school's worst offenders into tearful repentance. Through this simple act of sadistic flagellation, it was reasoned that you could beat compliance into a child. The obvious danger of modeling violence as a solution to violence was not yet widely considered. [1][2][3] Back then the formula was simple: correction by cowhide.

I often wondered about the Strap. Where was it made? Was there a leather belt factory somewhere that branched out into the flourishing world of corporal punishment? Had someone thought: *"Hey, you know this buckle is just blistering the hell out of my pinky when I beat my kids. I bet if we removed it, we could sell these to schools"*. Could you walk into a teachers' convention back in the day and pick up the latest straps right next to books on the latest educational theories regarding strap techniques?

Every kid in the school knew about the Strap. We knew that the worse your offense was, the higher the number of times you'd get hit. That was just common sense. We also

---

[1] Becker W. C., "Consequences of different models of parental discipline", *Review of child development research* (Vol. 1, pp. 169–208). New York: Sage, 1964.
[2] Patterson G. R., "Coercive family process", Eugene, OR: Castalia, 1982.
[3] Radke-Yarrow M. R., Campbell J. D., & Burton R. V., "Child rearing: An inquiry into research and methods", San Francisco: Jossey Bass, 1968.

knew more secretive things. For example, if you placed a single hair just right on the palm of your hand, the Strap could make you bleed. If it drew blood, lore maintained that you could sue the school board. Of course, no one ever knew of anyone who had successfully bled or sued. It was rumored that the principal would blow on your palm first just to make sure it was free of hair anyway. There seemed to be no way to escape the whip crack of justice.

By high school, the Strap had fallen increasingly out of favor. It wasn't used in my next school although it did remain legal in Canada until 2004 and is still legal in some parts of the United States.[4] I do however have clear memories of my high school teachers actively intervening in discipline. I saw students hit with rulers, pushed into seats, lifted up by their clothing, and roughly walked out of class. On occasion, cafeteria chatter would fall onto the topic of which teachers were the toughest and whether or not certain students could beat them in a fight. Our math teacher was an ex-quarterback. Our chemistry teacher was versed in Kung Fu. Our French teacher was a giant of a man. I clearly remember expecting that certain teachers would not hesitate to hit me if I crossed the line. The promise of violence was a very real component of my school discipline.

By the time I studied Education at McGill University, norms had changed yet again. By that point, it was constantly drilled into my head that under no circumstances should we hit a student. We were taught that if you were touching a student while giving a word of encouragement it was fine, but if you were limiting them or restricting them in any way, physical contact could be misconstrued. A student initiating a hug was acceptable, but a teacher initiating a hug was not. Within my four years of university, these norms changed further still, and by the time I graduated, these guidelines had evolved to the simple caveat: do not touch a student, ever.

In my first year as a teacher, I attended our local teachers' convention. Among the many sessions that I attended was one given by a law firm. Their caveat was even more resoundingly strict. They said, under no circumstances should you touch a student, particularly in response to violence or as part of an intervention. Now I realize that norms and laws vary from state to state and country to country, but in the 25 years since I graduated, the world has become increasingly litigious and more and more areas of the world have seemed to move towards this thinking.

- What then is a conscientious teacher to do should violence erupt?
- Where do our legal rights and responsibilities end?
- How can we be simultaneously mandated to never intervene while being expected to reasonably aid someone in need?
- At what point does our *duty of care* become an obligation to only watch?
- What are our responsibilities to ourselves and our students?

---

[4] Jacob S., Hartshorne T.S., "Ethics and the law for school psychologists (6th Ed.)", *Wiley*, 2007.

- More importantly, what tactics and strategies can be used in the absolute strictest of environments without resorting to violence?
- If we were to choose to intervene, what are our safest and most responsible options?
- Lastly, following exposure to violence, what are the best ways to process this highly traumatic experience?

STANDING IN THE DOORWAY

I was born and raised in Montreal. Language issues between the French majority and an ever-shrinking English minority would fluctuate, flaring up and cooling down like a lump of smouldering coal in front of a rotating fan. When I was 10 years old, I was jumped and badly beaten by four older boys on my way home from school one day just for being English. The incident would influence the rest of my life. A few weeks later I started training in Karate. I was angry. I wanted revenge. While I was in high school, I was smaller than average until my senior year when I sprouted. My training became more obsessive and I transitioned into what would become a lifelong study of Jujitsu. During my college and university years, to pay my way through school, I began working as a doorman at various clubs. Cash was tight and so I took jobs that paid too little, offered insufficient backup, and were plagued by far too much violence. I was embarrassed to tell people what I did back then. I never discussed it with friends or family. How could I be going to one of the best universities in the world by day and volunteering to throttle drunk people by night? So, I would excuse broken noses, black eyes, and bloody knuckles as training injuries and people just thought I was too intense.

In a much larger sense, I wasn't just "*working the door*" in those bars. I was also straddling a threshold between two worlds. In school, we had begun our teaching internship. During our weekly debriefs, the other students would share their fear and distress. They recounted the resistance or discipline issues they were facing in their classes as they struggled to learn how to control their students. Many of my colleagues were sorely under-prepared. Their issues seemed meek compared to the harsh realities of violence I was living on my weekends. At work, I was struggling to refine the traditional martial arts tactics and techniques into something practical. I needed to become the best I could be. Bouncing has a steep learning curve. I lost plenty of fights and felt the consequences of hesitation and poor decisions immediately. I began a deep dive into anything that would help. I read about the psychology of violence, communication, and body language. I studied meditation, visualization, and healing. I explored statistics and academic studies on fear responses. The door gave me the chance to field-test everything. When I worked the door, I was researching like a student. When I was in school, I was analyzing like a bouncer.

Over the decades since then, I have continued that journey of refinement, consolidation, and simplification. I would later work in personal security, working alongside veteran bodyguards and learning some of the secrets of their tradecraft. Later still, I would work alongside elite military and law enforcement. In this book, I will share with you these lessons as directly and simply as I know how in the hopes that these discoveries may help you too.

HOW AM I SUPPOSED TO REMEMBER THIS?

As a lifelong martial artist, I've taught a lot of self-defense classes and seminars. I've also attended a huge number. Some were great. Many were terrible. I can't even begin to recount how terrible with their *key-between-the-finger, magic pressure point, sell-my-gadget, one-hit knockout* nonsense. The worst of them invariably taught overly specific, overly complex techniques, and usually too many of them. One of the most common questions I would hear students ask was:

"How am I supposed to remember all of this in a crisis?"

This is a valid concern. Often it speaks to the nature of what is being taught. A 16-strike death karate combo vs. a simple wrist grab is way too much for someone to internalize in a day of practice. Sometimes, however, even the best information, no matter how well it is conveyed, can trigger the same concern. How are we expected to remember all of this in a crisis?

- **The short answer is you need to train it, a lot.** Start by freeing yourself from any imposed limitations or expectations to memorize a pattern.
- Look at anything you learn as being just a model. **Ultimately your goal is to resist and to be a hard target.**
- **Realize that training begins just by how you think.** The next time a tactical concern arises, like when you see a violent assault reported on the news, you have two choices: either you say to yourself *"Oh my. That's terrible"* as if the capacity and responsibility to try to understand it exceeds your ability, or else you ask yourself *"what could I have done in that same situation?"* Think of something. Think of anything.
- Remember, **you are rewarded for your result, not your method**. It doesn't matter if it looked beautiful or felt great. If it did the job, it worked.
- Often people recount terrible stories of aggression, which they finish with *"and I just didn't know what to do"*. **If you're alive to tell me the story you obviously did something right.** Realize that. If you could have done something differently, you would have. As for the next time, it's definitely a good idea to think about what we could do better. So, you debrief and explore options. **Training begins by switching your brain from just being a problem-detector into being a solution-seeking machine.** Everyone can identify problems. That's all that complaining is. It takes true courage to try to change things and that's where the training begins. Staying

survival-oriented rather than problem-obsessed is far more essential than the ability to specifically remember a given technique.

Another important element to remember is that when we think of intervening in a violent situation, it's quite natural for our mind to leap to thoughts of physically stopping the aggression. Often, our fears and frustration blossom into fantasies of action-movie-like arrests or superhero rescues. Initially, it will feel much more satisfying to think of using *"hard skills"* like hits and locks over the more subtle nuances of *"soft skills"* like avoidance and de-escalation. In reality, soft skills are the biggest part of any conflict. If we perform soft skills correctly as we'll see, we can often avoid the risks of physical violence entirely. I said earlier, we need to train a skill a lot. This is true of both hard and soft skills. The difference is that hard skills require knowledgeable partners, a space to train, equipment, and ideally qualified supervision. **Soft skills by comparison can be practiced all the time** in your everyday life and in your teaching, giving you many far easier opportunities for improvement and mastery.

When considering an intervention, there are multiple factors that will determine your success:

- **Physical attributes** do matter. We know that in physical endeavors, like escaping from a hold, that physiology plays a role. Despite the marketing myths often touted by martial arts, size most definitely DOES matter. It's a simple question of physics. That's why combat sports have weight classes. It does not however *guarantee* success. Expert performers often benefit from genetic factors like height, weight, or the size of particular body segments.[5] This is only part of the equation however.
- There is also **technical expertise**, such as awareness and sensorimotor coordination. While we all have differing abilities, our physical attributes can be hugely improved through continued training.[6] I was very small and light for most of my early training. I had to work a lot harder, but I simply wanted it more. My talent was not innate, it was hard-won by conviction and commitment. Combatively speaking, technical considerations can include the refinement and efficiency of your defensive movements and pre-combative elements like stance, distance management, and movement. We will be delving deeply into all of these in this book.
- **Tactical and Strategic Intelligence** is more important still. In competitive sports, knowing when to use the right movement can be the difference between moderate to elite performance.[7] How we observe events, what we perceive, and how that

---

[5] Wilmore J., Costill D. "Physiology of sports and exercise", *Human Kinetics*, The University of Michigan, 1999

[6] Ericsson K. A., Lehman A.C., "Expert and exceptional performance. Evidence of maximal adaptation to task constraints" *Annual Review of Psychology, 47, 273-305,* 1996.

[7] McPherson S.L. "Expert-novice differences in planning, strategies during collegiate singles tennis competition", *Journal of Sport and Exercise Psychology,* 22, 39-62

information is processed is essential in how our working memory and decision-making operate. Our bodies are filled with natural alarm systems. Often, in life, we are taught to ignore, discredit and stifle these alarms. Throughout this manual, I will outline some essential tactics to integrate into your everyday interactions that will make a huge difference should violence evolve. Until we get to the details, I will simply say that if something feels right or wrong, there are usually many reasons for that feeling. Trust your gut.

- **Emotional Expertise** is our final consideration. How we cope and manage stress can be the difference between activity and impotence. *Familiarity is the greatest antidote to fear.* A veteran who knows what to expect can often overcome physical, technical, and tactical lacking simply because of resolve. As we will see shortly, emotional skills can also be the difference between functionalizing and learning from an experience versus complete burn-out and there is a lot we can do to train our emotional expertise before violence erupts.

At the end of this book, I will address some elements of physical intervention. I realize for many readers these are simply forbidden. For some, they are a matter of curiosity. If you absolutely had no choice and did need to intervene, what could you possibly do? As you will see, there are valid and effective options that balance the responsible use of force with effectiveness while minimizing the risk of litigation. Before this, however, there is a lot we can do to learn to see violence sooner, to diffuse it before it can escalate, and to manage it if it does erupt that does *not* rely on physically contacting the subjects involved. Remember, technical, tactical, cognitive, and emotional components of mastery are much easier to practice. We can refine them all the time, whenever we think about them. As you'll see, we have opportunities to practice them in our day-to-day interactions and master them one step at a time. *"How am I supposed to remember all of this?"* Well, the short answer is by integrating the tactics that work for you in your everyday teaching. Not only will they get you ready for the possibility of violence, they will also make you a more effective teacher. Let's get started.

PUTTING THE "SELF" IN SELF-DEFENSE

I will begin our training program as I begin all of my training programs; by completing a brief value inventory. This simple step is the foundation of how I try to live my life and ultimately the most important thing you will likely read in these pages. Sadly, it's often overlooked.

In our desire to learn any type of *"self-defense"*, we invariably get lost in the *"defense"* part of the training. The defense part seems like the exciting part. Whether we train the physical, the emotional, or the psychological components, it's so easy to get lost in the *"how"* part of doing. In this very natural and well-intended pursuit, we invariably forget the *"why"*; why are we learning this? The secret to self-defense is in the *"self"* part of the equation, not in the *"defense"*.

So, let's strengthen our *"self"*. Take a moment to think of people you love: your spouse, children, friends, pets, and colleagues. This can include celebrities like actors and musicians. There is no particular order. If you think of your cat before you think of your sibling it doesn't necessarily mean that you love one more than the other and if you do that's fine too. Just let a list of faces flash through your mind of all of the people who are important to you. Anyone who brings you even the slightest joy goes on that list. Now think of the things that you enjoy; the activities, the foods, the possessions you own. If you could be anywhere and do anything, where would you be? What would you be doing? What would that list look like? Let all of those images just flash across the movie screen of your mind, again in no particular order.

Of course, I strongly encourage you to try doing a deep dive here if you feel up to it. Make the list as long as you can. Put absolutely anyone or thing on it that you have ever enjoyed. Just making the list can sometimes spark a fire of gratitude inside of you and make you feel more connected to the world. Sometimes it can give you more resolve and direction when you come out the other side of it. Sometimes it can make you realize you don't have that much that you care for right now. That's important to realize too because that means you deserve so much more than what you currently have. All that matters is that you take a quiet moment to realize that this list you've just made, this value inventory, **is unique to you**. There is absolutely no other person on this planet who will have this exact list. Your list represents the uniqueness that is you.

In learning to protect yourself, ultimately, you are learning to protect that uniqueness. I want you to please remember that you, *the individual*, matter more than any system. You are fighting to protect all of those memories, connections, and preferences that are on that list. The ideas and experiences that I share here are just for your consideration. Your own experience and intuition will always be most important. As Laurence Gonzales so aptly notes, the word *"experienced"* often just refers to someone who's gotten away with doing the wrong thing more frequently than you have. When it comes down to surviving, your motive will matter more than your method. *Why* you are fighting will matter more than *how* you are fighting, so rather than trying to memorize everything in this book, please take a moment to remember that you are the "*self*" you are seeking to defend.

STORY FROM THE FIELD:

"Pete Jensen PhD"

Pete Jensen is one of the many incredible professionals that I will introduce you to in this book. I am honored to call him a friend. He is an expert in leadership and performance. He has served as the Human Performance Program Chief at the U.S. Special Operations Command, where he led more than 200 strength coaches, physical therapists, performance dieticians, and sports psychologists, responsible for the physical and mental readiness and resilience of more than 30,000 special forces operatives, including Navy SEALs, Green Berets, Army Rangers, and Air Force Pararescue operators. I'll be sharing Pete's wisdom throughout this book, so I'll save the rest of his bio for later on because his resume is longer than Bilbo Baggins' burglar contract. It will also allow you more time to digest just how impressive he is.

Pete's advice to teachers is the same as he would give to new cadets:

"A teacher needs to realize how much experience they have. Even a new teacher already has a lot of life experience that is unique to them. This is something you can leverage. Even if you're completely new, you still have the ability to believe in yourself. You have the ability to have confidence. It's a choice. Just by having made that decision, you can rely on that belief and leverage it to do anything. Everything that you've done in your life matters. Even failure is a growth opportunity. This is how you build expertise."

IT'S YOUR RESPONSIBILITY

In my introduction, I noted that if you're reading this book, it's because you care. It's because you are trying. It's because somewhere, you have hope. Very often, even the hopeful among us get overwhelmed and dragged back into the bucket of apathy by the claws of despair. Have you ever had that feeling that the entire system is against you? Did it ever seem like you were fighting with futile fists against a drowning tide of bureaucracy? Subjected to those feelings long enough, even the strongest among us may surrender. I will once again quote Laurence Gonzales. Gonzales is the author of an incredible book entitled *"Deep Survival: Who Lives, Who Dies and Why"*. If you have an interest in the spirit of thriving and surviving, I cannot recommend this book highly enough. In it, Gonzales notes:

> *"Survival is the celebration of choosing life over death. We know we're going to die. We all die. But survival is saying: perhaps not today. In that sense, survivors don't defeat death, they come to terms with it."*

Wow. You might be thinking: *"This is pretty heavy for a book on non-violent intervention. I wanted to learn how to keep myself safe in my classroom and this guy is talking about death. What exactly did I sign on to here?"* I remember having that exact feeling in my early years of training in Jujitsu. My sensei introduced me to the concept of *jōjū shinimi*, which means to *"live as if you were already a corpse"*. I said to him:

> *"But I want to learn how to fight back. Isn't that the opposite of accepting death? The whole reason I'm training is that I don't want to die!"*

I was smiling and laughing, hiding my stupidity behind my humor. I thought I was so smart at the time. He just smiled and took a breath and said: *"It's ok you still have a lot of time to figure it out"*. He was so patient with my youthful ignorance. It took me a long time to figure out that accepting death was the complete opposite of giving up. It was actually about accepting the largest of responsibilities. Gonzales has summed it up so beautifully. In his study of survivors of the harshest of circumstances, he showed that a common baseline attribute was that they took responsibility for their survival. At some point, they said: *"No one is coming to rescue me. This is happening. I need to do something."* This is the deepest acceptance of death there is. There is no cavalry coming over the hill. There is no Hollywood ending. There is no excuse, only one choice. It's up to you.

So, if our first step is remembering what we are training to protect, our second step is to recognize that the responsibility to protect what we value lies with us. Yes, I would always love and welcome backup, support, and assistance, but I can't wait for it. Each of us is an *army of one*. We are our own backup. In staying connected to what we value through gratitude and in choosing to embrace our responsibility to protect that value, we are beginning to vanquish our first opponent: the helplessness that robs us of our resolve. We are more than enough of a spark to start the fire.

DISTANCE IS YOUR GREATEST ALLY

Now it's time to get physical with some tactical tricks that will help keep you safe.

When I was in college and university I was living on my own and needed to make as much money as possible on a part-time schedule. I decided to leave the meagre pay of retail and warehouse jobs to work as a bouncer. I had no experience other than my martial arts training and secretly wanted to test my skills. I didn't see it at the time, but the mental scars of having been beaten up when I was 10 years old were still driving me. I wanted to feel in control of my fears and I wanted to test myself at a higher level. My eyes were about to be forcibly opened.

The promise of easy money made me take the first job I was offered. It was a bar in the most lenient sense of the word: a grey box, lined with fake wood paneling and lit with neon beer lights, financed by a desperate congregation of regular burnouts, professional criminals, and young hoodlums. You could catch a disease by leaning on the walls. It housed a thriving drug trade and floors so permanently sticky that even the most tightly laced shoe occasionally was pulled off your heel. I saw that floor mopped on occasion but never saw soap or water changed in the bucket. This was back in the day when you could smoke indoors but somehow the smell of mold and stale beer trumped the cigarette stench. You could never fully wash the odor out of your clothing. A quick sniff of it in your laundry pile could instantly conjure that feeling of despair you felt while you were inside its walls. On busier nights I worked with a veteran named Pierre. Almost every dent or scratch in that bar had a story related to Pierre and a different unruly patron. Pierre taught me everything about working the door. He saved my life every weekend.

The very first lesson was about driving in the snow.

"When the weather is bad, you slow down", he would say. "If the weather gets worse, you go slower and you keep more distance between you and the next car. Distance gives you more time to react."

Everything with Pierre was that simple. Slow down. Keep distance. Any time he saw me letting someone getting too close he would remind me of this fact. Distance was a huge part of working the door. You were always in tight spaces. Patrons would walk up to you for admission and slip by you in tight corridors. You got into arguments in hallways too narrow for two people. You got into fistfights with people injecting heroin in bathroom stalls. You had to stumble and bulldoze through people and chairs and clutter. You were always trying to keep your distance in a space that offered none. I had to learn to shift away and evade people calmly, angle my body and use my hands to create fences to keep people away and I had to do it all naturally, eventually without actively thinking about it. In just a few more pages, I will show you how to add these super powerful tools to your communication and protection toolbox.

As classroom teachers, we don't have the same constant pressures that I had when I was working the door, but we are still faced with a similar challenge. We are always in tight confines with our students, sharing a common room and roaming mutual hallways. Aggression in schools happens far less often than it did in my bar days, but when aggression begins to simmer or when violence erupts, the space we're in can seem to disappear instantly. The very first step is to understand this simple fact: **Reaction time is based on distance.** The more distance we have, the more time we have to react.

What is even more important but somewhat less understood is that there is an absolute *minimum* amount of space that we need to react. It's not just that the closer an aggressor gets, the less time we get to react. **At some point, an aggressor gets so close that it will be impossible for us to react.** Generally speaking, that distance is about the length of our arm. Yes, there are things we can do even at the closest distance to improve our response time. We can simplify our options to one choice. For example: *"If he advances or tries to touch me, I will hit"*. We can visualize this response and become like a pre-loaded switch. Even then, once we let a hostile person get inside our personal space, we lose the precious time that we need to effectively process information. That means if we let someone get right in our face and then that person decides to sucker punch us, neurologically speaking we will not have the time to process what is happening. We won't have the time to cognitively select a response. Instead, we will be limited to triggering primal defensive reflexes or pre-loaded assumptions and both of these responses run a very high risk of being inappropriate for the situation and may end up either being insufficient or excessive force.

Naturally, we can't be ready for everything. Everyone can be surprised. Violence rarely happens all of a sudden. There are usually pre-indicators, signs, and cues that it's coming. Usually, our intuition tells us something is not quite right. It's precisely when we feel that, that we need to pay attention to our distance. When our gut tells us it's about to *"snow"*, we need to remember what Pierre taught me those many years ago: slow things down by creating and maintaining distance.

EXERCISE #1:

Pay attention to the distance you keep in your everyday interactions. Notice how it varies with your loved ones, your colleagues, and your students. You will likely notice that it even varies from student to student. Next, practice increasing it slightly. Often, people who are accustomed to being closer to you, will notice changes in distance and make efforts to recompress it. If you have made the increase too obvious, they may even be conscious of it and comment or even appear offended. Practice trying to make the smallest casual fluctuations and increases to your distance but do it as naturally and subtly as you can so that no one notices. This simple first step in increased awareness will begin to empower you with the effects of distance. It will also teach you to "*feel*" the changes.

EXERCISE #2:

Visualize an aggressive situation. Whenever I visualize something, I like to imagine that I'm sitting comfortably, watching the story play out on a giant movie screen. You control what you're watching. If you wish, you can pause, fast forward, or even rewind the film. If something starts to make you feel uncomfortable, you can skip it. If you want to feel the emotion more deeply you can zoom in and if you want to feel it less you can zoom out. The more you practice visualizing, the stronger those mental muscles will get and the more real and visceral a simple visualization can become.

On your mind's visualization screen, imagine you are watching a movie of yourself. You are standing near two other people who are becoming aggressive with one another. They are starting to argue and the risk of violence is possible. How far away are you from the aggression? Imagine what the experience makes you feel from that distance. Now imagine you were to take a step or two toward the aggressors. How would the feeling intensify? What about if you were to step back a bit? Does it feel any different? You might feel something physical like becoming more or less nervous. It might be cognitive like knowing it is safer for you. No matter what you feel, even if you don't notice a difference, just imagine the scenario as vividly as you can and note what you did or did not feel. There are no right or wrong answers here. The first step is simply to get in touch a bit with our triggers and comfort zones.

PERSONAL SPACE

"A key to your personal safety is to identify and protect the bubble of personal space around you."

The study of how we use and communicate with space is known as *proxemics*. Edward T. Hall conducted significant research on the psychological effects of space. He divided space into 4 essential zones:

- **Intimate Space:** This is 18 inches (45 cm) or less. This is reserved for the most intimate friends and family.
- **Personal Space:** This can range from 18 inches (45 cm) to 4 feet (1.2 meters). This is the usual distance we keep for casual conversations with familiar people.
- **Social Space:** This ranges from 4 feet (1.2 meters) – 12 feet (3.6 meters). This is a more formal distance that we maintain for business or communication with strangers.
- **Public Space:** This ranges from 12 feet (3.6 meters) or more. This is usually very formal like a presentation and can involve microphones and multi-media.

The important thing to note here is that these norms can vary for different reasons. If you're in a crowded bar or concert, it's unavoidable that people will invade your intimate space and make you accept distances that would ordinarily be completely abnormal in a regular social setting. Similarly, loud ambient noise or music can make you accept people getting closer as well. Sometimes, we take encroachment for granted. Because it's commonly done and justifiable in some settings, we can be lulled into lowering our guard. A classroom dynamic can have a similar effect. It's normal to form deeper bonds with our students and over time we will naturally become more comfortable with them. This can lead to the gradual erosion of distance in our interactions. If we were to modify Hall's classifications for our own needs, we would add a new category in third place which would be *tactical space*. This would begin at 3—4 feet (1—1.2 meters) and extend to as far as you can see. Tactically speaking we would like to always have aggression beyond arm's reach, but the further away it is, the safer we will be. I've witnessed many interventions where teachers or admin know the student well. As a result, in an effort to connect, they get too close. This is totally normal and well-intended, but violence can be unpredictable. Even a student with whom you have great rapport can hurt you intentionally or by accident when they are highly emotional. While it's impossible to always maintain tactical distance, if you sense the situation is escalating and emotions are getting heightened, try to increase and maintain as much space as possible. With a little practice and the inclusion of some of the strategies that I will show, you will still be able to create strong rapport and connection while minimizing the risk to yourself.

STORY FROM THE FIELD:

Dylan is an old friend of mine who has known me since I sported my rockabilly, Morrissey-inspired coif in the early 90s. He guarded the door at many clubs in our fair city and worked in private security. He is about as direct and brutally honest as a human can be and he wears the trials of his life clearly in his expression and across a face that has been remodeled by twenty years of boxing. When I asked him, what advice he would give teachers, he looked at me blankly and without delay said:

> *"Tell them to say no. There's nothing clearer than no. People can pretend to be confused by it or argue that they didn't know what you meant by it, but they always do. Anytime they don't comply, you know they're up to something. The problem is, sometimes we're not used to saying it. We need to practice it. We need to try doing it all the time. Just look at someone and say no and then stay quiet. That was the hardest part for me at first. Just stay quiet, but that's probably the biggest secret. You want to let it hang there in the air for a minute and stare at them. You can put up an open hand and signal stop at the same time but eventually, your stare will be enough. You will stop them with that word. Then you'll learn that anyone who doesn't listen is always trying to do something that you don't want and eventually you'll learn that if they don't listen, you need to act immediately."*

GOOD FENCES MAKE GOOD NEIGHBORS

In our last section, I noted that it wouldn't be natural to *always* maintain tactical distance. Sometimes, people need to get closer to us and we can always be caught off guard. Other times, we may simply not be able to increase our distance due to physical limitations. We may be cornered, in a crowd, or otherwise limited. Even when we can increase our range, distance may not be enough. How we position our bodies will also play a huge role.

In 1998, veteran UK doorman and self-defense expert Geoff Thompson published his seminal book, *The Fence: The Art of Protection*. This simple little book was the culmination of decades of working security at bars and clubs. When I first read it, it resonated with everything I had been taught and experienced firsthand. It promoted a simple universal self-defense stance, which he aptly referred to as *"The Fence"*. This posture is among the most important personal protection tools we can understand, on the street, in the schoolyard, or in the classroom.

"The Fence"

The first component of the Fence is to keep your hands up as a natural barrier between you and your aggressor. As we have seen, greater distance permits greater reaction time. Consider this: in research performed on elite boxers, the winners of matches were generally found to have better reaction time.[8] The same was found to be true of karate practitioners.[9] These same practitioners however were not found to exhibit higher than normal reaction times outside of the combative arena. Their faster reaction time was not based on raw physical speed. They reacted faster because they had more experience detecting specific cues and were more effective at choosing their response. Novice boxers were more likely to use their strikes to explore and test, striking to find their range.[10] By comparison, expert boxers were found to intuitively know to use quicker punches the closer they got to their opponent.[11] The expert boxers were not necessarily physically faster. Instead, they controlled the distance better which allowed them to process attacks more effectively and choose better responses. This is the logic behind the old adage:

"When you control the distance, you control the fight."

We saw earlier that there is a minimum distance that we need to process a threat. The Fence becomes even more important here because it keeps your aggressor outside of that essential processing range. The Fence gives us that life-saving bubble of personal space that we need to give our brain the minimal time it needs to process stimuli. When we let someone inside that bubble, it will be neurologically impossible to process and react to a sudden threat in time.

A second component of the Fence that is important to understand is that it appears **passive**. Our hands are always kept open, with the palms pointing towards the aggressor. This does a few important things at the same time:

- First, it supports efforts to de-escalate aggression. Imagine telling someone that you don't want to fight while simultaneously brandishing two tightly clenched fists. That's not exactly the most consistent message. By comparison, imagine how differently your intent would be perceived if your hands were passively open. Non-verbal communication, like posture and gesture, plays a huge role in our perceived credibility and persuasiveness.[12] We'll talk about this in more depth a bit later.
- One of the most common aggression cues we monitor is the position of an aggressor's hands. Hands that are suspiciously closed, near the body, under

---

[8] Bianco M, Ferri M., Fabiano C., Giorgiano F., Tavella S., et all, "Baseline simple and complex reaction times in female compared to male boxers", *Journal of Sports Medicine and Physical Fitness*, 51. 292-298, 2011.

[9] Mori S., Ohtani Y., Imanaka K., "Reaction times and anticipatory skills of karate athletes", *Human Movement Science* 21, 213-230, 2020.

[10] Hristovski R., Davids K., Aranjo D., Button C., "How boxers decide to punch a target: Emergent behavior in nonlinear dynamical movement systems", *Journal of Sports Science and Medicine,* 2006.

[11] Kap S., Ashker S., Kapo A., "Winning and losing performance in boxing competition: a comparative study", *Journal of Physical Education and Sport*, May 2021.

[12] Burgoon J., Birk T., "Nonverbal behaviors, persuasion and credibility", Human Communication Research, 17 (1): 140-169, 1990.

clothing or moving towards the waistband or pockets, can all be perceived as attempts to access or conceal a weapon. This is why law enforcement often shouts the command *"show me your hands"*. By pre-emptively offering our open hands in our Fence and by keeping them visible, we appeal to the aggressor's subconscious threat assessment. Open hands are one of the most universal signs of submission and passivity that you can project. By displaying our open palms clearly, we are showing that we are not armed and that we have no obvious desire to fight.

- Our gestures are being evaluated by *everyone.* We know they're being processed by the aggressor but they are influencing the onlookers as well. Even a justified defender can appear overly aggressive to a spectator. This is especially true when viewed out of context, for example, in a courtroom. Social perception matters in litigation. It's not enough to *be* justified to defend yourself. You need to look justified as well.
- Finally, should we ultimately be required to protect ourselves, nothing will be gained from warning our opponent that we're about to attack. I realize the idea of pre-emptively attacking an aggressor may be counter-intuitive or even offensive to some sensibilities at first. Many of us have been raised to wait until an attacker swings first. I simply submit that it is an established combative truth that it always takes less time to act than react. [13] If we remain reactive, we give a potential attacker yet another advantage over us. I won't delve deeper into this controversy for now. The previous points of maintaining distance for greater reaction time and projecting passivity to maintain social approval and support for our de-escalation efforts are more important at this time.

As simple as the Fence may sound, it can be hugely counter-intuitive. Some of us will have a hard time defining any type of limit. We may intuitively lower our hands when we get confronted in a subconscious effort to appear small and unthreatening. I saw it when I worked the door at clubs over and over again, in arguments, stare-downs, and pushing matches. Sometimes the arguments would fizzle out and the aggressor's ego was satisfied by asserting dominance and looking bigger than their victim. Other times it erupted with a sucker punch on an unprepared subject. Even if security pounced on the attacker immediately, he could often get a few hard punches or kicks in and cause significant damage to the subject first. Lucky for you, YouTube lets you sample a year's worth of doorman experience from the safety of your sofa, allowing you to see firsthand the dangers of lowering your Fence.

It was not easy to acquire these experiences. When I worked the door, you had to rely on second-hand stories which were often distorted or firsthand experiences that could easily be jumbled by stress. It took time and some degree of luck to learn how important

---

[13] Wisecarver C., Tucker M., "Force science reactionary gap", *U.S. Department of Justice*, Septembe 2007.

keeping your hands up was. What makes keeping the Fence up even more challenging initially is that many aggressors will keep their own hands low. They may flare out their arms and shoulders to look larger and more intimidating. Through subconscious influence we can be tempted to mimic their gesture, keeping our own hands low and letting them in way too close. The problem is if both people have their hands down, the person who decides to swing first will usually land a free hit and that is often enough to sway the result of the entire encounter.

EXERCISE #3:

Practice implementing your Fence. At first, it can be helpful to practice when you're alone. If you can, try it out in front of a mirror:

- Practice having your hands up somewhere between elbow and shoulder height.
- Make sure that your hands are open and that the majority of the time, your palms are facing your perceived aggressor to show them that they are empty.
- A big part of the Fence is keeping it natural—what I term *"the Casual Blur"*. We must become comfortable keeping our hands up and moving in a way that looks natural in the situation. You may be surprised by how awkward this will be for you at first. Our hand gestures should reinforce our speech.

Practicing the Fence may feel odd and downright unnatural. Some of us are simply born with more innate assertiveness. I can remember watching my son play with other kids when he was about 5 years old. He had a natural confidence, almost stubbornness that I envied. By comparison, I was a very shy child and I had to take a long and painful road to become more assertive. Of course, what we are born with is just the beginning. Assertiveness *can* be improved. Certainly, the way we are nurtured and supported plays a huge role. [14] That foundation is nurtured by our environment, our support systems, and even our geographic region.[15] It may vary according to gender since female assertiveness is more likely to be perceived as aggressiveness and socially discouraged and male aggression is more likely to be accepted and rewarded.[16] All of these factors have an influence, but

---

[14] Ezake E., Ozougwu A., Okoli P., "An investigation on parenting styles and gender influencing assertiveness on undergraduates", *International Journal of Innovative Research and Advanced Studies,* University of Nigeria, Volume 7, Issue 6, June 2020

[15] Sigler K., Burneett A., Child J.T., "A regional analysis of assertiveness", *Journal of Intercultural Communication Research 37 (2) 9-104*

[16] Maloney M.E., Moore P., "From aggressive to assertive", *International journal of women's dermatology,* 6 (1), 46-49

only *you* can decide how much you want to work on it and how much you'd like to develop your ultimate level. Remember, that **no skill or talent is innate**. There is no natural level of skill that we are stuck with. True talent and expertise come from deliberate, committed practice.[17] Now that we have a basic understanding of the Fence, we have a tool that can make an immediate difference to our safety and provide an instant indicator of our baseline assertiveness. Since this will be a sticking point for many of us, let's take a closer look at assertiveness.

---

[17] Ericsson A.K., Charness N., "Expert performance: Its structure and acquisition", *Science Watch*, 1994.

STORY FROM THE FIELD:

"Nico Van Huffel"

Nico Van Huffel is a very good friend of mine from Belgium. He began his career in 1999 at the Belgian Gendarmerie and then worked for 7 years as an inspector at the *Intervention Police*. He then worked for 10 years as Chief Inspector at the Intervention Police. Since 2001, he has been a Violence Control Instructor within his department and guest trainer at the National and Provincial Police Schools. Since 2016 he has become a full-time Violence Control Trainer and Educator at the Provincial Police School "PIVO". Beyond his impressive law enforcement resume, Nico is also an expert martial artist with decades of advanced training. I have had the great fortune to work closely with him in the improvement of law enforcement training methodologies, both training and teaching together. When I asked Nico what advice he would give classroom teachers, he told me they focus on 8 key elements of my approach with their cadets:

"Integrating the basic stance in everything that we do was a game-changer, for both basic police work and also for debriefing. We apply the concept to controlling people, doing vehicle controls, clearing buildings, etc. We use the name "basisopstelling" which means basic stance/approach/attitude. We integrate 8 key points:

1. Maintaining Distance (both physically and emotionally)
2. *Blading* (angling the body slightly to protect from impact)
3. *Zoning* (moving laterally from the threat rather than backpedaling)

4. *Fencing* (with our empty hands or also with our weapons)
5. Loading the Stance (keep not only our body but also our attitude ready to move forward)
6. Tactical Vision (how to use the eyes to watch the eyes, the hands, and our surroundings)
7. Verbal Commands
8. Breathing

We adapt these to every given situation, but these 8 points inform how we stand and how we present ourselves and are trained to become instinctive parts of our basic operating system."

We'll be going through these in greater detail shortly, but at this point, I'd like you to recognize that the same components that help keep a police officer alive will also help keep you safe in the classroom as well.

AGGRESSION vs. ASSERTIVENESS

"A key component of improving your safety is to consciously grow your assertiveness."

Assertiveness is a huge part of personal protection. Self-defense begins with defending your limits. Many people mistake assertiveness for aggression and then use that as an excuse for not setting their limits. They routinely let people walk all over them and then excuse it by saying: *"But I'm not comfortable being aggressive"*. Being assertive doesn't mean being aggressive. No one should try to be more aggressive but as we'll see we are all entitled to be more assertive:

- First of all, remember that assertiveness is *fair*. When you're assertive, you express your wants and needs but you are still able to consider the rights and needs of others. Sadly, the ability to have an open discussion and apply critical thinking are skills that are rapidly deteriorating these days. People are more comfortable clinging to polarizing viewpoints rather than engaging in open discussions and most things in society have been split into black-and-white opposition. There is so much mutual benefit, the potential for learning, and overall growth that comes from being open to criticism and staying receptive to differing views but to do that we must be able to assert ourselves. We can all benefit by learning to be fairer in our assertions.
- Aggressive people will try to bulldoze over you to enforce their views, but assertive people look for win-win situations. When we are assertive, we try to listen more

than we talk. Yes, we must still express our own needs and wants, but we also want to learn what the needs and wants are of whomever we're dealing with.
- Building your assertiveness should connect you more with those around you, not push them away. It should make you a better communicator by honing both your listening and expression skills. We'll be getting deeper into all of these communication skills later on but right now we must see this difference.

Assertiveness is also a better tactical choice. Aggression will escalate situations. By comparison, assertiveness defines your limits so you can better defend what matters to you. *The Fence* technique we saw earlier is a perfect illustration of assertiveness. It defines your personal space, your limits, and your comfort so that you can better defend them. It never seeks to impose, dominate, or harm. We're not pushing the aggressor away. We're simply stating *please stay this far back*. If an aggressor respects the Fence and de-escalates, there is no risk to them. The Fence is not a closed-fist threat. It's a peaceful open hand defining your limits. It also carries the power to better defend you should you need to, since it keeps your hand optimally positioned for counter-attacks. Very quickly we can see that the simple act of putting up your Fence is an exercise that develops and strengthens your *"assertiveness muscles"* and that training makes you take responsibility for your safety.

Increasing your assertiveness is also good for your health. It can reduce your feeling of resentment in situations and ultimately lead to you experiencing less stress.[18] We've all had the experience of not reacting the way we would have liked, not saying what we wanted to say and not standing up for ourselves correctly. Think of how that made you feel. After the fact, you could feel all of that frustration balled up inside of you and you were left complaining to confidants or muttering self-talk about what you should have done. This robs you of both your responsibility and your power. Think of how much stress just one situation like that can create. Now flip the script and imagine how much release and empowerment you would get by fully and confidently expressing yourself instead. Very quickly we can see that assertiveness is not just about improving our safety. It's also about improving our actual well-being, our health, and the quality of our relationships.

---

[18] Estami A., Ahmand R., Masoudi R., "The effectiveness of assertiveness training on the levels of stress, anxiety and depression of high school students", *Iranian Red Crescent Medical Journal*, Howsar Medical Institute, 2016

EXERCISE #4:

In 1975 Gambrill and Richey came up with a simple 40-question self-inquiry questionnaire known as the *Assertion Inventory*. This collection of simple questions allows you to assess your comfort levels with a range of interactions to get a better awareness of your level of assertiveness. Then following assertiveness training, the same questionnaire can help you assess whether you've made improvements and where you might want to focus your efforts to improve. In each of the following questions, honestly rate your comfort levels on a scale of 1 to 5:

1 = always do it
2= usually do it
3= do it about half the time
4= rarely do it
5 = never do it

To do this exercise, you will need 2 sheets of paper and something to write with. On the first sheet, go through the list, answering on a scale of 1 to 5, how likely you would be to honestly do each of these things. It will be helpful to label this sheet *"probability"*. Here are the questions:

1. Turn down a request to borrow your car.
2. Compliment a friend.
3. Ask someone for a favor.
4. Resist sales pressure.
5. Apologize when you are at fault.
6. Turn down a request for a meeting or date.
7. Admit fear and request special consideration.
8. Tell someone that you have a close relationship with about something they do that bothers you.
9. Ask for a raise.
10. Admit ignorance in some area of knowledge.
11. Turn down a request to borrow money.
12. Ask personal questions.
13. Ask a talkative friend to stop talking.
14. Ask for constructive criticism.
15. Initiate a conversation with a stranger.
16. Compliment someone who you are intimately involved with or interested in.

17. Request a meeting or date with a person.
18. Your initial request for a meeting is turned down and you ask the person again for a later time.
19. Admit confusion for a point under discussion and ask for clarification.
20. Apply for a job.
21. Ask whether you have offended someone.
22. Tell someone that you like them.
23. Request service when it's not forthcoming (for example at a restaurant).
24. Discuss openly with a person their criticism of you.
25. Return defective items to a store or restaurant.
26. Express an opinion that differs from that of the person you're talking to.
27. Resist sexual overtures when you're not interested.
28. Tell a person when you feel that they've done something unfair to you.
29. Accept a date.
30. Tell someone good news about yourself.
31. Resist the pressure to drink.
32. Resist a significant person's unfair demands.
33. Quit a job.
34. Resist the pressure to take drugs.
35. Discuss openly with a person their criticisms of your work.
36. Request the return of borrowed items.
37. Receive compliments
38. Continue to talk with someone who disagrees with you.
39. Tell a friend or colleague when they do something that bothers you.
40. Ask a person who is annoying you in a public situation to stop.

Now put that sheet aside and turn it face down or place it out of sight. On the second sheet, write the title "discomfort". On this sheet, you will re-read the questions and honestly evaluate how uncomfortable each situation will make you feel. It's important to not look at your first sheet of answers as they may influence the second round.

1=no discomfort
2=a little discomfort
3=a fair amount
4=much discomfort
5=a tremendous amount of discomfort

After you have re-answered these 40 questions, you can put the sheets side-by-side to compare. Now, clinically speaking, there are many different ways the assertiveness inventory has been used for research. For our purposes here it will be important for two reasons:

1. It will help **increase your awareness** of how assertive you feel you are. Even though this is a self-diagnosis, if you do it honestly, it will show you where you are strongest and where you struggle more. We need to start by knowing our weaknesses to be able to improve them.
2. It will show you your relationship between **ability** and **comfort**. It's important to recognize how much discomfort we experience in different circumstances if we ever wish to reframe our perceptions. Even if we ranked our ability to do something as likely, if our discomfort while doing that action is extremely high, that reluctance can become problematic when we're under stress. Often, the stress we feel is a more accurate indicator than the probability we think we will do something. Discomfort means those responses are less reliable and more prone to emotional influence. Realizing where we struggle more, helps us recognize that we may need more aftercare and de-briefing, which we will discuss later on.

For now, we've taken another important step towards acknowledging where we're at now while giving us some possible insights into what areas we might need to specifically focus on. As a side note, after you've completed this book and hopefully begun integrating a good number of the tactics outlined herein, consider revisiting these inventories from time to time to see if you would improve any of your answers.

GESTURE

Earlier, we discussed the power of distance and the role it plays in communication (proxemics) and our reaction time. We saw that it wasn't always possible to maintain ideal tactical distance and that the closer we get to a potential aggressor, the more important it is for us to use our hands to create a Fence if we want to avoid getting completely encroached. Now it's time to discuss the role of movement and gesture in communication. This field of research is known as *kinesics*. Back in the 1950s, the anthropologist Ray Birdwhistell first promoted the idea that non-verbal communication was systemic and socially learned. It is widely known that verbality is only one part of how we communicate. Some studies suggest that as much as 93% of all communication is non-verbal.[19] It should be noted that those estimates are often taken out of context and generously exaggerated. It doesn't matter what the exact number is for our consideration. It doesn't even matter if non-verbal communication constitutes the majority of how we communicate. All that matters is that it *does* play a big role. How we move and stand and gesture matters. As we break down under stress, we may struggle with complex verbal skills and our subject(s) may struggle to process them. Non-verbal skills can help us express our message more clearly. In noisy environments or with a subject who is experiencing auditory exclusion due to stress, non-verbal skills are essential. Non-verbal skills play an even bigger role when dealing with a language barrier. The great thing about these skills is that we can practice how we stand and move all the time. Research shows that teachers who more effectively use non-verbal communication are more likely to have a positive influence on their students' moods and are more likely to be positively received.[20] Moreover, the effective use of gestures with students with physical impairments was found to be more effective in increasing their self-esteem and reducing shyness.[21] Kinesics are an essential part of effective communication as a teacher and a powerful tactical tool against aggression.

When we look at The Fence from this perspective, we can see that it's also a great communication tool. Beyond keeping us safe, it projects passivity. One of the most important things we can do during any situation that is escalating is to:

Keep our non-verbal language non-threatening.

---

[19] Bambaeeroo F., Shokrpour N., "The impact of the teacher's non-verbal communication on the success of teaching", Adv Med Educ Prof., Apr; 5 (2): 51-59, 2017

[20] Bambaeeroo F., Shokrpour N., "The impact of the teacher's non-verbal communication on the success of teaching", Adv Med Educ Prof., Apr; 5 (2): 51-59, 2017

[21] Hedarpour S., Dokaneifard F., Bahari S., "The impact of communication skills on the handicapped students' self esteem and the reduction in their shyness", *New Ideas in Educational Science*, 3 (4): 65-73, 2008

We've seen that a key component of the Fence is to keep the hands open and passively pointed toward the subject. We want to show them that our hands are empty and that we have no aggressive intent. Now we're going to take this one step further. While there are times that will require us to be relatively still to appear non-threatening, we also want to avoid freezing (what is technically known as *tonic immobility*—that's our body's innate reflex to play dead to avoid danger). While playing dead may have served our ancestors against other predators, freezing up in a verbal de-escalation can get us seriously hurt. Most of the time, we would rather stay moving, even if only subtly. This will do a few important things:

1. **It will keep communicating passivity.** It is impossible to not communicate. Our body is ALWAYS communicating something. When we freeze, we may project fear, vulnerability, inattentiveness, disrespect or the inability to help the person in need. Non-verbal expression represents a big part of how we communicate, so when we stop moving and gesturing, we deprive ourselves of all of that potential communication and clarity.
2. **Action will channel your adrenaline.** During a crisis, your natural reflexes will dump huge amounts of stress chemicals into your body to make you better able to fight or flee. If we don't use those chemicals, they can overrun our bodies with jitters and a loss of control. By training ourselves to stay in constant motion, we will help to dissipate stress.
3. **It will help establish rapport.** Constant motion, however slight, will help funnel the aggressor's focus onto you, help you establish rapport, and better position you to de-escalate a scenario. Aggressors can be agitated and easily distracted. By constantly moving you are like a living worm on a fish hook—more likely to attract attention.
4. **It will improve readiness.** The main focus of this book is non-violent intervention. Nevertheless, should we be required to react, **we are more likely to respond more quickly if we are already in motion**, rather than trying to launch from a dead stop. Objects in motion tend to stay in motion. Objects at rest tend to get sucker-punched before they get moving.

A brief study of effective public speakers will reinforce just how subtle yet effective movement and gestures are. Great speakers are great non-verbal communicators as well. In the next exercises, we'll look at a few tips that will help you cultivate effective hand gestures that are also tactically sound.

EXERCISE #5:

Stand in front of a mirror and see how you can employ the following tips:

- Practice **keeping your hands visible**. Don't tuck them away or hide them behind your back. You always want them up between your hips and your shoulders. Remember that you may reflexively try to appear smaller if you lack assertiveness. In doing this, you may tend to bring your hands in close to your body or even hide them. Unfortunately, this can trigger an aggressor into thinking you are going for a weapon. It can also make you look like an easy target. So, regularly practice keeping your hands naturally up between hip and shoulder level and slightly away from your body. The more you do this, the more instinctive it will come to you.
- **Avoid pointing.** If you must direct attention, try using an open hand, with all of your fingers pointing in the same direction as if you were offering food in the palm of your hand to an animal. Rather than sharply pointing with one finger towards a subject, all of your fingers will be more gently sloped down so that the palm is angled towards the subject. Gesture and invite instead of pointing.
- **Reinforce** your words with your actions. This can be as simple as slowly bobbing your hand to the cadence of your speech every few syllables to emphasize a word or phrase. Think of your hands like an orchestra conductor's baton. It can include using your fingers to illustrate numbers as you list first, second and third points. It can involve gesturing size, like "*big*" or "*small*" with your hands as you say the words or can point directions. The most important emotion to gesture is passivity. Always keep those hands open.
- **Protect your body.** In conventional public speaking, we are widely encouraged to keep our torso open and exposed. Ordinarily, this shows that we are receptive to a subject. Normally, we try to avoid crossing our arms or closing off our body. In a conflict situation however, this can leave us too vulnerable. When facing aggression, we want to project that we are aware and ready. We still want to avoid crossing our arms so that our hands are ready to respond quickly. I can't tell you how many doormen I've worked with who crossed their arms to puff up their biceps and appear large, but then when aggressors got in their faces, they paid the price because their hands were all tied up.

Remember a Fence must remain up. A Fence will only be as strong as its consistency and ultimately your Fence will depend on your willingness to defend it. The minute you lower your Fence, you are at a disadvantage.

CHURNING

We've seen the advantages that something as simple as slowly but continuously moving your Fence can bring. The same is true of your body as well. It will be difficult to keep the arms moving without having some degree of motion in your trunk. Here are a few basic concepts to integrate:

"By leaning forward slightly and 'loading' your stance, your body will be better prepared to respond quickly."

- First, **play with the distribution of your weight**. We always want to feel strong and in balance, but because we are two-legged creatures, we are never truly in a state of stability. We maintain balance by constantly swaying and shifting and adjusting. To freeze in one spot requires a lot of energy. If you've ever worked a job where you stood all day, like a retail clerk, you know that you are always generally shifting and moving to change the demands on your body. Rather than deny this natural tendency, fuel it. Explore the way you can shift your weight.

    Generally, during interventions, I favor **loading** my stance, leaning with **more weight on my front leg than my back**. As Nico said earlier in his description of "*basisopstelling*" (stance/approach/attitude), Loading is not only a physical consideration but a psychological one as well. Although we might be frightened in a given situation, if we lean slightly forward and give ourself the simple objective of either entering or exiting should aggression erupt, then we are far more likely to avoid freezing. If instead, we allow fear to seep into our body and begin leaning back further and further, we are far more likely to cower and retreat.

- Whenever possible, I prefer having **my body slightly angled**. Although a correct Fence will go a long way to help protect your body, a slight rotation in the trunk will help a huge amount. This is what we term **Blading.** Our body is like the blade of a knife. We don't want to expose the flat front to our opponent. Rather we want to start turning the edge of our body forward. The key is to turn your body somewhere between 30-45 degrees. This will help protect the numerous vulnerable targets along your center line (your face, throat, solar plexus, and groin) by increasing the likelihood you deflect direct pressure. If we turn more than this, we risk exposing our back which again begins to increase vulnerability. Generally, we will keep our dominant hand in the rear (if you're right-handed, keep your right hand in the rear). This places maximum distance between our favored hand and our opponent. For police and military, this gives them more time to draw and retain a weapon. For a teacher, it might mean keeping objects like keys or phones out of reach. At minimum it places your dominant hand in the back, allowing for the most powerful hitting if necessary.

Whenever possible, maintain your Fence, Blade your body on an angle, and Zone away to one side of your aggressor's centerline.

- Beyond Loading and Blading, a third consideration is to zone. **"Zoning" is the subtle shift away from your opponent in a lateral or diagonal line**. In a crisis, most people have the reflex to retreat in a straight line. This is due in large part to tunnel vision. As our senses reflexively narrow to aid our survival focus, we lose peripheral awareness. When our eyes sense this, many people will naturally step back, as if they were staring through a camera lens, unable to zoom back any further. **Backpedalling is a dangerous habit in a conflict since it places you off balance and can weaken your resolve.** Attackers will also always be able to run forward faster than you can backpedal. Instead, practice slowly shifting to one side. Sometimes this can result in a circling action. This will cause your aggressor to constantly adjust and recalibrate their stance and expectations and will move you away from their optimal striking range.

STORY FROM THE FIELD:

"Jordan Bill"

Jordan Bill has trained in martial arts for over 25 years. I knew his father. One day his dad admitted that he was worried about his then 15-year-old son. He feared his boy was drifting in the wrong direction. He asked if I would train him in the martial arts to help focus his energies. I told him I was only teaching adult classes at that point, but that if his son could get up early and meet me at 5:30 every morning, he could work out with me. I hadn't expected a 15-year-old to show up, but there he was that first morning. Jordan trained with me without fail, in an ice-covered school parking lot behind my apartment. Every day, I came up with new ways to use the school jungle gym to push our limits, and every day he came back. At first, I was admittedly trying to break him but the harder I went the earlier he seemed to arrive. We climbed the monkey bars, shin kicked the rubber tire obstacles, dangled and balanced and fell and threw each other on the ice until our panting clouds of frozen breaths had been sufficiently exorcised. Finally, I let him join our adult group at my school because his desire to impress me was quickly exceeding my ability to hide how sore I was.

When Jordan hit adulthood, he began working in security. He was a doorman in different clubs and worked at private events. He balanced the pressures of being the bartender at a small bar where he worked alone and had to handle all the security issues that arose. He then branched off into private security and worked in bodyguarding. Jordan often employed a tactic that personifies the power of continual motion.

"One tactic I used a lot", Jordan said, *"was when guys would get in my face and would start getting angry, I would say "I'm listening, just follow me" and I would just go about my*

business, clearing tables and serving clients. I would constantly keep walking everywhere and then they would have to follow me. I would keep making eye contact and nodding, and would just keep them talking. This way, they would get to vent, but I could keep moving and that helped to avoid it getting more confrontational, and they would usually just talk themselves out and eventually calm down. The key was that I was always listening and always ready, but I was giving them a chance to tire themselves out."

Similar tactics are very effective in a classroom setting. Giving a student a task, or sending them on an errand is a great way to give an escalated student time to calm down while helping them to vent some extra energy. You can use your creativity here. I used to send problematic students on errands, making profound eye contact and saying *"This is very important. You need to bring this note directly to Mr. Peterson, ok?"* and they would run the note to the other end of the school. When Mr. Peterson got the note, he would open it to read: *"Jimmy needed a break. Nod and send him back directly. Thanks."*

Subtle, continuous motion is also a great way for you to dissipate your nervous energy, keep your aggressor distracted and stretch time, allowing them more opportunity to vent and de-escalate while giving you more time to prepare.

THE POWER AND DANGER OF TOUCH

The next powerhouse tool we will be looking at is the role of touch in communication. Known as *haptics*, this term has also come to include the role of touch in how we interact with technology like when we use a touch screen on our phone. So, if you google haptics now you may find a lot more information on technology interfaces these days, but we're only concerned with the original definition of the word here and we will be leaving our smartphones unusually neglected throughout this book.

Touch is the first sensation we process as a child. It carries tremendous power throughout our lives. It can be comforting like the embrace of a mother, intimidating like the push of a bully, welcomed, inappropriate or invasive. Here are a few basic guidelines to how we should use touch as educators:

- If you can achieve it through other means, like verbal commands, avoid touch.
- Avoid being alone with a student for any reason whenever possible.
- Favor contact that is casual, visible, and distant like a fist bump or a high five.
- Avoid permitting and never initiate hugs or more intimate contact that could be easily misconstrued.

That being said, there *are* circumstances where touch may be necessary. Some students will excessively try to initiate touch, asking for hugs, etc. While you should continue to avoid these, you should make note of it and mention it to the administration as this can be a sign of emotional need that indicates larger problems at home. It's also important to document your awareness of tendencies in your students when they may be unusual or inappropriate. It can become more complicated if a student is highly emotional, confiding in you, or having a breakdown. As a teacher, you should both keep a *personal journal*, where you can document these occurrences, your responses, and your objectives, as well as a *central log* shared by all staff, to help ensure a more informed awareness and treatment of each child.

When students are trying to initiate touch, you must maintain clear boundaries. Like a police officer, there are ways of showing that you are present and listening without needing to touch, but many people have a strong instinct to touch to console someone. This again points to the huge role non-verbal communication plays. In contexts where a student is escalating, possibly at risk of harming themselves or those around them, touch may become more necessary. Whenever possible, ask the student if it's ok if you can touch them first. Never assume that a specific type of contact is acceptable. Depending on what a student has survived in their lives, they may find any type of contact potentially threatening. If you see that your contact is making them uncomfortable in any way, stop immediately.

The one exception to this rule would be situations where someone is directly in your space. **If you are unable to create distance and move, perhaps cornered, then touch can quickly become necessary.** If we are correctly defining our space with our Fence but the aggressor is pushing into it, we cannot afford to compress our barrier continuously. Simply pushing back will only escalate matters. Instead, think of your Fence as being as elastic and springy as possible. More importantly, the moment an aggressor pushes in to contact our Fence, we should try to move laterally, Zoning away, preferably with a small sliding step: our left foot steps to the left, and our right foot follows (or vice versa). We always want to keep our legs stable and never cross them while stepping. The Fence serves to delay an aggressor so we can move safely away.

It's important to remember that we must always be using active, effective verbal communication, which we will discuss shortly. We cannot allow our Fence to be breached. The Fence must remain up. Every effort should be placed on keeping the hands near the aggressor's shoulders or bicep areas to allow you to better monitor the movement of their arms. Your goal should be to create distance as soon as possible. This is a dangerous range and the longer you stay there the bigger the risk of escalation.

STORY FROM THE FIELD:

Generally, we want to avoid initiating touch, but sometimes we need to touch and when we do, it can save our life. One night while I was working the door, I noticed a guy sitting alone. He was just staring at my partner who was working at the base of a flight of stairs that led to the upper floor. I continued to scan the floor, coming back to him a few times to monitor him, and noticed he wasn't changing his expression. He just kept staring blankly and had an empty shot glass and beer bottle in front of him. Then he got up and started walking toward my colleague. I tried to signal my partner but he was distracted, so I started walking quickly on an intercept path. Within a few steps, I noticed the subject's right arm wasn't swinging. When we walk, we naturally swing our arms. It counter-balances the sway of our trunk and conserves energy. To not swing your arm is unnatural and has to be intentional. I saw the subject had a knife in his right hand pressed snugly against his thigh. I surged forward, cuffed his knife arm, and pushed and pinned him firmly into a cluttered wall. I kept my hand firmly connected to his knife hand and leaned in hard. My life depended on knowing where that knife was at any moment. As I think of it now, I clearly remember the blue glow of the electric beer logo on the wall behind his head, blacking out the details of his face and giving him a neon halo. I tucked my head close to his ear to make it harder for him to hit me cleanly with his free hand in case he started fighting and just kept pushing him off balance until he was teetering. I said something like:

"Hey, you gotta be careful. You're gonna get caught."

I remember he was angry and confused at the same time. I wanted to distract him for a second to see if I could change his focus but I expected him to attack me and I was ready to yank him to the ground. I saw I partially had his attention.

"That's a really nice blade. You don't want to lose it. Where did you get it? They'll take it if they see it. Where did you get it?"

I could see him thinking but he was having trouble producing an answer. He was in that place between cognitive and primal. Then he looked down in thought and mumbled something. I couldn't make it out. I wanted to try taking the knife from his hand. Keeping one hand on his wrist with hard pressure, I reached down and took it out of his hand without any resistance and held it away from his reach.

"It's awesome. How do you close it? Where's the lock?"

He pointed to a button on the back of the knife. I unlocked the blade and closed it.

"Listen I can't let you have this in here," I told him. *"I can give it back to you when you leave or I can give it to you outside now."* I took some pressure off of him and started walking him outside, encouraging him to leave. He didn't resist. He was thinking about what I was

saying. I walked him outside, signaling the bartender to call the police. My backup had noticed what was happening and followed me outside. From there we were able to keep the subject from fighting and to keep him engaged until the police came. It turned out he had been bounced out a few weeks earlier when he had drunk too much and he had been embarrassed in front of his friends. Sometimes, if your life isn't going very well, something like losing face or being insulted can become an all-consuming threat to your perceived value, and getting revenge can seem like the only thing within your control. The reality is that we always have the ability to control our emotions. **We can't control circumstances but we can always control our responses to them.** In that instance, I was trying to remind the customer of that option. Everyone involved was lucky things didn't spiral out of control. When you play stupid games, you often win stupid prizes.

Situations don't always work out as smoothly as this one did. When they do, no one has to get hurt. I could have easily become physical the minute he had a knife, but there is always a huge risk in any fight and it's much worse when there's a knife. Violence ruins lives. It can maim or kill you. It can leave lasting legal problems. It can cause crushing financial debt as a result. It rarely just ends on the spot. I chose to try getting the patron verbal and fortunately I was able through soft skills and touch to monitor the threat, command his focus and keep him calm. Touch can be a very powerful and valuable tool even in extremely dangerous situations but it must be used mindfully.

STAND STRONG

In nature, predators will look for the easiest prey. These can include the old and the young. For example, more than 50 percent of the individuals killed by serial murderers are under the age of 30 while only 10 percent are over the age of 60.[22] By comparison, a study of what attracted predators to victims for basic assault shown a predilection to older victims. Predators will favor people who appear weaker and look like they will put up less of a fight. The serial killer Ted Bundy said in a 1985 interview that he could *"tell a victim by the way she walked down the street, the tilt of her head, the manner in which she carried herself."* Attackers will also often look for those who are alone or otherwise distracted.

While Bundy admittedly evidenced a high degree of self-awareness in his crimes, many criminals are much less conscious of their drives. They are nevertheless governed by a high degree of instinctive understanding which they simply aren't aware of. In 1981 Betty Grayson and Morris Stein conducted a study on inmates who were convicted of assault on strangers. The subjects were each shown a video of over 60 randomly videotaped strangers walking through a dangerous part of New York City. They were asked to evaluate and rate each potential victim on a scale indicating who they were most likely to select as a victim. Almost all of the convicts selected the same ideal targets although no common reason was given. Later analysis of the tapes by the researchers shows that the major difference between the perceived victims and nonvictims was an overall coordination in their movements.[23] There was no consideration of gender, age, or race. The criminals chose people by how they stood and walked intuitively. The subjects that moved with short choppy steps, taking up very little space and carrying their body weight off balance, were universally perceived as being weaker and easier victims. Subjects that walked with confidence, balance, and large strides, were universally the least desirable to potential aggressors.

A little bit earlier we discussed **Fencing** (keeping our hands protectively yet passively up), **Blading** (turning our body on a defensive angle of roughly 30-45 degrees), and **Zoning** (moving subtly and slowly in a lateral or diagonal path away from the threat). Aside from making you far more defensible, these same skills also make you less likely to be targeted or victimized, to begin with. Now we will take a look at how we move through our everyday life.

---

[22] Crocket, Z., "What data on 3,000 murderers and 10,000 victims tell us about serial murderers", *https://www.vox.com/2016/12/2/13803158/serial-killers-victims-data*, Dec. 2016

[23] Grayson B., Stein M., "Attracting assault: victim's non verbal cues", *Journal of Communication Volume 31: Issue 1, p 68-75,* Winter 1981

EXERCISE #6:

Take a moment to visualize yourself standing still. The same rules for visualizing always apply. Imagine you're watching this image on a large video screen. You can move the camera, zoom in, pause or fast forward and control what you are seeing and feeling. I want you to imagine yourself standing powerfully, standing perfectly. Your spine is straight and strong. Your head is upright without any pride or ego. It's simply natural, relaxed, and aware as you look around your surroundings. You are fully comfortable. Imagine taking a full, long, deep breath into your lungs. How would your shoulders look? Notice how they are open, permitting full comfortable breaths. No part of you is hunched or shielded or closed. Correct posture encourages better breathing which in turn helps keeps you cognitive in a crisis. Your feet are apart, strong and stable. **In our mind's eye, we are entitled to be perfect, free of limitations or fear.**

Now, if you're able to, please stand up wherever you are, and let's see how close to that ideal we can get right now. Start by shaking out those legs and placing your feet comfortably apart. Keep your weight balanced right in the middle of your feet without shifting or fidgeting. Imagine someone gently lifting up your head by an invisible thread of energy, stretching your spine fully open. Let that perfect energy thread gently stretch you up to your full height, opening up all of your body. Feel your ribs each lifting from the one below it until at last your shoulders fall back slightly, opening up your chest for a full and healthy breath. Feel the weight of your arms hanging comfortably from your shoulders. I often focus on a gentle squeeze between my shoulder blades as a simple physical trigger to remind me to open up my chest. Finally, move your head around like a bobblehead until you find its point of center and balance. Let that imaginary thread help take some of the load off of your neck.

You are entitled to stand with this degree of comfort and balance anytime you want. You deserve to feel balance and strength and confidence in absolutely every situation but fear and self-consciousness will try to rob us of this. To remember our inherent potential, we must first experience it. Like anything else, if it's unfamiliar, it can be uncomfortable at first. It takes practice. The good news is that this practice has already begun. By allowing yourself to see the way you want to be, and then by taking small steps to practice physically feeling those changes, you are creating new habits and changing how both you and the world around you will perceive you.

EXERCISE #7:

Once you have a feel for how to stand a little more confidently, it's time to get things moving. Remember that study of convicted criminals who had assaulted strangers; they were all universally attracted to people that moved in a manner that was small, uncoordinated, and clumsy. We do not want to be among those targets. Again, we'll begin with **visualization**. On our mental movie screen, I want you to visualize yourself walking. Imagine yourself maintaining that straight, confident posture. As you walk, I want you to notice **three** things:

1. Notice that **your head is upright**. Your body is straight and strong and balanced. Your weight is not shifting all over the place.
2. Notice **your strides are long and strong**. Feel and hear the smooth and steady rhythm of your walk. Step, step, step, step.
3. Notice the **long and fluid swing of your arms**. Long strides need long arm swings for counterbalance. Take the space you deserve in the world.

Take a minute to imagine how you would look walking this way.

Now the next part may be awkward but I would like you to stand up once again and try this out in person. Remember our goal is to move with balance, long strides, and long arm movements. Be tall, steady, even, and strong. Even if you're walking in an extremely small space, focus on being even in your rhythm and as graceful as possible. For many of us, this is so unnatural that it will need a lot of practice. If we're really shy, that means practicing when we're alone. Then try taking it to the street and practice walking in public. An added rule of walking through crowds is to move to the rhythm of the crowd around you. Let yourself relax a little and feel the rhythm of the crowd, just like you're driving through traffic. Keep the pace.

As a side note, anything that integrates posture and movement will let you hack into shortcuts for improving your movement. Dance training, Tai Chi, Pilates, weight lifting, martial arts and Yoga are amazing ways for you to open your body and inject a little more confidence into your movement.

STORY FROM THE FIELD:

Jamal is a long-time friend. We trained together in my early years. He taught me the Indonesian martial art of Pencak Silat. He also worked as a bouncer, is ex-military, and now works in private security. When I told him I was writing this book, I asked him what one tactic or tip would he recommend to a school teacher that might encounter violence. There was a second of silence on the phone, then he said: *"Learn to stand tall. Practice standing taller every day. Whether I'm working or going about my everyday life, the minute I catch myself off balance or slouching, I straighten up and take a deep breath. I try to connect with gratitude and think how lucky I am to still have the health to do this. It's an incredible privilege to have a brain that can notice something like this and a body that we can control and change. I just breathe and enjoy being stronger in that moment. In every job I've taken, I've had to learn to stand and walk more efficiently. In the military, I had to adjust to the weight of the gear. As a doorman, I had to learn to be strong without being overbearing. As a bodyguard, I had to move smoothly and responsively and adapt all the time to the crowds and spaces around me. I am always working on how I stand and move. Whenever I get distracted or shaken up, I go back to these basics. They're my anchor and my compass."*

Jamal went on to say that so much of the work he has done was just about standing. Working the door, personal protection, and even his time in the military. Standing wrongly could not only get you picked on needlessly, but it can also have devastating effects on your physical health, spawn chronic injuries, impede your breathing and diminish your energy. How you stand can even affect how aware of your environment you are. A simple investment in bringing mindful awareness to *how* you stand can bring huge pay-offs.

THE QUIET EYE

"I couldn't beat people with my strength; I don't have a hard shot; I'm not the quickest skater in the league. My eyes and my mind have to do most of the work."
-Wayne Gretzky-

Most of us take our vision for granted. In reality, we have a superpower quietly sleeping in our eyes. One of the biggest differences between the most elite performers in the world and the vast majority of average people is how they use their eyes. By studying their vision tactics, we can learn to take a huge performance shortcut, saving us wasted time, or possibly even a lifetime of inefficient use.

Every martial arts instructor I've ever trained with had something to say about what was the best way to use my eyes. They all had different advice:

- My Kung Fu Sifu was quite emphatic that I look just above the eyes, at the middle of the forehead. He said this would prevent me from getting lost in the opponent's stare but still allow me to maintain an awareness of them.
- My Kempo teacher insisted that I stare at the throat and aim there so if my opponent lowered their chin or bobbed down, I would still hit their chin or face.
- My Jujitsu sensei said I should stare at the shoulder axis and diffuse my vision to better predict how the limbs would move.
- My Russian Systema master told me to not look and to rely more on feeling.
- My Tai Chi teacher said similarly look at nothing so you can see everything.
- Then every bouncer or law enforcement professional I ever worked with said, always look at the hands.

There were bits of truth in all of their advice. I did want to avoid getting lost in an aggressor's stare; There are some intimidating people out there and losing even a second in distraction can cost you. I also wanted to diffuse my field of vision and see more; there is a lot of value in using your peripheral vision to widen your awareness as we'll discuss shortly. I also knew you could sometimes predict limb movements by watching the trunk. However, whenever I found myself in a real-life dangerous situation, I kept finding myself looking for those hands like all the veteran bouncers and cops had told me to do. Then, I started to notice that many of my martial arts teachers, no matter what they claimed they were doing, were actually watching the hands too. They said to look at nothing, but they were staring directly at the knife hand in every demo. Every one of them I mentioned it to seemed to get insulted and insisted it was still best not to look at the hands. The reality was quite different from the theory. Most of them were expressing an ideology but the police and military veterans were sharing combat experience.

It wasn't until I discovered research on the science behind our eyes that I had clarity. Enter Joan Vickers. This researcher from the University of Calgary has pioneered a new understanding of the role of the eye in target acquisition. She discovered that elite performers use a relatively long-lasting fixation before initiating a complex motor movement. She terms this technique, *"The Quiet Eye"*. Through advances in technology, Vickers was able to physically track the gaze of athletes and measure the fixation of their eyes under conditions of stress. While most athletes scanned a target or even looked at the target while they were shooting a ball, the most elite would fixate for at least 100ms before shooting. Law enforcement and military researchers took notice. They started researching the role of longer target fixation when shooting and found it made a huge difference in accuracy under stress.

Now there are a few points that we need to understand about this research. First, the Quiet Eye is only one part of the equation. Elite performers who were using the technique were only able to have the time to apply it because they had evolved the ability to read cues earlier and to more accurately see openings.[24] This gave them the time they needed to stare a little longer. We'll be addressing aggression cues and spotting danger shortly. Early detection depends on keeping more distance. Once again, we see the importance of controlling the space around us.

Vickers found that during interceptive timing tasks, like blocking a ball or receiving a pass, effective performers tended to maintain a long, continuous fixation gaze to track movement. We need to track with our eyes to detect variations like spinning, direction changes, wind or other variables. When a movement becomes unpredictable, the fixated eye moves side-to-side to compensate.[25] Sometimes these predictions are made before an object even starts moving based on postural cues.[26] That means that all of my teachers who said never to look directly at a threat were wrong. They were teaching what they thought we should do rather than what they were actually doing. In the real world, elite tactical performers watch the hands because the hands are what are going to harm you.

Stress also consumes our cognitive processing resources. Our brain fixates on the threat stimuli which makes it harder for us to process new information.[27] [28] That means that during the crisis, our brain will have a harder time processing information and making

---

[24] Vickers J., "Origins and current issues in Quiet Eye research", *Current Issues in Sports Science 1, 2016*

[25] Land, M. F., Vision, eye movements, and natural behavior. *Visual Neuroscience,* 26, 51-62. 10.1017/S0952523808080899, 2009

[26] Causer, J., & Williams, A. M., "Improving anticipation and decision making in sport", *The Routledge handbook of sports performance analysis* (pp. 21-31). London: Routledge. 2013

[27] Corbetta, M., Patel, G., & Shulman, G. L., "The reorienting system of the human brain: From environment to theory of mind", *Neuron, 58, 306-324. 10.1016/j.neuron*, 2008.

[28] Corbetta, M., & Shulman, G. L., "Control of goal-directed and stimulus-driven attention in the brain", *Nature Reviews Neuroscience,* 3(3), 201-215. 10.1038/nrn755, 2002.

decisions. Techniques like the Quiet Eye train us to dedicate our attention where it matters most and allow us to better regulate our emotions under stress. The more stressed we are, the more time we need to process a threat and the longer we need to look at it.

Now, Quiet Eye research is still in its infancy. In the 20 years since it was clinically observed, a debate has arisen about the link between enhancing the visual processing of target information and eye movement. Is eye movement helping individuals ignore distracting context information, or is the Quiet Eye just a by-product of people who have cultivated better prediction skills? In the end, it doesn't matter whether the chicken or the egg came first and there are two major reasons why:

1. First, what I know for certain from my experience in the martial arts and personal security is that **when we consistently identify a behavior in a successful individual, it benefits us to emulate it.** Modelling is an essential part of learning. That's why the vast majority of elite performers have role models. [29] Modeling behavior gives us an example of how people do things. Steven Covey in his classic book "*7 Habits of Highly Successful People*" noted that successful people often aren't self-aware of *why* exactly they are so effective. What they may believe is the key to their success may in fact be far less relevant than habits that they take for granted. This is what all of my teachers did: they taught me how they *thought* I should use my eyes rather than realizing how they actually used their eyes. This is one reason why modeling is so successful. It bypasses the need for self-awareness to some extent and allows us to simply imitate mastery. When we see someone performing something well, subconsciously our brain learns how to organize our behavior. We intuitively become more efficient by watching, more confident, and ultimately better able to achieve reflexive ease and flow in that activity.[30]

2. Most of the teachers I had in the martial arts were not native English speakers. Whether Japanese, Chinese, Russian, or Thai, these instructors often struggled with their words. I learned most through copying their movements. If I exceeded other students in my class, it was first because I studied my teachers' movements more closely and then openly tried to emulate them. As teachers, we need to realize that all of our students are watching. Whether or not they intend to, they are absorbing and to some extent emulating. The first thing that we learn as we start to improve our tactical vision, is that we are also being watched. As classroom teachers, we are often faced with the challenge of teaching students whose first language is not English. Modeling can be an incredibly helpful tool to bridge that gap.

---

[29] Morgenroth T, Ryan M.K., and Peters K., "The motivation theory of role modeling: how role models influence role aspirants' goals", *Rev. Gen. Psychol. 19, 465-483/ doi: 10/1037/gpr0000059*, 2015

[30] Lee S., Kwon S., Ahn J., "The effect of modeling on self-efficacy and flow state of adolescent athletes through role models", Psychology, *14 June 2021*, https://doi.org/10.3389/fpsyg.2021.661557

My work in the security field also supports the Quiet Eye theory. In the beginning, I tried to look at everything. Anything bright or loud or close or moving commanded my attention. My field of vision was like a movie directed by a butterfly on Red Bull having a seizure under a strobe light. I tried to look at everything without a plan and ended up missing a lot. Over the years, I've seen that most amateurs do the same thing and you just can't maintain that frantic pace. You become hyper-vigilant and burn out. Then you have a choice to make: either tune out completely and stop trying (which many unfortunately do) or else learn what to look for and become more selective. All the pros around me constantly told me to "*scan the eyes of the crowd*". Look for people that are out of sync with the room. When something seems odd, those people become visual anchors in the room that you come back to continuously. Then, whenever you have persons of interest, you oscillate between their eyes to monitor their intent and their hands to pre-emptively detect their actions. Even when you look away from them, you train yourself to maintain awareness of them in your peripheral vision. It's a simple formula: scan the eyes, and monitor the hands. With a little practice, it becomes a habit.

Now as classroom teachers, we're not facing the same level of constant threat as a bouncer or a bodyguard. Hopefully, our students aren't rowdy drunks looking to jump us to avenge a bad grade from the week before. The Quiet Eye is still a powerful classroom tool:

- The next time you're invigilating an exam, you have a very obvious scenario to test your eyes. Try scanning the room, looking at your students' eyes first. Just sweep from one side of the room to the other in whatever sequence that feels natural. Relax your eyes and let yourself feel what you're seeing. Anytime something feels off, glimpse down at their hands. This is a great way to catch students cheating on a test.
- If you're a Phys. Ed. teacher or monitoring recess, the same skill will help give your scanning a simple sequence to make sure you're more methodical. Most of us have bad scanning habits initially. We look at the same things in a small loop and neglect blind spots. We need to practice scanning like a security camera, working from one side to the other. You need to teach yourself to be systematic.
- The next time things feel off in your class and you can feel there is tension from some drama that is running through the school at the time, or you see that students are unfocused and suffering from high or low energy, try using a Quiet Eye scan. By looking methodically at the eyes and then glancing at the hands when you feel the need, you'll be surprised by what information you may collect. The Quiet Eye teaches us to look objectively. Often, we will get a feeling that something is wrong in a certain part of the class or with a particular student. Looking at eyes and hands also helps us notice actions and posture. You'll see which students are working normally, and who is looking angry, sad, distracted, etc. Spotting irregularities sooner will help you monitor the mood and climate of your class and give you the

ability to intervene pre-emptively. That may mean building rapport with a student, giving them extra attention, or asking questions to find out what's happening or to help the students vent. We'll look at a few steps you can take in our next exercise.

"In potentially violent situations, it's a good habit to pay attention to the subject's eyes and hands."

The Quiet Eye becomes even more important during moments of escalation, where aggression or violence is possible. Knowing how to scan helps us avoid getting ambushed. Learning to look is not about paranoia or becoming hair-triggered. It's the complete opposite. **Effective tactical vision is about developing efficient calmness and putting your energies where they matter.** Even if we never experience classroom violence in our lifetime, the simple practice of scanning your students in the classroom or as you navigate the hallways will allow you to improve your awareness of your surroundings. Effective vision keeps you connected to your environment. It shows aggressors that you won't be an easy target. As the legendary samurai Miyamoto Musashi said:

"For simply observing things, the eye is naturally strong but for seeing things as they truly are, the eye is weak."

EXERCISE #8:

The next time you're in your classroom, pay attention to how you look around the room. I've been a guest speaker in a lot of classrooms. I've seen teachers who keep their heads down in their work and only look up occasionally, ignoring their students most of the time. When they do look up, they often tend to look at the same one or two spots. They might only look at students they perceive to be problematic or only at their favorite students. No matter where they look, most don't actually process anything they are looking at. They look but don't see.

Try these two simple steps to strengthen your vision and processing skills:

1. First, scan your room sequentially, then look back down at your desk. Try to recreate a mental image of what you just saw from memory. Practice rebuilding a mental model. How clear and complete is that mental image? If you have black holes in your memory, look up to those areas for a second and then back down to fill in the blanks.
2. Second, try to sweep from one side to the other. It doesn't matter if you go left to right or right to left or even up and down rows. Do whatever feels natural but do it the same way every time. When I teach professionals, we use the motto: *"Left to right, up and down, over-under, inside and out"*. As you scan, look briefly at the eyes of every student. If any of the eyes or facial expressions trigger your intuition because they seem odd or stand out, look down at that student's hands. This simple tactical sweep will become natural very quickly. Think of how many opportunities you have in a given day to practice this. You are entitled to achieve effortless, unthinking mastery in very little time.

STORY FROM THE FIELD:

"Luc Cantara"

Luc Cantara is a world-class bodyguard and personal protection expert who has worked for heads of state and some of the highest-ranking public figures in the world. He began his career working for 10 years in night club security before beginning his work with the Royal Canadian Mounted Police where he served for 31 years. 23 of those years were in close-quarter protection and for over 10 years he also worked as a national instructor in self-defense and body guarding. He has protected sitting U.S. presidents, Prime Ministers and royalty. Luc is a bodyguard pro.

To give you some back story on the incident we're about to discuss, the Prime Minister of Canada at the time, Jean Chrétien, had had a number of security incidents in the years preceding our story. In 1995, the province of Quebec where I live held a referendum to separate from the country. They voted against it by an insanely narrow margin of 50.58 percent. That meant that roughly half the province was full of unhappy citizens. As a result, a disgruntled knife-wielding separatist broke into the Prime Minister's residence with the intent to kill him. Chrétien's wife thankfully heard the intruder and locked the bedroom door while Chrétien armed himself with a statue until his security arrived. The following year, as Chrétien was leaving a flag day celebration, his security allowed a mob of protesters to surround the Prime Minister. With his reflexes extra heightened following the attempt on his life, Chrétien famously grabbed one protester by the throat and the nape of the neck and threw him to the ground, then he grabbed the bullhorn of another protester that was shoved into his face and steered him away. This move affectionately became known as the *Shawinigan Handshake*, named after Chrétien's birthplace of Shawinigan, Quebec.

It's now two years later. Luc and his partner were protecting Chrétien. Tensions remained high. In bodyguarding, there are different formations the guards will take around the principal (client). During medium to high-risk occasions, it is common for the core team to use a box formation, where four guards are stationed like corners of a square, each about 2 steps away from the principal. The back can rotate 90 degrees to become a diamond, where one guard, slightly offset, offers more direct frontal protection, one flanks either side directly, and a fourth blocks the rear. In 1998, Luc and his partner were working on a *"close support"* detail, which is when support officers create an outer ring of protection around the box. As Luc said "*they are bodyguarding the bodyguards"* so this will give you some idea of the threat level. When Luc arrived at the hotel where Chrétien was staying, the head of hotel security notified him that one stranger had been mulling around the lobby for 90 minutes already. Luc immediately took notice of the subject as he prepared with his partner. Sometime later, the elevator opened and the Prime Minister and his security detail emerged in formation. As Luc went into position, he noticed the stranger immediately dart towards Chrétien. Luc raced forward, intercepting the subject by creating a human barrier. The subject recoiled his head to spit. Luc grabbed him by the throat, redirecting the spit onto his arm and chest, and drove the subject back through a doorway as the Prime Minister's detail hurried him to his car. Police officers moved in for the arrest.

Now, I realize that as school teachers we would not throat-grab a student for spitting on us. If a student were trying to spit on you in the classroom, I will show you how to shield your head in our physical intervention section at the end of the book. I would advocate protecting your face, creating distance, and using strong verbal commands to control the escalation. Naturally, for Luc, bodyguarding a Prime Minister with a history of attempted assault and assassination, the response needed to be more resolute. What we need to learn from this situation is not how great a throat-grab works. Rather, it's that awareness begins by seeing. It requires continuous observation. You need to accept the potential risk and actively look at and process what is in your surroundings. If you see something that seems unusual, accept it and take responsibility to keep looking. By maintaining constant awareness, Luc was able to intercept someone faster than they could spit.

As one of my mentors used to say, 95 percent of the job is standing in the right place and looking at the right things. A bodyguard's only goal is to protect the client. Despite what Hollywood often portrays, they can't afford to get tied up in fights with aggressors because this creates a breach in security and leaves their clients vulnerable. As classroom teachers, our threats and risks may be far lower and less common, but the same tactic remains true: we must learn to stand in the right place and look at the right things.

EXERCISE #9:

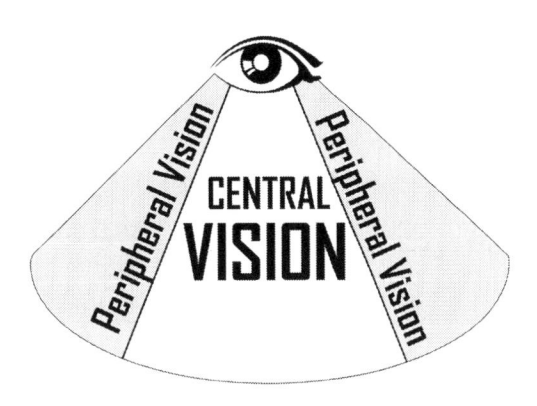

"Field of vision"

Now here is another great drill that will teach you how to use your eyes like a bodyguard. We have two main types of vision:

1- Our *central* (or foveal vision) which concentrates on what is directly in front of us, and
2- Our *peripheral* vision (which registers what is to the side of our central vision).

Our central vision is much clearer and more sensitive to light. Our peripheral vision tends to struggle with details and appears a bit hazier. Our central vision also enjoys the majority of our cognitive processing attention. Our peripheral vision only plays a support role in our overall perception, but it's far more important than many people realize. Our peripheral vision might trigger a flinch response if it registers a blur racing in from the side but on its own, it's not very detailed and can be hard to decipher.

If we ever experience the loss of central vision, from aging or injury, our ocular motor center shifts, placing greater reliance on our peripheral vision.[31] Similarly, we can also learn to shift our cognitive focus intentionally from our central to peripheral vision should we wish to.

Wherever you are, whether you are sitting or standing, I want you to pick a focal point at least three meters away from you. It could be anything: a clock on the wall, a tree, a chair. The best thing would be an actual person because this will add a layer of real-world psychology to it. Now, once you have your focus, I want you to see how far away from that focal point you can look, while still maintaining slight awareness of it in your peripheral vision. For example, if you picked a clock as your focal point, see how far away from the clock you can look, while maintaining some awareness of the clock on the side of your field

---

[31] Treleaven A.J., Yu D., "Training peripheral vision to read: Reducing crowding through an adaptive training method", *Vision Research Volume 171 pages 84-94*, June 2020

of vision. Stay there for a bit and see how much information you can gather about the clock at the limit of your peripheral vision. Can you just see a rough shape? Can you discern any color? Now you are actively working those peripheral muscles. Next, practice moving your head back slightly toward the clock so it's a little easier to see it in your peripheral vision. You will notice you now have more information about the clock as your central vision gets closer to it.

This type of peripheral strengthening is important, but it's just part of the technique. There is a time to rely on our peripheral vision and a time to focus on a subject with our central vision. Now, as you maintain awareness of your focal point in your peripheral vision, I want you to take a glance back at it, for example turning to look directly at the clock for one second, then look away again. You'll notice, by indulging that brief direct glance at the object that when you look away again, you will have more information in your mind's eye. You will have added more information to your "*mental map*". You will remember it in your mind's eye and use that new information to build a more complete image of it. This is also a great way to help support keeping your cognitive brain center in control.

In a hostile situation, this is the exact type of vision we use when scanning a crowd. The focal point (our clock) is like a subject's hands. I can't always stare at their hands to monitor their actions or else I will fixate and lose awareness of their eyes and the intent they reveal as well as everything else in my environment. So, I need to scan the entire room, using their hands as one of my visual anchors. I will scan past their hands but keep them in my peripheral vision. I might glance for a second directly at the hands to gather a bit more information for my mental imaging. If the hands become a threat, I may look at them a little longer when I glance and look a little longer at the subject's eyes and face as well, but I will never stare at them at the complete exclusion of the room around me.

The same vision will apply to trying to determine if a student is cheating on an exam. If you simply stare at them, they may hide their intention every time you look. By comparison, if you keep them in your peripheral vision, you will gather more information without appearing to notice them. Then when you glance back at them, your gaze will be more targeted. Your movement and cognitive processing will also be more efficient because you are already "*on task*", you are more likely to actively register what you are scanning. There will be less delay in your cognitive processing. You will be more likely to see what you are looking at. Even if you glance for a second, then look away, your brain will continue to digest what it just saw and create a more complete image.

The first time you try this drill, it can be exhausting. Your eye muscles will not be used to it. They will quickly get stronger with practice. Your brain will also feel overwhelmed because the skill will still be at a very conscious level. The more regularly you practice it, the more automatic and easier it will quickly become.

EXERCISE #10:

Create a small pack of 26 slips of paper, each about the size of a playing card. On each of these slips, write a single capital letter from A-Z. Shuffle the deck and place it face down on your lap.

- Pick one card and place it about a meter in front of you so you can clearly read the letter with your central field of vision.
- Pick up a second card with your right hand and hold it out to your right side.
- While maintaining direct eye contact with the central card, try to read the second card with your peripheral vision. If you can't see it comfortably, you can slowly move it toward the center until you can make it out. You still want to make it challenging. After you've guessed, you can turn your head to verify it, then look back at the center card to see if your mental image of it is stronger after having looked at it.
- Now put that card down and raise a card to your left side with your left hand. Repeat the drill, guessing, confirming with a glance, then returning to center vision with more information before putting it down.
- Switch from right to left as you move through the deck. For an added challenge, you can keep the peripheral card moving slowly up and down or even shake it more vigorously to challenge your processing skills.

This simple drill is fantastic for building reading focus but will also create transferable improvements in your peripheral vision that translates to everyday awareness.

EXERCISE #11:

Phys. Ed. Teachers have some of the best peripheral vision and processing skills you can have. The reason is, they have to. Gym teachers with poor peripheral skills usually have dodge-ball motivated career changes. There is nothing that will build eye strength and awareness like scanning a screaming gymnasium filled with 30 kids bouncing and throwing balls in every direction. Through constant exposure to that kind of environment, you can develop incredible natural skills. So how can we do this in the comfort of our own homes with less risk of accidental head impact?

- Choose a focus point on the wall in front of you. In training, I like to use a small piece of masking tape and place it at eye level.
- Stand about 1-2 meters from the wall.
- Grab a small, soft ball (a balled-up sock will do, or a ball of tape).

- While maintaining focus on your central target, move your ball hand to your side, until it's outside of your peripheral vision.
- Practice tossing the ball into your field of vision from the side and try to catch it with your free hand.

For added challenges, you can toss the ball on a higher arc so there is a larger gap between your release from one hand and your catch with the second hand. This larger gap in feeling between releasing and catching will challenge your orientation skills. You can also bounce it lightly off of the wall and intercept it with a catch to introduce unpredictability. For the hardest variation, have a partner toss the ball for you so you will have no warning. This simple drill is something that I use with all of my students, from civilians to military to law enforcement, to build peripheral vision strength and processing skills. It is also a staple for bodyguard training and it's a cheap and easy addition to family game night.

EXERCISE #12:

While you're in your classroom or walking the halls, practice oscillating between central and peripheral vision. Try to see how much information you can be aware of and process. This becomes much more difficult when you're also performing a task like walking through a crowd. Remember you can glance at your peripheral target at any point. This will give you more information and also give your eyes and brain a little break. A huge part of tactical vision is managing it and knowing when to use central vision and when to use peripheral.

STORY FROM THE FIELD:

"Carlos Diaz"

So far, we've been focusing heavily on the use of the eyes, so that you'll have some very clear, concrete strategies, to try integrating into your daily habits. Truly observing your environment should include all of your senses, however.

Carlos Diaz is a former United States Army E-4, Specialist. He was an Infantry Rifleman, Scout Sniper for a Reconnaissance (RECON) platoon who served in Afghanistan. I have had the honor of training with Carlos. He notes:

"You need to learn to take the time to STOP, LOOK, LISTEN, SMELL. In the military, we use the term SLLS (pronounced SEALS). Using all of your senses helps you absorb any irregularities that are out of place at any given time in your environment. This is such a small physical action, but if you look deeper at it and embrace the concept, using all your senses will change how you experience your environment. I start every day, from the moment I wake up and put my feet on the floor, by trying to experience everything around me fully."

"We're taught you must crawl before you run, right? Don't you think you should metaphorically look where you'll step first? Be an Observer. In the military, we use the term "Patterns of Life". In my time as a Recon Platoon member, I was taught to always look for daily patterns, individual routines, habits, etc. When we would notice and watch the common population of a given community, we took the time to understand their culture, and to be more informed in all facets of their lives."

"The hardest part of Afghanistan was the fact that the same people you would see during the day that were friendly towards you, could be plotting your death. It was like the moment it turned a certain time of day or a certain day of the week, it would get quiet, then whistles of mortar fire and alarm signals were going off. For me every time a bomb dropped closer to me, it was a mark made by violent enemies inching forwards to achieve their goal. I was an American in a country in which they did not want us and they wanted to kill us."

As teachers, we can benefit from the same tactics. Anyone who has worked in a school environment for any period of time knows that feeling that something is wrong. How many of us just dismiss it and let it go? Let's take a moment now to reset our perceptions. Take a deep breath in. Smell your environment. Listen to it. Notice the taste in your mouth. Feel the air current on your skin, the connection of your body to your chair or your feet to the floor, even your clothing on your skin. Look at everything. What does your environment make you feel right now? Your intuition is a powerhouse tool. It integrates all of your life experiences into a very precise detection system. Take a moment to appreciate what it's saying. You may be surprised by what it teaches you.

TO LOOK OR NOT TO LOOK

When situations become more escalated, sometimes we can become more aware of where we're looking and for how long. Over the years, this has been another area where I've received conflicting advice from experts. I've heard some teachers say:

> *"Always look your aggressor straight in the eyes to show them you're not scared"*, or
> *"Always look them straight in the eyes or else they'll perceive it as a sign of disrespect".*

Meanwhile, other instructors said:

> *"Never look them straight in the eyes or else they'll perceive it as a challenge"* or
> *"Never look them straight in the eyes or else you'll acknowledge there is a conflict and that will make it harder to avoid."*

Again, all of these statements contain some element of truth. The problem is, they're evaluating a symptom rather than the entire situation. The first thing we need to do is not worry about what the attacker might perceive. We can never control how another person will interpret something. Of course, I would ideally like to avoid provoking them, but my first goal is to ask: **what do I need**? What I need is information. I need to know as much as possible about what is going on and about the environment that it's occurring in. As I said earlier, it's impossible to always be ready. We all get surprised, but the minute I notice danger, I need to focus my attention as effectively as possible on that threat and that means using my eyes to gather information about my aggressor(s) and the environment around me. That being said, I don't exist in a vacuum. I need to also consider my aggressor. It's true, they can construe my eye contact as invasive or dismissive, challenging or disrespectful. So how do we balance both?

As a basic rule, **I want to make eye contact**. I need to gauge my aggressor's intention as well as I can. Eye contact must be done respectfully. Our goal is to simply look, not to stare with anger or hostility. Research has shown that something as simple as making brief eye contact with strangers walking past you on the street can increase your ability to interpret their intention and direction.[32] We've already seen that interviews of incarcerated violent offenders revealed that they all selected the same types of subjects. Even though they weren't aware of it, they preferred a target that was disjointed and awkward. When we make eye contact, we are better able to make predictions about strangers. We are also better able to move through our environment. That will immediately contribute to making us look more organized and graceful and make us less likely to be targeted, to begin with. I've worked with a lot of survivors of violence and one of the first things I notice is that the majority of them have the habit of averting eye contact.

Research has also shown that most people make less eye contact with someone who is looking back at them.[33] That means that looking someone in the eyes, even briefly, helps you to define your limits. It's like fencing with your eyes. It shows them that you are aware of them. It makes it harder for the aggressor to build a sense of dominance and gather information about you. Yes, there are definitely alpha predators who will win a staring match with you and feed off of any attempt to be defiant. The good news is that by looking at them directly, you will be able to detect this immediately. If they stare back at you defiantly, look away casually but begin to focus your peripheral awareness actively toward them. It's better to know what type of potential aggressor you're dealing with soon. This is why we don't want to stare at our aggressors. Tactically speaking, staring can create fixation and cause me to lose awareness of my overall environment. It can also increase the risk of being misconstrued as a challenger. Worse than that, if I lose a staring match, it can expose me to feelings of vulnerability. Instead, I want to look directly at the eyes, then look away to a secondary focal point in my environment. If I was far enough away, this can mean glancing at their hands, or other individuals who could be potentially aggressive, then back to the subject's eyes, and so on. Even at extremely close ranges, I can oscillate for a second or two on the eyes, then look at the forehead or slightly to one side of their face.

Effective eye use is a skill we can train every day. It can help us increase awareness, maintain control and discipline and project confidence in our students. Take a few moments every day to pay attention to how you use your eyes.

---

[32] Pelphrey K.A., Viola R.J., and McCarthy G., "When strangers pass: processing of mutual and averted social gaze in the superior temporal sulcus", *Psychol. Sci. 15, 598-603. Doi: 10. 1111/j.0956-7976.2004.—726.x*, 2004

[33] Laidlaw, K. E. W., Foulsham, T., Kuhn, G., and Kingstone, A. (2011). Potential social interactions are important to social attention. *Proc. Natl. Acad. Sci. USA* 108, 5548–5553. doi: 10.1073/pnas.1017022108

STORY FROM THE FIELD:

When I worked in club security, eye contact was a constant dance. While scanning the floor, sometimes I would notice people staring back at me. Sometimes, people would get built up by alcohol and by the urging of their friends saying: *"I bet you could kick his ass"* and so the staring would begin. Other times, like in the story I recounted earlier, people would feel slighted from something that happened to them in the past and they would come in, build up their courage with drinks, and start staring with fixation. Sometimes people just had a bad day and decided they didn't like my face. That happened a lot. I have become convinced I have a highly punchable face. Like the stranger in the hotel lobby that was waiting for the Prime Minister, most of these individuals have a period where they pace around to build up their courage. If you know what to look for and you trust your intuition, you will see and feel that something is just wrong before it happens.

On one particular night, I noticed someone staring at me. He was sitting with a few friends but he wasn't engaging them much. He was just looking past them at me most of the time. At one point, our eyes met for a second, so I gave him a cordial doorman smile and a nod and kept scanning. For the next while, I could feel he was puffed up, accelerated, and waiting, so I avoided making direct eye contact again. He started to drink faster at one point. That's rarely good. I tried to appear uninterested and unaware while I scanned my environment. It was a quiet night and I was working alone. I went over to talk to the bartender to let him know of the potential situation. I asked the barkeep not to look anywhere but just to be ready. Then I got a drink of water. Pre-fight jitters kicked in and I immediately wanted to go to the bathroom, but I couldn't leave the floor. The employee bathroom was also in the kitchen and you needed to walk past the client bathrooms to get to it. Tactically, that could give an angry client an excuse to follow me and the opportunity to ambush me in a tight space. I didn't want to risk it, so I just focused on my breathing and calmed myself down as well as I could. I avoided looking at him directly to not give him an excuse to accelerate, but he eventually got agitated by that too. He got tired of waiting for me. He got up and started to walk towards me. At that point, I looked directly at him. He was staring back at me and about 20 feet away when he nodded his head up and shouted: *"What the f@#k are you looking at?"*. My hands were already clasped in front of my waist and I brought them up into a Fence and responded *"Nothing at all sir. Are you having a good night?"* He got close, but had his hands low. I scanned down to make sure he wasn't holding a bottle, glass or other weapon. His hands were clenched into fists. They appeared to be empty but you can never be sure. He stopped about 2 meters in front of me, hands low, shoulders very contracted. His chin was down. His face was very angry.

"That's none of your f#%king business", he spat.

"Fair enough. Can I get you anything?" I was still smiling politely. Although I was smiling, I was only thinking if he even twitched to attack me, that I would drive forward and through him immediately. In these situations, **you need to fill your short-term memory with one simple plan to stay on task**. Either you're going all the way in, through him, to overwhelm him, or else you're creating distance. There is no in-between. You're in or you're out. The trick is to **not** show what you're thinking and to project politeness and to still try to do everything in your power to avoid the conflict. My only concern was trying to keep things polite. If he moved closer or was holding anything in his hands, I would have ordered him to stand back. At this point, he was doing neither to escalate the threat.

"Yeah, you can do something for me. You can wipe that f#@king smile off your face!"

Now my face became neutral. I looked over the aggressor's right shoulder and saw my bartender was watching. I made direct eye contact with the bartender and shook my head *"no"* with a long, slow left-to-right motion as if I was responding to a request, but my bartender didn't know what I was doing. Truth be told, even if he hadn't been watching, even if no one was there, I would have looked in the same direction and made the same gesture to imaginary backup. Signaling imaginary back up to stand down was a tactic I used all the time. I did this casually, for one second, keeping the aggressor in my peripheral vision, then I looked back at the client directly and smiled as calmly as I could. The aggressor registered what I had done. He took one step back from me cautiously and looked over his shoulder until he saw the bartender looking back at him. There is a natural reflex in us to follow the gaze of others. If you want to test this out, just stop in the hallway and stare up at the ceiling. Watch how many people do the same as they walk by.[34] When the client looked to see where I had looked, he took a step back. If you ever have to divert your gaze, you reduce your reaction time. To compensate, you want to create more distance by stepping back or to the side. When he did this, he showed me he had street smarts. He had probably been in a few fights. It's exactly what I would have done. Even if no one had been there, the confusion and distraction would have given me a break. When he glanced back, I shifted back and away from him to disrupt his control and expectations. Sometimes, when you do this and you watch the subject turn back, they almost seem to lose balance and need to shift and adjust their stance because you're not exactly where you were a second ago. The bartender had both hands on the bar and was staring a hole through the back of the client's head. He wasn't angry. He was just looking blankly.

The aggressor looked back at me then back at the bartender then back at me again. He was visibly agitated. He hadn't expected this and he was distracted. This interrupted the flow of how he had imagined things would evolve.

---

[34] Milgram S., Bickman L., Berkowitz L., "Note on the drawing power of crowds of different size", *Journal of Personality and Social Psychology,* October, 1969

"I hope you have a great rest of the night", I told him. *"Just let me know if you need anything"*. I was polite but intense and quiet. I became curt and more focused. My comments implied the conversation was over.

He shifted a little bit more and looked back at the bartender one more time. I could hear the gears in his drunk brain grinding. He was fully distracted and his expectations had been drastically redirected. Sometimes, this type of shifting can be a nervous precursor for someone building up the motivation to hit you. In this case, his shifting was more nervous than aggressive though. He was fidgeting and thinking more than ramping up. He stepped back another step. When people move toward you, usually they want to escalate. When they start moving away, usually they want to avoid fighting. Sometimes they will try to act defiant as a *"face-saver"*. Sometimes they will insult you and spit and rant because they're embarrassed. You need to expect that and just let it go. It can take a while for aggression to dissipate and there are many junctures where it can be reignited, so if there is no danger to you, let it go. As the old Arab proverb says:

"The dog barks. The caravan passes."

If you ignore taunts and insults, aggressors will often walk away eventually. In this case, his expectations had been interrupted. He hadn't anticipated the bartender as backup. The bartender wasn't particularly imposing. He was small and slim, but he was a second person nonetheless and the client didn't know if he had a weapon or would call the police. A second person is always a problem. Don't believe the movie fantasies. Fighting two people is never easy. At minimum, they're a witness. Even though the bar was full of people, the reminder that a specific person was watching him was what reminded him of the consequences.

Another important thing to understand is that I tried to avoid eye contact to not escalate things, but it didn't matter. Sometimes, even when you do everything right, some people are still going to escalate. Still, you always want to *try* to avoid escalating things. It doesn't always work out like it did that night, but it often does. It also gave me more time to prepare myself which allowed me to act from a place of calmness.

In a classroom setting, if a student begins to escalate, something as simple as pausing the interaction to request something from another student can remind the aggressor that they're not alone. Sending another student to the front office on a task can remind the aggressor about the office, administration, and ultimately that there are consequences to their actions. Sending another student to get another teacher can bring you much-needed backup, which provides both an interruption and greater security.

HAVE A PLAN

How you use your eyes is important, but it's even more important that you have intention. If I only look but don't see, if I don't process and acknowledge what I'm seeing, then all of the looking in the world won't matter. It's like having a shelf full of books but never reading them.

You need to look with a purpose. You need to have a plan. The plan should be as simple as possible. I suggest just having two basic options like:

- I am going to try talking this student down and direct him back to his seat.
- If he advances more, I will make my Fence stronger, my commands stronger, and move away. If he sits down, I will move away and monitor him in my peripheral vision.

I try to stay at step one as long as I can. I try to talk the student down. I try to get them back into their seat. I listen, I redirect, and I use all of my body language tactics and all of the verbal skills we'll see shortly, but in the back of my mind, I am visualizing the worst-case scenario. If they advance more, I know what step I will take next.

Then the next situation would be the same. I would be strong and commanding and define my space. If the subject continued to advance, I would retreat to the door. I don't want it to get to that point. I want to de-escalate. I want the student to go back to their desk, but at that moment, I focus only on the immediate threat. Either they choose action *"a"* and I respond with response *"a"* or they don't and I respond with response *"b"*. I keep every decision that simple or else my brain will start to spin with *"what ifs"*. Left unfocused, our thoughts will race off on tangents and very often we start to over-consider their size, anger, and capacity. We get overwhelmed by their power. When we adhere to a simple *"a"* plan or *"b"* plan, we remain focused on *our* power.

I've had students recount violent encounters who admit they just fixated on one simple goal like: *"I just knew I had to keep my Fence up. I don't remember what I was even saying, but I know I couldn't let him past my Fence. I just kept it up and kept moving to maintain distance. I knew if my Fence would fail, I would have no choice but to fight."* This is a classic example of an *"a"* plan (keep up my Fence at all costs) and a *"b"* plan (or else I needed to fight).

If we look at sports research, we can learn a lot about how we process things under stress. We know that through a combination of looking and relating to what is seen, an athlete can create an accurate forecast of what they think will happen.[35] They need to look at what is in front of them and know what they're looking at. Elite athletes can predict

---

[35] Urgesi C., Makris S., "Sport performance: Motor expertise and observational learning in sport", 2016.

the outcomes of action by reading physical cues. These include the opponent's intentions through (partial) signals, which can be temporal (when they will happen), spatial (where they will perform it), and executive (what kind of action they will choose). [36] An elite performer's reaction is limited to their domain. A world-class soccer player knows what to look for in soccer but they may not necessarily be faster in other reflex tasks outside of their sport. That's because their brain creates sport-specific movement based on motor and visual experience. In other words, it runs through a sequence of movements based on their experience and fills in any missing visual information[37][38] The expert athlete has an anticipatory advantage. They collect visual information from the opponent's movement and create a model in their brain that's based on their experience with similar motions. This helps them to predict what will happen next. A boxer will know that one motion at a distance is a preparation for a strike, but that at one distance, the strike is likely to be a jab, in another position a cross, at closer range an uppercut. All of this information has been gathered from extensive experience and is hard-wired into their nervous system.

So, what does this mean to classroom teachers? In the beginning, if we don't have much experience, then we don't have much of a mental model to rely on. We don't have an anticipatory advantage. That means that every reaction we have will be new and based on whatever stimuli we are actively seeing. Authentic responses like these take more time and we know that means we will need more distance to have that reaction time. [39] As we learn to observe, the more we practice new behavior, the more experience we'll collect for our mental models. That means in the beginning, when we have no experience, distance is even more important. Over time, we'll be able to predict things more effectively and we may be able to operate a little closer. Every time a student gets too close, if we learn to notice this feeling and we train ourselves to casually step back and put our hands up in a natural Fence, it also allows us to subconsciously digest everything that happens:

- How does a person normally move at this range?
- What do they do with their hands?
- Where do they look?

All of these things get subconsciously digested and linked to our experience of that action. We create a mental model of our experience at that distance, just by mindfully

---

[36] deGelder B., "Nonconscious emotions: New findings and perspectives on nonconscious facial expression recognition and its voice and whole-body contexts", Barret L.F., Niedenthal P.M., Winkleman P., (Eds), *Emotion and Consciousness*, p 123-149, 2005.
[37] Komatsu H., "The neural mechanisms of perceptual filling-in", *Nature Reviews Neurosciences, 7 (3), 220-231*, 2006.
[38] Pessoa L., Thomson E., Noe A., "Finding out about filling-in: A guide to perceptual completion for visual science and the philosophy of perception", *Behavior and Brain Sciences, 21 (6), 723-748*, 1998.
[39] Munro H., Plumb, M.S., Wilson A.D., Williams J.H.G., Mon-Williams M., "The effect of distance on reaction time in aiming movements", *Expert Brain Research*, Nov, 183(2) 249-57, 2007

employing the strategy. The clearer the model, the sooner we will detect actions that don't fit and the sooner we will get a warning sign. This is how we teach ourselves to see what we're looking at and to hone our intuition.

Remember to have a simple plan ready like: *"If the student continues to advance, I will create distance and reinforce my Fence"*. Ideally, we would like to create a simple trigger based on a single cue from our aggressor. If the aggressor does "x" I will respond with "y". Distance has been shown to have a negligible effect on action time when pre-cued movements are used since you are not actually selecting a reaction in the moment. Instead, you are triggering a pre-selected response. This is why an expert boxer can evade punches at incredibly close ranges. They don't see each punch coming and then choose an authentic reaction. Rather, when they feel a certain impact or throw a certain punch, they know there are only a limited number of possible outcomes. They know from experience where they are most likely to be hit from and so they move pre-emptively in anticipation. They make an educated guess. When the opponent then throws that high-probability punch from their limited selection of options, it appears as if the expert is psychically predicting them or moving with superhuman speed. In reality, neither is true. This is not a real reaction based on them seeing what is happening. Rather it is a **reflexive assumption based on pre-cued movements learned through training repetitions.**

Remember to stick to the plan. Simple plans improve reaction time. This even applies to things like dealing with an irate parent. Imagine you have a parent who disagrees with your teaching style. They are blaming you for their child failing. There has been a recent escalation in emails and now the parent has shown up at the school unannounced. My *"a"* plan would be to delay the meeting. Explain that you are currently with students or tutoring or otherwise engaged. Explain that you would be happy to meet with them in person but that you just need to schedule a time. Deferring allows you to better prepare for a time when you feel less ambushed while also increasing the likelihood that the parent will de-escalate slightly. I would commit to deferring the meeting. I would not allow myself to meet unannounced. I am simply not able to. I would be polite and apologetic but I would not meet with them.

If you are unable to succeed with your *"a"* plan, how do you wish to proceed? Remember, if you are unable to defer the meeting, that means you are having difficulty asserting yourself and you have volunteered for a huge disadvantage. Nevertheless, your *"b"* plan could be to simply stay factual. No matter how emotional the parent gets, stay factual. Comments like:

"Understood",

"Noted",

"I appreciate you expressing your concern" and then returning to the facts would constitute the majority of what I would say. If I wasn't able to defer the entire meeting, then I would attempt to defer the majority of the decisions to a later date. I would simply be there to listen and then I would commit to looking into the matter and a follow-up plan.

I would not allow myself to be forced to make huge decisions on the spot. You could set a goal like committing to monitor the incident more closely, to keep the parent updated, or even to consult a resource person on staff. We will discuss additional protocols like logging the incident and reporting it to the administration a little later.

Whether the meeting is deferred or spontaneous, backup is always a smart tactical decision. It's a good idea to bring in another member of staff as a witness. You can explain that it's standard protocol to have a witness as part of your school's policy. This will help keep you safe and will reduce the likelihood of the individual escalating too far. If they do, you will have both a witness and another person to help keep you safe.

THE POWER OF WORDS

Now, I'd like to give you some verbal tools to add to the mix. It's difficult to focus on any one aspect too much since everything overlaps and compliments one another so much. The first step is seeing what makes sense to you. Then you can experiment and decide what you like most. Even if you can integrate just a few of these strategies, you will massively improve your readiness for violence while simultaneously becoming a better communicator not just in the classroom, but in life in general.

Now we've all heard the old expression:

"Sticks and stones may break my bones but names will never hurt me."

While I get the intent of this message, the reality is that words do hurt. They are powerful. They can damage our self-esteem. They can harm our self-image for life. They can trigger lasting anger. Cyberbullying, which is just words, has led children to suicide. In the case of violent situations, the words we choose and the way we use them can get us killed. They can be the difference between escalating things and defusing them. We'll be looking at many aspects of verbal de-escalation. The first is what are termed *Alpha* and *Beta* commands.

Alpha commands are any command that is simple, direct, and specific, like *"take 2 steps back"*.

Beta commands are commands that are ambiguous and less clear like *"get back"*.

Many of us don't realize it, but we may lack specificity when we give our commands. Some of our language behaviors are modeled by our environment and influenced by culture and a host of other factors. Sometimes, we weaken our commands in an effort to sound more casual, approachable, or modern. Other times, we've become accustomed to only give commands when things have already escalated too far and we're ready to explode. This leaves our language choices to be made by an emotional brain. The result is that we explode and scream *"Quit it! Knock it off!"* Worse still, if it seems to work well enough in the moment, the decision gets embedded in our toolbox, not because it's efficient, but rather because it didn't seem to fail overtly. That's why we need to heed the advice of the philosopher Seneca:

"Times of security should be used to prepare for harsh circumstances."

I always tell my students that **we can't wait until we are at knifepoint to decide what we're willing to do to survive or what the moral ramifications of harming someone**

are. We need to do that thinking long before the possible fight. Similarly, as teachers, we can't wait until we're in a classroom escalation to realize what words come out in our anger. We need to consciously improve our efficiency when we're calm and test out our language repeatedly in regular circumstances when we have cognitive control if we ever hope to make lasting changes.

The first thing that's interesting in the domain of Alpha and Beta commands is that the majority of the foundational research was not done in tactical circles. Rather, it was completed in the classroom. Alpha commands are a teacher's tool that has been co-opted by tactical circles, so there is ample research and material available on this topic catered just to your needs. **Alpha and Beta commands are essential to being the best teacher you can be**. That means that every day you teach, you have an opportunity to refine these essential skills and become a better teacher while at the same time cultivating a skill that will make you a better interventionist.

Research has shown that there is a direct link between a teacher's effectiveness and the quality of the commands and instructions that they give. Simply using clear commands increases student compliance.[40] This has also been tested and proven to be true with health professionals in hospitals, with law enforcement officers during crisis interventions, and even with elderly patients in long-term care homes.[41] Clear commands become even more essential with individuals who have an increased chance of being confused by instructions. This includes dealing with students who have a specific learning difficulty, are in a state of emotional escalation, struggle with language barriers, trauma, or are under the effects of narcotics and alcohol.

Alpha commands should have **one verb**, requiring one action in each phrase. For example, avoid bundling commands together such as:

> *"Ok, everyone please take out your binders, open them up to a blank page and print your name on the top left corner of the page."*

Instead, it would be far more effective to ask:

> *"Ok, everyone please take out your binders now."*

Then, wait for everyone to comply. If some students are lagging, you can reiterate:

> *"John and Tina take out your binders now please."*

---

[40] Peterson C.A., Reschley D.J., Starkweather-Lundn A., "Training teachers to give effective commands: effects on student compliance, academic engagement, and academic responding", *Iowa State University Psychology Dissertation,* https://dr.lib.iastate.edu/handle/20.500.12876/6399

[41] Christenson A., Buchanan J., Houlihan D., Wanzek M., Command Use and Compliance in Staff Communication with elderly Residents of Long-Term Care Facilities, Minnesota State University, https://doi.org/10.1016/j.beth.2010.07.001, 2011

You want to resolve the first concern before proceeding to the second. It's so easy to get comfortable with how we talk or teach and to take things for granted. It's tempting to just bundle a few commands together. It feels like it will save time. The reality is that sometimes we can get away with bundling commands and those who didn't understand or who were confused may figure it out by watching what everyone else is doing in context. This doesn't change the reality that bundling commands is always a bad habit. It weakens understanding, increases the risk of losing control, and ultimately, it requires more effort in the long run.

STORY FROM THE FIELD:

Tom Dafniotis is one of the best examples of the use of Alpha commands I have ever witnessed. He is a veteran Phys. Ed. Teacher who I've been fortunate enough to work with over the past few years and who I am honored to call a friend. Tom has a reputation for being able to handle even the most problematic discipline issues.

The first time I witnessed him in action, I was already well-versed in Alpha commands and I had considered myself quite good at them. After all, I had used them against people trying to aggressively cause me bodily harm. What better test could there be? I was a guest self-defense instructor at the high school where Tom worked. I could hear his group approaching long before I saw them. This wasn't because they were loud with the normal clamor of a young high school group excitedly approaching the gym for a self-defense class. Instead, the corridor became unusually quiet. Above the silence, I heard Tom almost whispering.

"Alright everyone, so as I told you we are very lucky because we have a special guest today..."

His voice was calm. He described in detail what was about to happen. He told the students that he expected them to be on their best behavior and to listen, to raise their hands if they had questions, and other basics. He gave them one request at a time and waited to get a confirmation after each. Then suddenly his voice rose to a strong command.

"John, face me." Then there was a moment of silence. *"Thank you."*

He continued with his instruction. *"We will enter one group at a time. Enter quietly. No talking. Sit down immediately around the edge of the mat please."* His words were slow, clear, and deliberate.

Then I heard him counting students. *"1,2,3,4 please enter"* and the four appointed students entered. They looked a bit sheepish. Excited but quiet they found the edge of the mat. *"1, 2, 3, 4 next, go"* and so it continued.

As he approached the final group of students, I caught my first glimpse of Tom in the doorway. He was tapping each student on the shoulder with his index finger *"1,2, 3, 4 you may go now"*. Once everyone had entered, Tom followed and said hello. Then he looked at the students who had jumbled up along one edge of the mat. *"Guys why are we all huddled together? Space out around the edge of the mat please"* he insisted and he gestured with his hands. Some moved. Then he walked to one side of the mat where there were the most students and again with a shoulder tap he counted *"1, 2, 3...could you 3 please go to the opposite corner of the mat?"* and they did immediately.

Initially, I thought, ok I guess this guy likes symmetry. It honestly felt this was stricter than I was accustomed to. Before passing the group over to me, Tom said *"if at any point I tap any of you on the shoulder, please leave the mats and wait on the side until I come to you."*

Then I started to teach. Before long the group was getting hyper and loud and more than a few times Tom intervened and within 10 seconds had them quiet again. By the end of the hour, I felt that his group was among the tougher ones that I taught. I had honestly lost control more than a few times and he had reigned them in effortlessly. Every time I saw his group after that, I came to appreciate how Tom conducted them masterfully. I quickly came to realize he was using Alpha commands much better than I was. I realized that while I was very comfortable using them in aggressive contexts, I had a tendency to lower my guard a bit with the younger groups and Tom showed me how effective consistency with commands truly was.

DON'T QUALIFY. BE QUALIFIED

Another detail to be conscious of when you're giving commands is whether you are qualifying your statements. When we qualify our commands, we weaken them. We need to become aware if we are using phrases like:

- *"Would you mind"*
- *"Would it be possible"*
- *"How about"* or
- *"Could we"*

While the intent of using these phrases is to make the commands less aggressive and to make them more positively received, they ultimately make your statements less confident and less likely to be followed. I struggle with this one the most. I often tend to qualify statements and I can tell you from experience that if you do everything else right, you can get away with it in general situations but when things become critical and violence is imminent, it becomes even more important that you tighten up your speech patterns.

Research on police officers showed that officers who used Alpha commands were perceived as being more in control of a situation. Officers who used Beta commands were perceived as being less in control. It didn't matter what the reason for the stop or arrest was. We've all had the experience of having had a teacher who couldn't control their class. If you think back to how they gave orders, they probably used a lot of qualifiers that made their statements too weak to be respected or else were desperate, emotional, and over-the-top. Both extremes show a lack of control and the students can smell the weakness like a shark senses blood in the water.

Now, while we can quickly come to cognitively understand that Alpha commands are stronger, the difficulty comes when stress kicks in. Police officers routinely experience high levels of stress caused by aggression and the risk of violence. Studies on officers have shown that the quality of their commands tends to deteriorate drastically under stress.[42] If it happens to them under stress, it will happen to us. While it is widely established that cognitive processing is deeply hindered by stress and it logically follows that language skills will be equally tested by these decreases, training *will* improve your performance even under the worst of conditions. Just because command quality often deteriorates under

---

[42] Schwarzkopf N., Houlihan D., Kolb K., Lewinski W., Buchanan J., and Christenson A., "Command Types Used in Police Encounters", *Law Enforcement Executive Forum*, 8 (2), 99-141., 2008

stress doesn't mean that it must. A little bit later on, we will discuss how to control our stress levels, specifically through breathing. At this point I will simply introduce the idea that effective verbal commands will also be a great tool to help us ensure more effective breathing and that better breathing will in turn help us stay cognitive and in control of our commands.[43] As we will see shortly, talking can keep us calm and cognitive.

---

[43] Kenneth Gibson J., "Stress p and verbal commands for law enforcement in high-stress situations", *Walden University*, 2021

DON'T THINK OF A LARGE WHITE POLAR BEAR

"Whatever you do, don't think of a
large white polar bear sitting in the room."

In the world of *Neuro Linguistic Programming*, there is a famous attention direction drill that begins by saying:

"Whatever you do, don't think of a large white polar bear sitting in the middle of the room."

Of course, what's the first thing your brain does? It needs to create an image of what the big, white polar bear would look like. Then we need to battle to remove the image we've just created from our thoughts. Our brain processes through images. When we read or hear a word, we create an image of that thing in our mind.[44] This is part of the reason it can be so hard to control cravings. If I'm trying not to snack on chocolate and I think: *"Whatever you do, don't eat chocolate"*, the first thing my brain does is visualize chocolate—sweet, smooth, life-affirming chocolate and of course visualizing chocolate makes that craving just a little stronger and controlling that impulse just a little harder. By comparison, if every time I crave chocolate, I replace that craving with a more positive thought, like, *"I want to eat more fruit so I feel healthier"*, then I am more likely to eat fruit,

---

[44] Sutherland S., "When we read, we recognize words as pictures and hear them spoken aloud: Words are not encoded in the brain by their meaning but rather by simpler attributes such as sound and shape", *Scientific American*, July 1, 2015

which in turn will satisfy my appetite, make me feel healthier, give me more sustainable energy, making it a little easier to avoid that chocolate.

In exactly the same way, imagine you were confronted by a knife-wielding attacker on your way home tonight. You decide the last thing that you want to do is risk your life for a little bit of money and credit cards that can easily be canceled so you blurt out:

> *"Please, I don't want to fight. I didn't even get a good look at your face and I promise I won't call the police. Just don't kill me."*

While you had great intentions, what did your language just do?

- *"Please, I don't want to fight"*. Both of you are now visualizing what a fight might look like. This may introduce unwelcomed images into our thinking.
- *"I didn't even get a good look at your face"*. Maybe he forgot to put on his mask. Maybe he forgot to consider this. You may have just reminded him he could be identified. Now, he begins to panic.
- *"I won't call the police"*. Again, this is not the best thing for him to focus on if you're trying to keep him calm. Now, he's thinking about being arrested and all the possible repercussions. You may just have motivated him to escape at all costs now and get rid of any witnesses.
- *"Just don't kill me"*. Again, now both of you must visualize what killing you might entail. Not the most reassuring image for either of you to focus on. Maybe this will make him angry.

By comparison, imagine if you had said:

> *"Ok, ok. Let's just take a breath. I'm on your side. You just tell me what you need. I'll do everything I can to help you. I just want to get home and see my son."*

This time, all of your words are painting positive images. Breathing to calm down and regain lucid thought. Being on his side. Listening to him. You going home to see your loved ones. None of these are threatening to him. All of them show hope and belief for a better future for both of you. They start to turn you from an anonymous target to a person with an identity and care for him. Mostly, it shows you are listening to him and respecting him.

One of the schools I work at recently installed cameras. I'm not a fan as we'll discuss a bit later on. They came with a zero-tolerance vaping policy. A teacher had caught a student vaping. The teacher was much smaller than the student. The student was agitated, becoming aggressive and challenging the teacher to take the vape from him:

"What are you going to do about it? You want it? Take it then!" It was an overt, angry taunt.

The teacher with the best of intentions responded: *"What are you going to do? Hit me? Don't be stupid. There are cameras everywhere. You're already in trouble. Don't make it worse."*

What did the teacher's language just achieve:

- *"Hit me?"* She just introduced the idea of hitting her.
- *"Don't be stupid."* She just insulted the student. De-escalation 101. Don't swear. Never insult the aggressor.
- *"There are cameras everywhere. Don't make it worse."* While she had good intentions, she has implied the student is already in trouble. This will not help calm him down.

That's a lot of innocent mistakes in a small amount of time that might change the entire direction of the conflict. By comparison, imagine if the teacher had said: *"John, please put the vape away. I'm trying to help you but you need to work with me. There are cameras everywhere. Put the vape away before someone else notices. Come with me. Let's see what we can do."* Now, rather than trying to wrestle the pen off of the student which was creating resistance, you're appealing to them to cooperate. You're introducing a positive image of working together and you're encouraging them to come with you, away from the audience or the isolation, perhaps to a front office, where you can sit them down, and allow them to cool down a little. You're also better able to move them to a more public space where you have more backup, putting you less at risk and giving you more psychological leverage. The result may be the same. The student may get suspended in this case, but there are two major differences:

1. You massively reduce the risk of escalating it into something worse.
2. You show them it's nothing personal. You will work together even though the outcome may not be ideal. When they return from suspension, you initiate contact to check in with them. Show them you care about their safety and that you don't want them vaping. Remember, this student will come back into your environment in a few days. You don't want them to become a vengeful enemy. You want them to be an ally. Always follow up on every disciplinary action. If you handle the situation correctly, this can be an opportunity to create a deeper connection.

We've already seen that Alpha commands are clear and simple. By comparison, Beta commands are ambiguous, confusing, and often jumbled. The next step is to make those Alpha commands even stronger. All of our commands can either ask someone to *start* doing something or else *stop* doing something. Start or stop. When we look at Beta commands, research shows that it doesn't make much difference if we use *Start Beta* or *Stop Beta* commands. If I say:

> *"Listen, I don't know if it's possible but do you think you guys could **stop** talking?"*, or
> *"Listen, I don't know if it's possible but do you think you could please **be** quiet?"* the result is about the same.

One was asked to stop talking. One was asking to start being quiet but both were Beta because they were weakened by too much qualification. A jumbled confusing command is equally weak in both circumstances.

By comparison, in the domain of Alpha commands, *Start Alpha* commands are generally *more* effective than *Stop Alpha* commands. For example, if I say:

> *"Brian, stop chewing that gum immediately"*, the command is simple and clear, and therefore Alpha but it is asking Brian to stop. He could theoretically swallow that gum, spit it out when I'm not looking, or stick it under his desk. Technically, he would be complying with what you asked, particularly if the stop command triggered resentment and resistance. It gives him too much latitude.

By comparison, if I said:

> *"Brian, I need you to spit that gum out in the garbage pail"* I'm not focusing on what I don't want him to do (which gives him a lot of room to interpret). Instead, I'm directing his attention to exactly what I want him to do. This could be made better by moving towards the garbage pail to show him that you are watching him and waiting until he has completed the task. You could point at the garbage pail at the same time or you could bring the pail to his desk, to keep him in his seat, to give him even less wiggle room, and to get it done as efficiently as possible. I could even say: *"Brian, stand up please"* and wait for compliance. *"Please come here"* and direct him to the front of the class next to the garbage pail. As Brian approaches, create distance for tactical safety and move away. *"Please spit your gum into the garbage."*

Earlier, we looked at how powerful tactical vision techniques like the *Quiet Eye* can be. We noted how the more you practice correct vision, the more consistently it will emerge. We also saw that it's unlikely you will be able to always maintain constant Quiet Eye focus. In fact, research has shown that the *"unquiet eye"*, or general unfocused vision, may be just as useful in non-targeting situations if for no other reason than it gives your cognitive processing a break.[45] In the same way, the more you practice Alpha commands, the more natural, constant and automatic they will become. Still, it's unrealistic to expect us to *never* use Beta commands. Beta commands come out naturally in casual speech, especially where we have deeply rooted habits. Beta commands can seem softer and help build rapport. Sometimes, Beta commands in general speech will emphasize the seriousness of an Alpha command because of the stark contrast they provide. Just remember that anxiety will also make processing speech and implementing cognitive strategies more difficult.[46] When we get stressed, we're more likely to see any stimulus as threatening.[47] Once we start losing control, we can quickly spiral so when we sense aggression building, it's time to tighten up control of our language and to steer a situation away from escalation, it's time for Alpha commands. Unless the habit of employing Alpha commands is trained to become reflexive, they are unlikely to come out. So, be mindful of your everyday instructions and make a continual effort to simplify and strengthen your speech. Replacing one bad verbal habit with a powerful one may make all the difference in a crisis.

EXERCISE #13:

Think of recent instructions you may have given to your students or others:

- How do you feel they were received?
- What did your audience's facial expressions look like while you were giving the instructions?
- What did their body language look like?
- Did everyone pay attention to your instructions?
- Did anyone need more clarification?
- How rapidly and accurately did the group respond?
- Do you feel your commands were as clear and concise as they could have been?

Choose one element of your speech that you wish to improve.

---

[45] Foulsham T., "Functions of a quiet and un-quiet eye in natural tasks – comment on Vickers", *Current Issues in Sport Science 1*, 2016

[46] Mathews A., & Mackintosh B., "A cognitive model of selective processing in anxiety", Cognitive Therapy and Research, 22(6), 539–560. https://doi.org/10.1023/A:1018738019346, 1998

[47] Bishop S., Duncan J., Brett M., & Lawrence, A.D., "Prefrontal cortical function and anxiety: Controlling attention to threat-related stimuli", *Nature Neuroscience, 7, 184-188.* doi:10.1038/nn1173B, 2004

EXERCISE #14:

Think of a situation that you encounter frequently where you are required to give commands. Get a sheet of paper and write down a brief script depicting how you would typically deliver those commands. Honestly write down the language that reflexively comes to mind. Once you've written your script, take a good look at it word by word.

- Is every command as simple and direct as it can be? Remember to only have one verb/action per command.
- Are you focusing on what you *want* them to do rather than what you don't want them to do? Remember the most effective type of commands are "*start*" commands rather than "*stop*" commands.

STORY FROM THE FIELD:

There are exceptions to every rule. While it is a general rule that we should always strive to keep our language positive, it's important that you also work in a way that suits your nature. Case in point, Jordan Bill, the veteran bouncer and bartender that I introduced earlier. Jordan often would employ the exception to this rule—complete negativity. On some occasions, when he had an aggressor who was still lucid enough to logically process language, he would say things like:

> *"Listen, I have no doubt you can beat the crap out of me. Obviously, you're going to win. But where does that leave you? You beat the crap out of me. They call the cops. Then you spend the night in jail. Maybe you get charged. I go to the hospital and you go to jail and that's your whole night. Obviously, I would rather not get the crap kicked out of me but if that's what you want to do, if you want to lose your whole night and spend it talking to cops, get arrested, maybe charged, have that on your permanent record, then obviously there's nothing I can do to stop you. It's your call. I'd rather just finish my night and forget about this whole thing. But, it's up to you."*

Jordan has a very deep voice, an even tone, and a dry self-deprecating wit that allows him to deliver this with a bored baritone. You can't fake this type of script. It has to be who you are and how you feel. One of the most important takeaways from Jordan is that sometimes the most effective way to use a principle is as a guideline that can be violated. In the end, you, the unique individual, matter more than any system, strategy, or principle. Remember that motive matters more than method.

TONE

The words we use are just one component of how we speak. There is also our *paralanguage*—all of the support structures that help convey the intent and meaning of our words. They include our *tone, pitch, volume*, and speaking *speed*. It also includes the pauses between our words, gasps, sighs, grunts, and other non-verbal vocalizations. We employ paralanguage all the time, without thinking about it, but we can also consciously employ paralanguage to help convey our message more efficiently.

I've conducted training around the world. I've taught students of all ages from children to seniors, civilians to basic military, special forces, beat cops, specialized teams, bodyguards, and everything in between. A lot of this training addressed the role of paralanguage. Very often, no matter how politely I present suggestions for improving this part of our communication, people get defensive. It can be very personal to evaluate how we sound and it can be difficult to change habits that we use hundreds if not thousands of times every single day.

I struggled with my own paralanguage for a long time when I was younger. I have a Canadian accent from a province where English is spoken by less than 8 percent of the population and where conducting business in English is illegal. To attend English school, you need to have at least one parent who was born here and they had to have attended their education in English. It's Orwellian at best. The French that *is* spoken by the majority is bastardized and has wandered far from the original seed planted over 400 years ago by French settlers. As an English speaker, I bastardize that bastardization even further having learned to speak from resentful English-speaking teachers who were forced to conduct classes in French and often ill-equipped to do so. Then, I inadvertently throw those fractured expressions into English and mash the two languages together at random. I also had a lisp when I was younger that I've worked hard to correct. I still retract my s's and tend to make more of a "*sh*" sound when I try to make "*ss*" sounds and as a result, I naturally feel that Sean Connery was the best Bond. Some things are tough to change. At the same time, I've made massive improvements to my breath control, how I project my volume, my pacing, and the use of my pauses. I've been consciously working on how I speak for 30 years and made a lot of important corrections but it's still a work in progress and I'm always improving. Initially, it can be awkward to deconstruct the way we speak, but once you begin to honestly explore improving your paralanguage, the benefits and rewards will offset the awkwardness and self-consciousness. No one is a perfect speaker and everyone who becomes a great communicator has to work at it.

Tone is one of the easiest places to start. Our tone is largely affected by our genetics. It's governed by the shape and size of our vocal cords, the volume of our lungs, and even our height and weight. It's also influenced by mimicking our parents and the people around us, so there are regional and cultural factors at play as well. Some of us will have structural abnormalities, different emotional baseline states, even allergies, all of which can factor in. Tension and stress will also tend to cause our vocal cords to contract and make our voice more nasally. Nevertheless, tone can always be improved and there are some simple things we can do to train our voice and to maximize our potential.

EXERCISE #15:

Take some time to warm your voice up. This can include:

- **Massaging your throat** for a few minutes.
- **Stretching your throat.** Raise your chin up to the sky and breathe deeply. Practice stretching your lower jaw, jutting it forward past your upper jaw a few times. Practice extending the tip of your tongue past your lips like you are trying to touch the tip of your nose.
- **Taking a deep breath in.** Then breathe out with a long, slow hum. Practice maintaining the longest, most even hum possible. Every time you exhale, try to vary the tone of the hum. Not only is this a great way to strengthen your voice, but it will also build up your lung capacity and teach you how to manage the release of your breath.
- **Practice speaking in different tones.** As strange as it sounds, if you practice reading out loud and play with the tone you use, you will discover you have a lot more range than you might realize. Unless you explore it, you're unlikely to discover it.
- **Practice breathing exercises.** A little later, on I will give you some great breathing exercises. At this point, it suffices to just take a few minutes to breathe deeply. Simply bringing awareness to your breathing and playing with long full breaths can create huge changes in your lung volume, breath awareness, and control.

Remember, under conditions of stress, your brain function will be deeply affected. You will not process information the same way as you do in less emotional states. While it's true that stress will try to rob you of your best tone, through awareness training and breath control you can massively counter these effects just like professional singers do every time they take the stage. Your aggressor will also usually be suffering from as much altered brain function as you, if not more. **Your aggressor is far more likely to be ahead of you in their primal trigger state.** They may be struggling to process what you say. By mindfully controlling your tone, you will help the receiver more accurately and efficiently process the words you are saying. Paralanguage improves understanding.[48]

---

[48] Helrich H., Weidenecher P., "Impact of Voice Pitch on Text Memory", *Swiss Journal of Pscyhology 70 85-93, 10. 1024/1421-0185*, 2011.

STORY FROM THE FIELD:

"Mike Malpass"

There are few people who I respect and am inspired by more than Michael G. Malpass. Mike is a veteran martial artist and former heavyweight kickboxing champion. He has been in law enforcement for over 24 years as a beat cop, a tactical training officer, and a member of SWAT. He is a pioneer in defensive tactics who has developed numerous training programs over his career. Mike is the author of *"Taming the Serpent: How Neuroscience Can Revolutionize Modern Law Enforcement Training"* and *"Fall Seven, Rise Eight. A Kaizen Approach to Law Enforcement and Life."* I've worked closely with Mike in developing intervention programs and he has been a huge influence on my work. Here is a story that Mike graciously recounted to me:

> *"This situation occurred about fifteen years ago while I was assigned to the SWAT team. A squad of patrol officers had encountered a fifteen-year-old male. When they made contact with him, he pulled out a folding knife and placed it against his neck, and was threatening to kill himself. At the time of this incident, the male subject had not committed a crime and the initial reason for stopping him was to check his welfare as he was walking in the middle of the roadway. When the officer initially cleared the radio dispatcher to advise of the situation, I happened to be in the area on other business. I arrived to see the male subject sitting on the front porch of a house with several officers surrounding him and shouting commands. The young man had a knife in his*

right hand and was holding it with the point of the blade shallowly inserted into the left side of his neck. His posture was bent over from the waist placing his body weight onto the blade and drawing a small amount of blood."

"The juvenile did not appear to be overly distressed, in fact, he appeared to be eerily calm like the demeanor you get when you don't even have the energy to be angry or upset anymore."

"The officers were all yelling various commands and standing within ten feet of the knife. The commands ranged from "drop the knife" over and over again, to "get on the ground" or "show me your hands."

Shortly after I arrived, another member of my SWAT team who was also in the area, arrived on the scene. Several problems could be quickly identified:

1. All the officers are **too close** and due to this close proximity they could be easily enticed into a lethal shooting of a young man who obviously needed help.
2. Four people shouting emphatic commands does nothing but **confuse** and exacerbate a situation that is already getting out of hand.
3. No one was trying to communicate with the boy. Instead, they were commanding him to do different things.
4. Officers were preparing to use a taser on the boy from behind him not realizing that the shock from the taser could pitch the boy's body weight forward thus impaling him on the knife.

"The total intensity of the scene was dialed up and momentum was building toward action when what was needed was a chance to slow things down and gather more information to see how we could help. In other words, we needed to exit-cop mode safely, and open up the lines of communication to see if there could be a peaceful resolution to the problem."

"Dave, the other member of my SWAT squad and I directed the officers to move back and take positions that would put a barrier between themselves and the knife-wielding subject. Dave and I also took positions that placed a barrier between us and the subject. This was now our scene and our responsibility. Dave armed himself with a taser but was only going to use it if the subject stood up and started walking toward officers, hopefully not with a knife against his neck."

"While I had been to schools on negotiations and dealing with people in distress, I always found some of the initial formalities of the training a little too technical. Obviously, you have to build rapport and for me, it usually started *with a statement that has nothing to do with the immediate problem at hand as a measure of how much cognitive bandwidth the subject was currently using or willing to use. I said something to the effect of, "man, sometimes life goes by so fast, you never get to take a breath and see where the hell you are at. Does that ever happen to you?"*

"This doesn't always gain a response but a non-response also tells me some things. In this case, he turned his head sideways and made eye contact with me, and nodded his head slightly."

"At this point, he can only see me and Dave as everyone else is giving him room. Dave and I are about twenty feet away and are using a barrier to inhibit the subject's movement toward us to buy us time to respond. I am armed with a rifle but I am not pointing at him and Dave has a taser also not pointed at our subject. We are confident in our capabilities and don't need an overt show of force at this point."

"Given his head nod in response to my statement, I responded with something to the effect that "we had plenty of time right here and now to slow down and take some time to process." He didn't respond verbally but instead, let out a long slow sigh of breath. I was then able to get his name and find out that recently both his parents had been killed in a car crash and his girlfriend had broken up with him because he wasn't able in his grief to go to the many summer parties happening around the neighborhood. We talked for about an hour and then he agreed to give up the knife and allow us to get him some help from a medical professional. We had built up a good rapport with him and he agreed to let fire personnel treat his wound then take a trip to the hospital for a psychiatric evaluation as long as Dave and I accompanied him."

"The key takeaways from this are that **life does in fact happen relatively fast at times and the human brain doesn't process information well when this is happening**. When it is safe to do so, slowing things down by buying space and time and remaining calm, can make all the difference in the world between an incident like this turning violent or a peaceful resolution. There are no guarantees in life but time, distance, and calmness, used correctly, can slow things down relatively speaking and provide the best opportunity to enact a peaceful resolution. The final learning point is, **if you give your word, keep it**. We stayed with him until he agreed the doctors were going to help him and he thanked us for being there for him when it seemed like no one would. If you don't keep your word and this incident occurs again in the future, he will be less likely to believe anyone he is talking to."

PACE

The next aspect of paralanguage to look at is your pace. We all have a natural **rate of speech**. I think and speak very quickly. As a teacher, a coach, and a public speaker, faster rates of speaking often help me to boost the energy in a room and command attention. Faster speaking does *not* help me with comprehension, however, so I had to learn to slow down. There was a long period in my life when I was more concerned with energy than content. The first place I learned to slow down was during conflicts. When situations accelerated around me and became stressful and emotional, it was even more important that I slowed down, but this took a lot of conscious effort and practice to improve. Most people freak out under stress. They start babbling or else they become monosyllabic grunt machines and get silent at all the wrong times. That's an ineffective state I like to call "*Caveman Hostage Negotiator*". The reason this happens under conditions of stress is that our basic fluency becomes impaired.[49] Any time we experience higher levels of emotional stress, the areas of our brain that control memory and complex thought become inhibited, and the hypothalamus, pituitary and adrenal glands are triggered.[50] Stress makes us breathe faster and makes our vocal cords get tenser which can affect our tone and speed. Very verbal people tend to babble. Very quiet people tend to stay too quiet and pause too long. Making things even more complicated, when we speak faster, we are more likely to be perceived as being more stressed which can in turn escalate our listeners.[51] By comparison, when we fail to respond quickly enough, we can be seen as non-cooperative. Either of these extremes can irritate an already escalated aggressor.

---

[49] Buchanan T.W., Laures-Gore J.S., Duff M.C., "Acute stress reduces speech fluency", *Biological Psychology Volume 97, pages 60-66,* March 2014

[50] Saslow L.R. et al, "Speaking under pressure: low linguistic complexity is linked to high physiological and emotional stress reactivity", Published online Dec. 20, 2013. Doi: 10.1111/psyp.12171

[51] Francis R., "An examination into the effects of speech rate on perceived stress in monolingual and bilingual populations", University of Chester, Rachel_Francis[1].pdf (mmu.ac.uk), 2018

EXERCISE #16:

The good news is that we can change our pacing.[52] This begins by being aware of how fast we normally talk. On a scale of one to ten, 1 being a sedated-sloth-moving-through-a-swimming-pool-filled-with-molasses-slow and 10 being you had 4-coffees-and-a-Red Bull-before-6 am and are beginning to see the movement of molecules hyper-fast, how slowly or quickly do you think you normally speak?

- What gives you this impression?
- Do people regularly tell you that you speak slowly or quickly?
- Do they complain about it?
- How do you think your regular rate of speech enhances or injures how well you are normally understood?

The next step is to try playing with your rate of speech. In one of your next everyday interactions, try to change your rate of speech.

- If you think you are on the slower side of the spectrum, try slightly increasing how quickly you speak. If you feel that you normally speak too quickly, try to slow it down just a little.

Ideally, you would like the change to be so slight and subtle, that your listener won't specifically notice. They may notice an overall difference in feeling but you don't want them to say *"Why are you talking so quickly or slowly?"*. They may however remark *"Are you feeling a little tired today?"* or *"Is something wrong?"* or even *"It sounds like someone had their coffee this morning."* The change may even be so subtle that they don't notice anything. The only thing that matters is that you try to control your rate of speech.

In my former life, I was a call center manager and trainer. In that job, I had the responsibility of training a wide variety of employees from young students paying their way through school to seniors supplementing their retirement salary. Their language skills varied massively, with every manner of tone, pitch, confidence, and accent you can imagine. In that job, I was constantly managing paralanguage. I would have 30-minute periods in the day where we might try to speak a little more slowly and deliberately as an office. Other times we tried to speak a little quicker. Arbitrarily playing with our rate of speech kept the job interesting and forced us to bring deliberate mindful focus to

---

[52] Meyer A.S., Wheeldon L., van der Meulen F., Konopka A., "Effects of speech rate and practice on the allocation of visual attention in multiple object naming", *Front. Psychol.*, https://doi.org/10.3389/fpsyg.2012.00039 *20 February 2012*

aspects of our speech that were otherwise so reflexive we took them for granted. That awareness always brought change and improvement and usually correlated to a spike in sales. Attention and focus lead to growth.

The Chinese philosopher Chuang Tzu said:

> *"The wise person hears of the correct way and thinks of it always.*
> *The average person hears of the correct way and thinks of it occasionally.*
> *The fool hears of the correct way and laughs. For if they did not laugh, it would not be the correct way."*

I often use the maxim with my students. Any time we try to adopt a new habit, we tend to go right to the extreme of thinking of it like some type of new diet that needs to be constantly enforced. In doing this, we focus on the effort and inconvenience involved in changing rather than the benefit. As we all know, most of us struggle to0 we talk. That will be extremely difficult to sustain. We just need to think of it occasionally and explore, experiment, and try. In Chuang Tzu's words, we don't need to be wise. We just need to be average. Every effort that we make improves awareness and contributes to lasting change.

As educators, our day is filled with opportunities to communicate. Dedicating a few minutes here and there to play with your rate of speech can bring a new appreciation to parts of your job that you had taken for granted and it can help keep things interesting. This is another one of those skills that can give you immediate advantages in the classroom while giving you more tools for your crisis intervention toolbox should the day ever come that you need them.

●●

THE POWER...OF PAUSES

Our next skill is tightly connected to pace but it also carries a host of other advantages as we'll see. It's the skill of using pauses. At its simplest level, pausing breaks speech up into bite-sized chunks and lets the listener digest it more easily.[53] In every circumstance the listener needs time to process what we are saying. This becomes even more important if the speaker is talking quickly. Pausing gives the listener's brain time to catch up to yours. If you are a particularly fast-talker like I am, massively slowing down your rate of speech can be difficult. Learning to inject pauses can be a much easier fix.

The key to adding pauses is to make sure that they fall at the end of units of speech. Naturally, we don't want to pause in the middle of a word. That will just make you harder to understand. In the same way, we should never pause in the middle of a phrase. For example:

- In regular speech, if we were using longer...sentences, we would not want to pause where I just did.
- If we were using longer sentences...we would want to pause between two phrases.

Think of it as finishing a part of your thought. The pause will give the listener time to digest a full thought that they can make sense of.

Of course, as we've seen, the more stressed we get, the more we should try to keep our thoughts short. We should also try to focus on using Alpha commands. Ideally, we would therefore be pausing at the end of a complete command:

"John please take 2 steps back...Lean against the wall...thank you."

---

[53] Bae R., "The effects of pausing on comprehensibility", *Iowa State University Dissertation*, 2015

STORY FROM THE FIELD:

I was teaching staff at one of our area hospitals. Normally, we trained in a physiotherapy gym but due to some renovations. we were forced to temporarily relocate to the gym in the psychiatric day ward. The ward was voluntary and usually housed very mild cases, but it also took walk-ins from the street which could vary in intensity quite drastically. The security could be lax. On this particular day, a man in his twenties walked in and started pacing in front of the reception desk. The receptionist was somewhat accustomed to dealing with people in various emotional states so it wasn't yet something that was out of the ordinary. She later recounted she was on the phone at the time and she assumed he was just pacing a little as he waited. The minute she put the phone down, he turned explosively and lurched at her. He knocked her paper tray everywhere and spilled her cup of water over onto her keyboard. Reflexively, she moved back from her desk and started pulling out tissues to mop it up. In that moment of distraction, the stranger grabbed a pen from her desk and started rhythmically stabbing the palm of his hand, muttering in gibberish. She paused, naturally startled, then motioned for her phone but realized it had fallen onto the floor. As she slowly went to pick it back up under the guise of reorganizing her desk, he pushed behind her desk, causing her to roll back in her chair up against the wall. Now she was effectively trapped and he was far too close and between her and her phone.

There was no security nearby at the time. I was on my way out from my class, sweaty, lugging a hockey bag filled with gear. I had to walk through the reception area to leave. This is when I came upon the scene, catching a glimpse of the subject from behind. I could see the receptionist leaning all the way back in her chair against the wall. Her hands were up. Her face was quite calm all things considered. She had worked there for some time. It took a minute for my brain to process what I was seeing. I slowly put my bag down in the narrow hallway and took a step forward in the small gap that remained on the floor but at that moment the subject turned around screaming. I don't think he had heard me coming. It was just bad timing. He saw me and his eyes grew more intense and he walked towards me, holding the pen in front of him. It didn't register that it was a pen. I thought it was a knife at the time and only noticed that his hands were bloody. I stepped back into my hockey bag, stumbled a step into the wall, and then slid back along it until the bag was between us both. I was trying to figure out where the blood was coming from. My hands immediately went up into a Fence and I said:

"Hey weren't you here earlier?" I had no idea if he was. It was just the first thing that came to my mind. He looked down at the hockey bag, then kind of swayed left and right and looked behind himself and then back at my bag. He was always muttering but I couldn't understand him.

"Didn't I see you a little earlier?" I asked, trying to put a cordial smile on my face. In fact, I was thinking *"not today"*. I thought I might be killed and I was teetering on the edge of self-pity. I was so exhausted. It was terrible timing. I didn't feel particularly strong. I could feel my breath wanting to race away from me and I tried to slow it down. He turned to the receptionist and scream gibberish, then snapped back to face me and just shouted a guttural noise. I paused and repeated: *"I think I saw you outside, as I was coming in"*. My heart felt like an angry little monkey trying to punch its way through my ribcage. At this point, I managed a slightly larger smile. His eyes were darting all over the place but the times they did look at me, I felt as if my words were registering somehow. I felt like he could see me. He seemed to be trying to think about what I was saying but my words were competing with a few different radio stations that were playing simultaneously in his brain. I also remember thinking I had to look calmer. I was trying to quiet down a lot of negative self-talk. I tried to make my eyes kind and looked right at him for a few seconds. I knew I didn't want to move closer toward him and I was very aware of the hockey bag between us. It felt like we were silent for a long time. I was afraid to say something stupid but it became clear that if he started to walk past the hockey bag, I would need to attack and I was trying to conserve my energy for that.

"Would you like someone to help you?" I paused. I could see the words sinking into his brain as his eyes focused and flickered. Then his eyes started flicking left and right as if he was looking at my left eye and then my right alternatingly. He wasn't looking around the room as much anymore and I could feel the weight of this newfound focus. I had experienced this type of eye movement before with some clients at the bar. When eyes that are darting around in a state of disassociation suddenly start to fixate on you, it can feel like a crushing weight. I just kept thinking about calming my breath. I tried to focus only on one of his eyes or else to scan the environment quickly. I managed to see the receptionist. She was picking things up from the floor. I didn't have the presence of mind to notice this included the phone. I was consumed by the stranger's intensity. At this point, I looked back at him. There was a lot of blood on his hands. I remember his hands being fully gloved in blood and it thinning near his elbow and dripping to the floor. I had the hopeful thought that maybe he would pass out from blood loss. There was so much blood I still couldn't tell it was a pen. My crisis-brain focus was being swatted all over the place with every odd detail. I was struggling to focus on staying calm and looking at his eye and the environment in a slow loop. It felt like an eternity.

"Are you hurt?" I asked shifting my expression from a smile to a look of sincere concern. This gave me an excuse to look at his hands. I looked at his eyes, then back at his hands and I pointed to them slowly and softly. He finally looked at his hands. Now I was sure the words were getting in.

"Put that down and we can wash your hands." I paused. I still didn't know what he was clenching in his bloody hand but I knew I didn't want to get stabbed with it. For a second

I thought I had made him mad. It was very quiet. Then I pointed over to the chairs in the waiting area. *"Sit down and we can wash your hands. Just put that down and sit down."*

I paused again. He paused. He stared at me blankly. Now I actually wished his eyes would start shifting again but instead, they just stayed so completely locked on me that I had to keep taking breaks to look at his hands. I expected him to pounce. His intensity was smothering. It seemed like his stare was muffling all of the sounds in the room. Then, just like that, he dropped the pen on the floor. It bounced out of sight. I heard it but didn't see where it went and he turned abruptly and marched to the wall, muttering more loudly now. He sat down and started rocking. At that point, a member of the security team came in through the front door. He was coming back from lunch. He froze for a second and we explained that we had someone that needed medical attention. He was on full alert. He radioed in a code White, indicating there was a violent incident. That would bring backup. I waited until they came. I stayed to keep the subject calm and assured him we were getting him help. He stayed very quiet, muttering a few low sentences. Backup came and protocol took over. They contained him, cleaned and wrapped his palms, and brought him inside where he would get help. By the time I picked up my hockey bag to leave, my body was drowning in adrenaline. I slung the bag over my shoulder and I felt it squish into my t-shirt. I was saturated with sweat. I was shaking so much I could hardly open the door. I remember how good the sun and fresh air felt.

That incident was not the most dangerous I had ever faced, but I remember the pauses so clearly. They seemed so long. The stress was oppressive, but it was those pauses that let me regain control of myself and the situation. I remember a lot of self-talk occurring. A lot of situations are like that—little mental tug-o-wars filled with self-doubt and fear and even anger. I doubted myself and then had to reaffirm myself in the moment. The brain works very fast in situations like these. I remember consciously breaking eye contact because the intensity of his mental state was so strong that it was eerie. I was completely taken by surprise. I had been looking forward to a walk down the hill to the metro station on a beautiful summer day. I was only thinking of the sun as I approached the lobby. I could not have been less ready.

Even now, as I think back to watching the staff tend to his palm, I realize that could have just as easily been my face, pierced and punctured and being patched up by those workers. Things could have played out very differently. Pauses saved me that day. They gave me the time to slow things down and regain cognitive control, both of myself and the situation.

TAKE A BREATHER

Another advantage of taking pauses is that it allows you to catch your breath. Stress can make your heart rate spike instantly. In that escalated state, even the smallest amount of exertion can leave you gasping. When I worked in bar security, I was usually exhausted just from being up all night and trying to sleep during the day. I relied on too much caffeine to stay alert and on a given night my energy and awareness had a few peaks and crashes. Whenever I found myself in an aggressive altercation, I learned early on that using pauses was a great way for me to catch my breath, orient myself, and to get into the zone. Pauses let me warm up quickly and get into character. They let my body systems come back online.

• •

EXERCISE #17:

From these experiences, I learned the importance of working breath limitations and recovery into my training. I started doing brief periods of intense cardio in my training to get gassed, then instead of waiting to recover before becoming verbal, I would try to use talking as a way to regain my breath. I would recite the St. Crispin's day speech from Henry V while skipping. I would say my lesson plans out loud as I jogged along the river. Anything that would get me gassed and challenge me to be verbal.

What I quickly learned is that in the most gassed states, when my lungs were burning like ghost peppers in my chest, the easiest trick was to:

- Take a short inhale, like I was sniffing with a runny nose.
- Speak a small phrase on my exhale.
- Then, repeat it over and over until I regained my breath.

Speaking in small blurbs, with breaths in between, did a few things:

1. It allowed me to get my breath back in small sips. We've all had the experience of being out of breath and then trying to take a huge breath in but it seems impossible. That's because our emotions want a huge inhale but our lungs are full of CO_2 so there's no room. By taking a short sip in, we slightly indulge the emotional and physical need for oxygen but then by talking, we prioritize a longer exhale, so we

can empty the carbon dioxide to make room for our next breath. Think of it like taking smaller bites when eating. Smaller bites are easier to chew and digest. So are smaller breaths.
2. By taking a shorter inhale, then trying to speak a slow, fluid, phrase, I continue to have the breath I need to speak and I can use my speech as a way to help ensure fuller exhales.
3. By pausing to breathe in between phrases, I also break my speech up into bite-sized pieces for the listener, with each pause giving them time to process my words and giving me more time to formulate my strategies.

Speaking and breathing in interchanging bursts has changed the way I approach stress vocalization. So here is a simple exercise to practice this skill:

- **Begin with taking a deep breath in by the nose.**
- **Hold your breath.** While you hold your breath, try not to add pressure to your face. Don't bloat your cheeks or strain your eyes. Try to keep the pressure in your throat and below as if you could close an imaginary valve in your throat. Pretend you are trying not to show any of the effort required for you to hold your breath. No one should be able to tell you are holding your breath. This will mentally help you assert control over your body and it creates the good habit of not showing your opponent your stress.
- **When you need to exhale, practice reading this text out loud.** Rather than just reading as you normally would, however, break it up into small chunks. Breathe out as you read a phrase. Pause. Breathe out more on your next phrase…then continue until you need to inhale.
- **When you do need to inhale, just take the smallest sip of air in through your nose and then immediately continue exhaling on your next phrase.**
- **Repeat this for a few minutes then breathe normally.**

When we are stressed and running out of breath, we have the reflexive habit of wanting to breathe in too much. In reality, however, what we usually need to do, is get rid of the gases that are in our lungs to make room for more oxygen. Although oxygen deprivation makes us fixate on the idea of breathing *in* and can make us want that extra deep breath, we rarely need as much breath as we think. I equate it to fasting. When we fast, we naturally get very hungry. It's normal to fixate on food. When we finally get to eat again, the last thing we want to do is have a huge meal. Our body won't handle it well, especially if we've been fasting for multiple days. Instead, we need to ease ourselves into eating again, having small meals that are easy to digest, maybe just a vegetable broth or fluid, then soft foods and work our way up. The longer we fast, the slower and more carefully we need to reintroduce food. It's the same with breathing. When we are deeply out of breath, every part of us wants to gasp and suck in all the air in the room but this will just add more tension to your body and force you to exert more energy that in turn requires more oxygen. Instead, we need to train ourself to realize that we rarely need as much air to recover as we think. By immediately exerting control over our breathing, we can better handle our emotions and impulses and regain cognitive control much more quickly from the fear and emotions that are trying to hijack us.

STORY FROM THE FIELD:

"Stewart Breeding"

Stewart Breeding is a master-level fitness trainer and strength coach. A combat veteran with the 82nd Airborne Division, he is the author of Limitless (2010), Biohacker (2017), and Total Warrior (2021). I can think of no other human being that I have ever met who embodies the superhero Wolverine more completely. Compact, seething in intensity, his diamond-hard stare convinces you immediately that he is a coiled spring set to release. Stewart begins training with renewed intensity when most individuals choose to quit.

When we discuss breath training and breath control, we are talking about uncomfortable things and no one expresses the importance of embracing discomfort quite like Stewart, so with his gracious permission, I will quote from his book Biohacker (which I highly recommend). To me, this is what the correct attitude should look like:

> *"Years of training in the suck has rewired my brain and body. Self-pity and agony are just triggers now. Once pulled, they release the beast. They're no longer an excuse to quit. This option no longer exists in my nervous system... Evolution is pain and suffering multiplied to great lengths of time. This is not some sadomasochistic radical concept. It's just truth. Without pain and suffering there is no need for transcendence into higher levels of performance."*

RESISTANCE ISN'T FUTILE

Having a trick to recover our breath in a crisis when we need to talk is helpful, but the real secret is to prepare in advance. When an elite performer encounters breath stress, they tend to be more familiar with what is happening. They know what to expect because they have volunteered to push until they have encountered that stress repeatedly. All of the feelings are familiar to them because they've experienced them before in their training over and over again. This helps them stay goal-oriented and manage the stress better neurologically. The less experienced practitioner however will tend to become distracted by the symptoms of breath stress and lose efficiency.[54] When they encounter it in their training, they take it as an indicator to stop rather than to keep pushing through. Whenever I use breath deprivation drills with small children in a class, they often look at me stunned and say things like: "*my heart hurts*" or "*my chest feels funny*". Sometimes they are on the verge of tears. Then I just smile and say, "*that's ok. I feel the same way, but it will go away and it will get easier every time.*" The second time they feel this burning, it's no longer a surprise. I may even ask them if they feel burning in their chest and they will nod. I make it clear that it's normal and in doing this, every time we train it, we take away a little more fear and replace it with familiarity. I turn the scary pain into a dragon's breath and have them make intense faces and hiss out the fire. Practice makes fear into something familiar and the more we experience these symptoms, the less fearful they become.

The simple practice of holding our breath will create a host of physiological responses in our bodies. Of course, the moment we feel the absence of oxygen intake, our body has the strong desire to breathe. This can trigger panic as our heart rate increases or becomes irregular and the pressure in our lungs begins to build. By intentionally practicing breath-holding, we quickly become much more familiar with the symptoms of the stress response and we learn to stay calmer under pressure.

Breath-holding also promotes a lot of benefits as a health practice. Holding the breath has been shown to help regenerate brain tissue.[55] Breath-holding, followed by re-oxygenation, creates an *"oxidative"* stress in cells and tissues which helps trigger cell division and regeneration. Breath-holding has been found to change the activity in more than 5000 genes (that's over a quarter of all the genes found in human cells). This can

---

[54] Paulus M.P. et al, "Subjecting elite athletes to inspiratory breathing load reveals behavioral and neural signatures of optimal performers in extreme environments", https://doi.org/10.1371/journal.pone.0029394, January 19, 2012.
[55] Lust K., Wittbrodt J., "Hold your breath!", doi: 10.7554/eLife.12523, December 16, 2015.

include a boost in immune function and anti-inflammation.[56] In numerous meditation practices, breath-holding is also used as a way to bring deeper mindfulness to your breath cycle. Often, in states of hypertension, I use a sequence of breath holds to increase my focus before trying to enter a state of long, slow breathing. I find it a helpful shortcut to bring me immediately into the present.

EXERCISE #18:

Try to simply hold your breath. Inhale naturally through the nose then hold. At first, it's enough to just see how long you can keep your lungs full. Just observe the various feelings it creates in your body. As you approach your threshold and feel greater stress, remind yourself that you are in control and that you are sparking a host of beneficial health effects just by holding your breath. Something as simple as holding your breath to your absolute capacity turns something fearful like not being able to breathe, into a safe and strengthening game. Breathe naturally afterward to recover. When you feel ready, try another hold.

By performing a few simple breath holds, observing your response, and then allowing yourself to recover, you begin to turn the fears associated with breath deprivation into something more familiar. At the same time, you will increase your breath-holding capacity and better prepare yourself for some of the stresses of conflict. You can perform this anywhere, anytime that you want increased awareness and a quick physiological reset. It works much faster than a coffee for a quick wakeup and is a lot healthier for you on every level.

---

[56] Eftedal I., "What the immune system is up to while you're holding your breath", *NTNUhealth*, 21 December 2016.

JUST BE AWARE

Ultimately, the most important breath exercise we can perform is to take a few minutes every day to just focus on breathing. There is so much research on breathing and so much information out there, that sometimes I find people make the whole thing way too complicated. Here are a few lessons that took me a long time to learn:

- There are a lot of different specific techniques out there and it is fine to play and explore **all of them**. Just remember, we're all different. Remember at the outset of this book when we created our value inventory? I said then that our **motive matters more than our method**. *Why* we are doing this, matters more than *how* we are doing it. The simple truth is that some of us will respond better to some techniques and we just won't like others. No one can tell you what will work best for you. Only you can discover this. In fact, breath training may actually be a placebo.[57] If the objective of a given breath technique sounds credible then that may be enough for it to have a therapeutic effect even if the rationale is scientifically incorrect. The reason is that breathing promotes relaxation and mindfulness which in turn improves our overall health on many levels. Moreover, breath control increases a sense of self-efficacy and mastery, which increase cognitive control and help us regain emotional regulation.[58] So, the next time you see someone claiming this breath technique or that method is the magic formula for something, remember that research has shown it's less a question of *how* you breathe and more a matter *that* you breathe. Maybe they really believe their method works best because it worked best for them. Maybe they're just trying to sell you something. Don't buy it. Believe in what works for you.
- One simple way to increase awareness is to simply **count your breaths**. Trying to slow your breath to take 4-6 breaths per minute is an easy way to get a reliable standard for your breathing exercise. Start by taking a slow, comfortable inhale, hold for a fraction of a second, then release the breath. When you exhale, there is no need to add force. I like to visualize that I have a slow leak, so I don't risk adding force and stress to the breath. Then repeat. Use a timer on your phone for one minute and find out what your baseline state is. Most healthy people can

---

[57] Carssen B., de Ruiter C., van Dyck R., "Breathing retraining: A rational placebo?", *Clinical Psychology Review, Vol. 12, pp. 141-153,* 1992.
[58] Stromberg S.E., Russel M.E., Carlson C.R., "Diaphragmatic breathing and its effectiveness for the management of motion sickness", *Aerosp., Med. Hum. Perform.* 86 452-457, 2015.

immediately slow down to 4-6 breaths per minute. Repeat this for a second minute. See if it changes. You can use this measurement as a future reference point. Any time you stop to perform a minute of deep breathing, always remember how many you were just able to do under ideal conditions. Knowing your baseline state can be a helpful way to measure how stressed you are and can help you get back to your baseline state more quickly.
- Another way to measure your breaths is to count without judgment. Spiritual traditions use meditation beads for this purpose. Similarly, a rhythmic sound like a chime can help you set a simple **breathing cadence**. You can find a variety of meditation chime apps for your phone that make trying this out easier than ever. If counting the number of breaths (4 per minute etc.) is causing you stress, then you might prefer signaling the breath without measurement. Every time you hear a chime, breathe, or every time you finish a comfortable breath, count another bead with your fingers.

Regular breathing practice stimulates the pre-frontal lobe and strengthens your cognitive processing[59] Remember, it doesn't need to be complicated. Breathing can reduce your overall anxiety in as little as 5 minutes a day.[60] Even a single breath practice of a few minutes positively impacts your blood pressure and heart rate so even if we just implement occasional practice, the payoff can be huge.[61] Find an exercise that works for you and slowly try to integrate it into your routine. If you stop liking it, change it. Stronger breathing over time will make an important investment in your wellness and overall health.

---

[59] Bhatia M., Kumar A., Kumar N., Pandey R. M., Kochupillai V., "Electrophysiologic evaluation of Sudarshan Kriya: an EEG, BAER, P300 study", *Ind. J. Physiol. Pharmacol.* 47 157–163, 2003.
[60] Chang S.B. et al, "Effects of abdominal breathing on anxiety, blood pressure, peripheral skin temperature and saturation oxygen of pregnant women in preterm labor", *Korean J Women Health Nurs* 15 32–42. 10.4069/kjwhn.2009, 2009.
[61] Wang S.Z. et al, "Effect of slow abdominal breathing combined with biofeedback on blood pressure and heart rate variability in prehypertension", *J. Altern. Complement. Med.* 16 1039–1045. 10.1089/acm.2009.0577, 2010.

MIRRORING

Mirroring (also known as the *Gauchais Reaction*), is the action of imitating the body language and paralanguage of another person. This can occur subconsciously as a by-product of interest and attraction or it can be done intentionally to help build comfort and rapport. If you take a quick look in the corridors of your school, you'll likely notice the various cliques and social groups that exist there. Among each of these groups, you will often notice that the students dress similarly, use similar speech and language and express themselves with similar gestures. This is a natural adaptive by-product of spending so much time together. When we like someone, we tend to emulate them. In turn, by projecting familiar habits and qualities, that person is more likely to feel comfortable around us and find us approachable.[62]

While some level of subconscious mirroring is always occurring, it can be very helpful during extremely tense and emotional circumstances to dedicate awareness to consciously mirroring the other person. It's always important to trust your instincts. If a subject notices that you are mirroring them, it can be perceived as mockery.[63] **The key to mirroring is to be subtle**:

- **Adapt to their speed.** If the subject is speaking extremely fast and escalating, increase your rate of speech slightly. I always try to stay just below their speed to reduce the risk of being perceived as mockery while also helping me to control the tempo of the conversation. If you don't match their speed to some degree, they may find you frustrating, but by increasing your rate to a level just below theirs, you begin building rapport.
- **Just keep them talking.** If the subject is speaking very slowly, or exhibiting long periods of silence, slow down your rate until it's closer to theirs but ask questions and encourage them to answer. If you can get them talking, keep them talking. Listen and prompt them. Avoid interrupting. **A verbal subject is more likely to be a cognitive subject**.
- **Prioritize your safety.** If the subject is using extremely fast and erratic gestures, be careful about just increasing the speed of your gestures indiscriminately. If we

---

[62] Weatherholtz K., Campbell-Kibler K., Jaeger F.T., "Socially-mediated syntactic alignment", Language Variation and Change, 2014; 26(03): 387, 2014

[63] Kavnagh L. et al, "When it's an error to mirror: the surprising reputational costs of mimicry", *Association for Psychological Sciences*, 22(10) 1274–1276, 2011.

just start moving our hands erratically even if we're trying to match their speed, we might end up escalating the encounter or triggering aggression.

- **Keep your Fence up.** Limit hand actions to a small range of motion that keep them between the hips and your shoulders at all times.
- **Avoid crossing your arms.** Closing off your body can place you at a tactical disadvantage. It ties up your hands making it slower for you to defend or counter-attack. Covering your body can also make your aggressor more suspicious and less trusting of you.
- **Nod your head.** Small head nods can be done quickly to mirror the subject's speed without sacrificing your safety. Nodding is also an affirmative action. As we saw earlier, Alpha commands are stronger than Beta commands, and *"start"* Alpha commands are better than *"stop"* Alpha commands, because they tell the subject exactly what to do. Start commands are also preferable because they are affirmative. Research on hypnosis and the psychology of influence has shown that positive language, accompanied by a quick yet smooth triple nod, can greatly increase the likelihood of agreement.[64] [65]

EXERCISE #19:

The next time you're having a conversation with a student or colleague, take a moment to observe the habits of the other person:

- How far away are they standing?
- How are they leaning?
- Are they tilting their head?
- What type of gestures are they using?

A simple way to encourage the subject to keep talking and to give you more time to observe them is to try injecting a few triple head nods. This shows you are listening and registering what they're saying.

Once you feel ready, try incorporating a single gesture or habit from your conversation partner. I don't like the word *"imitate"* because we're not trying to mock or copy. Rather, we want to be inspired by their gesture and integrate our own version of their action. The movement still needs to feel natural for us or else it may stand out too much. It can be as

---

[64] Erickson MH: Further clinical techniques of hypnosis: utilization techniques. 1959. Am J Clin Hypn 51:341–362, 2009
[65] de Shazer S: Keys to Solution in Brief Therapy. New York, WW Norton, 1985.

simple as leaning in the same direction or folding your arms in a similar manner. Even if this is a friendly conversation the person may use large and rapid hand gestures. Some people are very excitable in their regular speech. If this is the case, remember to try to maintain a casual Fence through your gestures. Gestures can be a great way to maintain space between you and your subject. Your hand motions can become more rapid to match them more closely but always keep them between your shoulders and hips at all times and avoid crossing the arms.

AGGRESSION CUES:

The body is always communicating. Even when a subject is consciously attempting to lie to you, their body will usually manifest aspects of their physiological state. This is extremely obvious when a subject is emotional or aggressive. Most of these *"aggression cues"* are quite intuitive. Over our lifetime we've experienced them every time we've seen someone get emotional and we've come to form strong subconscious associations with them whether or not we realize it. When things start to go badly and we intuitively feel like something is wrong, often it's because we are subconsciously registering the presence of these aggression cues. By consciously training your awareness to identify these cues, you can massively enhance your intuition and help you make more accurate interpretations sooner.

We **never** want to mirror or imitate aggression cues. If we mirror signs of anger, we will likely trigger an escalation. Berkowitz has extensively studied the role of aggression cues and found that when environmental aggression cues are present (for example, the presence of a weapon or threat) they tend to provoke the continued escalation of aggression. This is known as the *"weapons effect"*.[66] It reinforces the importance of keeping our hands open in our Fence at all times and it warns us that the presence of aggression cues in our aggressor can tempt us to escalate. We must be extremely conscious about not inadvertently mirroring aggressive actions.

Here are a few essential aggression cues we should learn to identify. To keep things simple, we will start from the top of the body and work our way down:

1. **The stare** can be used many different ways but all of these would be unusual or inappropriate in an ordinary day-to-day conversation. They can include:
   - **Staring blankly at you.** This is a sign of the amygdala hijacking the cognitive brain and of the subject entering a state of primal fixation.

---

[66] Berkowitz, L., "Whatever happened to the frustration-aggression hypothesis?", *American Behavioral Scientist*, 21, 691-708, 1978.

- **The subject scans you from top to bottom.** This can be done in a sexually inappropriate way or can be done to assess how much of a threat you might be and how much of a challenge you'll present if they proceed with violence.
- **The subject scans the environment, specifically looking behind themself.** This is usually done to see if there are any witnesses around or anyone that might come to your aid.

2. **Pupil dilation** can be harder to notice. As the subject enters a primal aggression state, the pupils can widen to absorb more information. Survivors of attacks from extreme offenders like serial murderers, often recount the attacker's eyes seeming to become entirely black. Sometimes you may not even know why, but the way someone is looking at you will just make you feel uncomfortable. In every case, trust your intuition.
3. **Lowering the brow.** This is a reflexive attempt to protect the vulnerable eyes as the aggressor prepares for conflict.
4. **Flaring the nostrils.** This is a by-product of a rapidly escalating breath rate. Some researchers believe it may also be a primal reflex to smell the testosterone and hormone levels of the opponent.
5. **Grinding or brandishing the teeth** is a natural by-product of aggressive contraction. Sometimes it can be as subtle as the subject jutting their chin forward like they are chewing on something or the lips curling back and revealing their teeth to the gum line.
6. **The chin lowering excessively.** This occurs by virtue of them lowering the brow and for the same reason—in this case to protect the vulnerable throat.
7. **Clenching the neck and shoulders.** As the emotional center of the brain gets activated, the subject will turtle up in many cases to be more resistant to impact. The shoulders can also rise and fall quickly, evidencing aggressively heavy breathing.
8. **Puffing up the chest.** Sometimes the subject will square up to you and flare their arms at the sides, usually with the hands in a low position, in an attempt to appear larger and more intimidating.
9. **Making fists is an obvious precursor to aggression.**
10. **Reaching into pockets or the beltline.** This can be an attempt to access a weapon and subjects doing this should be treated with extreme caution. Unless you are obligated to physically intervene, you should immediately increase the distance between you and the threat. Ideally, try to place obstacles between you both. We will discuss this a little later in our treatment of tactical positioning.
11. **Stomping the ground with their feet.** This can be an aggressive discharge of energy. This can also be a method of trying to build up physical and emotional momentum to initiate an attack. If you've never seen this type of response, the first time you witness it, it can startle and confuse you. If an aggressor starts stomping the ground, give them as much space as possible.

Of course, there are other possible cues like **shedding clothing** or obvious factors like a subject saying *"I'm going to knock that smile off of your face"*, but the important thing is that we have some rough idea of what aggressive behavior looks like so that we can:

1. Learn to see aggression building earlier and
2. Make sure that we do not inadvertently mirror it and possibly make things worse.

In a security setting like bouncing or bodyguarding, these aggression cues might trigger us to pre-emptively attack. For a classroom teacher, however, we know that physically intervening may not be permitted. In these cases, aggression cues tell you when to:

- Increase the distance between you and the threat.
- Place obstacles between you and the aggressor.
- Call for backup.
- Confirm your exit routes.

Since these cues are very logical and self-evident, with just a little effort, you will begin to clearly and reliably notice these behaviors.

One final point of mention is that **aggression cues are just rough indicators**. The same behaviors could manifest for other reasons. Just because someone reaches under their shirt doesn't mean they always have a gun. For a law enforcement officer, where a decision must be made to shoot or not shoot, the stakes are higher. Thankfully, the classroom teacher usually has a simpler decision like deciding to create distance or possibly escape. Because these cues are just rough estimations, the more of them that you notice, the more reliable they become as predictors. Ultimately, the most important tool in our survival toolbox is our intuition. If something feels wrong, listen to your senses and get backup.

• •

EXERCISE #20:

Think of any aggression you have experienced in your life. It could be an argument with a friend, colleague, or stranger. Try to recall the sequence of events that led to the altercation:

- Do you recall how the situation escalated?
- What aggression cues can you recall?

- How did you know the other person was angry?
- Was there a point you could have made a different decision that would have changed the outcome? Could you have made things worse? Could you have made things better?

Debriefing our own experiences with aggression will help us identify and replace harmful language, behavior, and gestures, and improve our control of hostile situations, both in the classroom and our everyday life.

PREDICTING AGGRESSION IN YOUR SCHOOL

Predicting aggression cues in an individual student during an escalation is a valuable defensive skill. A far more important ability is to learn to predict and pre-empt violence before it can develop within the school environment.

Research suggests that one of the most important risk factors for school violence is the level of violence in the neighborhoods where students live. Realistically, there is very little that a school teacher may be able to do to transform the many neighborhoods from which their students all hail. Teachers do still have the power to motivate change, however. The most effective protective step they can take is to encourage and invite increased parental involvement and volunteerism.[67] **The increased participation of parents has been shown to have a direct effect on decreasing school violence.** This isn't always easy of course. We've all had the experience of dealing with parents who refuse to participate in their child's schooling. If we're honest, an uninterested parent can make us feel underappreciated and taken for granted but imagine for a moment what it's making the child feel like. We've dealt with parents who are overtly aggressive and who deflect blame squarely back on the school and the teachers. They refuse to accept fault or see the needs of their child. We've also likely experienced parents that are so retentive and obsessive that they question every move you make as a teacher. All of these scenarios can be immensely discouraging and there is a very real risk and temptation that we give up on these kids as a result of it and just avoid engaging these parents at all. If we do, however, these students are the ones who suffer the most. As difficult as it may be, we must engage the parents to fully support the student.

There is an old expression that says you don't just marry the spouse; you marry the in-laws. Anyone who has been married knows how much truth there is in this. Similarly, I believe that a teacher has a responsibility to educate not just the student; they must also teach the parents. Often, this must be done with as much if not more sensitivity and subtlety since many parents resent the intervention. Some parents will openly lay the blame on the teacher saying *"it's your job to teach my child"* when their marks are too low, but in the same breath they'll remind you that *"you're not their parent"* if you dare to venture too close to topics of discipline or assessment. This can be a tough tightrope to balance on. The fact remains, **every child deserves to be protected**. They deserve to be championed. We need to put our teacher egos aside and remember the commitment we made to every student when we accepted this vocation. **We cannot consistently**

---

[67] Afkinich J.L., Klumpner S., "Violence Prevention Strategies and School Safety", *Journal of the Society for Social Work and Research* Volume 9, Number 4, 2018.

perform in a manner that is inconsistent with how we see and value ourselves. Our interactions with parents are an important indicator and opportunity for improving our essential assertiveness. If you cannot clearly and calmly assert your limits with parents, this points to an underlying sense of insecurity. Anything that is confidently believed can be calmly asserted. If we are unable to calmly assert, we need to work on the reasons why otherwise we will weaken our overall ability to defend ourselves.

Inclusivity is another huge factor in preventing violence that is within our influence.[68][69] The feeling of not fitting in or not being equally represented can lead to increased issues of resentment and aggression for students that range from vandalism to violence. Even more troubling, subjectivity in school discipline and disproportionate punishment according to ethnicity and race is a surprisingly prevalent issue.[70][71] As we'll see a little later on in our criteria for a healthy school, something as simple as acknowledging religious holidays, culturally significant events, and representing diversity in activities, décor, and the subject matter goes a long way to create a more integrated environment.

Another topic we will delve into a bit later that begs mentioning here is the problematic issue of zero tolerance practices and punishments.[72] The lack of flexibility in such a policy causes more problems than it may solve. While zero tolerance policies can sometimes create the illusion of short-term improvements in discipline issues, overall, they have been shown to decrease the perception of safety among students and staff alike and model a negative fear-based discipline template for conduct.

Regardless of what interventions you decide to use, remember that distributing the efforts over a longer period is much more effective than just bombarding students with changes all at once. In an analysis of over 200 violence prevention programs in schools, one of the most important elements that emerged was the frequency of the efforts. **Multiple sessions in succession were found to be more effective than a single session.**[73] This is

---

[68] Eddy, C. L. et al, "Does teacher emotional exhaustion and efficacy predict student discipline sanctions?" *School Psychology Review*, 49(3), 239–255. https://doi.org/10.1080/2372966X.2020.1733340, 2020.

[69] Felix E. D., You S., "Peer victimization within the ethnic context of high school", *Journal of Community Psychology*, 39(7), 860–875. https://doi.org/10.1002/jcop.20465, 2011.

[70] Girvan E. J. et al, "The relative contribution of subjective office referrals to racial disproportionality in school discipline", *School Psychology Quarterly: The Official Journal of the Division of School Psychology, American Psychological Association*, 32(3), 392–404. https://doi.org/10.1037/spq0000178, 2017.

[71] Girvan E. J., McIntosh K., & Santiago-Rosario, M. R., "Associations between community-level racial biases, office discipline referrals, and out-of-school suspensions", *School Psychology Review*, 50(2-3), 288–302, 2021.

[72] Cornell D.G., Mayer M. J., & Sulkowski, M. L., "History and future of school safety research", *School Psychology Review*, 50(2-3), 143–157, 2021.

[73] Wilson S.J., Lipsey M.W., "The effectiveness of school-based violence prevention programs for reducing disruptive and aggressive behavior", *Document No.: 211376 Date Received: Sept, U.S. Department of Justice Commissioned Paper,* 2005.

consistent with research in sports[74], the classroom[75], and even law enforcement training. Given the same amount of time allotted, training that is distributed (spread out over time with intervals in between) vs. massed (taught in a single block) is consistently found to be more effective. The German psychologist Hermann Ebbinghaus found that newly taught information is quickly forgotten. This is what he termed *"the forgetting curve"*. So, it's hardly surprising that the same holds true for teaching social norms and values. The difficulty is of course that distributed training requires more exceptions, more work to schedule, and often more budget which is why blocked training continues to be favored.

Statistically, there appear to be overarching gender-based differences in violence and I've seen different approaches used accordingly. Males statistically appear to be more prone to physical violence, whether male-on-male or male-on-female. Females tend to be more prone to verbal and indirect aggression like cyberbullying. First, I would caution about how we interpret statistics. This is not always the case and biasing your expectations can be dangerous. I have seen large increases in physical violence among female students in the environments I have worked in, so assuming that a given demographic is *"safe"* from certain expressions of aggression would be a huge error. Secondly, these variations may point to an underlying sexism and the existence of problematic stereotypes which lie at the root of the problem. While stereotypes may direct *how* the aggression manifests right now, the ignorance that permits the very existence of these same stereotypes may well be what is motivating the hostility to begin with.[76]

Finally, I would submit that the largest key to pre-emptively avoiding school violence is to **maintain a strong rapport with your students**. They are your eyes and ears. I always engage the students wherever I go. I listen to their experiences and make it known that they matter. As a result, they always keep me informed about everything that is going on in the school. By staying on top of the school climate, I'm always in the best position to see problems before their start and to help teach the students how to make better choices sooner.

---

[74] Kwon Y.H., Kwon J. W., Lee M.H., "Effectiveness of motor sequential learning according to practice schedules in healthy adults; distributed practice versus massed practice"
[75] Killian S., "Distributed practice and massed practice: What works best?", *Evidence Based Teaching*, August 9, 2019.
[76] Toldos Romero M., "Adolescents' Predictions of Aggressive Behavioral Patterns in Different Settings", *The Open Psychology Journal*, 4, (Suppl 1-M6) 55-63, 2011.

EXERCISE #21:

Think about your own school environment. While it can be overwhelming to think of the massive task of changing the entire school, the reality is that **change begins with you, one small step at a time**. What *one* change could you begin to implement today in your environment to make your classroom or workspace more inclusive, more welcoming, and more integrated? It could be as simple as opening a dialogue to involve your students, asking others for feedback, adding to the décor, creating a new practice, or reaching out to a parent. Start from a place of gratitude and see where it takes you.

THE OODA LOOP

The entire goal of learning to see aggression cues, whether they are in the individual aggressors in front of you, or pre-indicators in your school environment overall, is to be able to intercept and re-direct them before they can develop. At this point, I would like to introduce one of the most important tactical frameworks I know.

In the 1950s, Colonel John Boyd of the United States Air Force developed a decision-making model known as the OODA Loop. He noted that a key factor in combative encounters was that soldiers needed to:

- **Observe** a threat,
- **Orient** themselves relative to that threat,
- **Decide** what to do and then finally
- **Act**.

Boyd recognized that there were two ways to win. Either:

1. You learn to process your OODA Loop **faster** than your opponent, or
2. You **interrupt** your opponent's cycle and don't let them complete it.

Throughout this book, we have already seen the importance of maintaining maximum distance to provide optimal reaction time. This helps us complete our OODA loop.

Similarly, by learning how to use the Quiet Eye and principles of tactical vision, we seek to strengthen the accuracy of our **Observation** phase. All of the contextual examples and verbal skills, seek to prolong our **Orientation** phase, to allow us to make better **Decisions** and to **Act** accordingly.

While many people tactically obsess over improving physical reaction speed, I am a larger proponent of trying to **stretch time** whenever possible so that we have more chances to process and react. We need to remember that we will rarely have much time to prepare ourselves for aggression. Often, we will be ambushed by it. That can mean that the aggressor had time to escalate and to choose the time and location of the attack. They have created a mental model of how they expect that attack to play out. Anything we can do to violate those expectations can make their OODA loop hiccup and reset. Simple things like maintaining distance and keeping your Fence up can interrupt the aggressor's plan and help you stretch time and make better decisions. Similarly, concealing your own aggressive intent with a passive stance and gestures and asking questions to interrupt an aggressor's patterns and to re-engage their cognitive mind can go a long way to fully derail their momentum and lead towards de-escalation.

I'm going to give you a more violent example of how OODA Loops worked in my life. I'm including it here because, despite its brutality, it's the clearest example of this principle working when your life can be on the line. Afterward, I'm going to discuss how we can adapt this understanding to a responsible power setting like the classroom.

STORY FROM THE FIELD:

Dylan is an experienced doorman who has worked in some of the toughest clubs in the city for over 15 years. In Dylan's career, he has seen people stabbed, shot, beaten, and maimed. Like anyone who has worked the door long enough, he's also made his share of mistakes and ended up on the receiving end more times than he can remember.

"We've all had that feeling that something bad is about to happen. Call it intuition, a gut feeling, or a subconscious realization. It doesn't really matter what it is. It only matters that we listen to it. When you work in violent environments, you have more opportunities to learn from it. If you're lucky like I am, you get to survive your mistakes. There have been a lot of people who are smarter than me, stronger than me, better than me, that simply made one bad decision at the wrong time and they aren't here anymore. For whatever reason, despite the mistakes I've made, I survived. That means I've been hurt, beaten down and I've seen people get worse. So, I've been able to learn from my mistakes and from theirs."

"Working the door, I saw that the person who attacks first, massively controls the direction of that fight. If that person has a little experience and they attack first, usually they will win the exchange. The best street fighters I've seen almost always attacked first and finished things very quickly. It was never fancy. Never pretty. They never gave their opponent a chance to counter. I eventually learned that when everything told me I was about to get jumped, it was safer to simply attack first. I realize that may sound terrible to an outsider, but it's the truth. I also learned that if I wanted my attack to be as effective as possible, it was best if I totally suckered someone. So, I got into the habit of asking a question. I would say things like: 'What about him?' as I would point over his shoulder or 'Is he with you?'"

"The key was to wait a second. Sometimes the words just wouldn't sink in. You would see no change. Maybe they would just continue swearing at you. If it sank in though, you'd see it in their eyes. Maybe they'd blink or look behind them or look down as they thought. That would be the moment when I would hit. If I hit them when they were distracted, usually I could hit them cleanly and they'd go down. Morally I know this sounds terrible. Violence is terrible. The reality is, if I wasn't certain they were about to attack me, I would create distance. If I felt they were about to attack, I would attack first. You had to ambush them before they ambushed you. Once you did it a few times and felt how much better it worked, and how much less you were hurt, there was much less hesitation. As I look back, I also consider it the more humane option, because it let me finish things without it escalating to a point where everyone got seriously damaged. It was far better to drop someone with one or two clean hits than to get into a protracted struggle where everyone got mangled and innocent bystanders were placed at risk."

Now Dylan developed this awareness through working in a very particular environment. Honestly speaking, when I worked in those environments, I was exactly the same. Looking back on how I had to be in that job from the current security and safety of the sofa where I'm writing this, I know that I was a different person then. I had to be. The lessons it proved to me however have stayed with me. I always prefer to attack first, the only difference is these days I may attack pre-emptively with a movement, a gesture, or a verbal strategy rather than a punch. A single short sentence or question is all it takes to completely infiltrate someone's OODA Loop and catch them with their guard down. Of course, the same strategies can sometimes be used to intercept someone with kindness, as Mike Malpass did in our earlier story with that boy who had a knife to his throat.

The key is that the subject has to want to take that invitation. Sometimes, the subject will choose the path of *most* resistance. Sometimes they will be so far gone that none of your strategies will get in. Sometimes we are not just facing an aggressive student who we have a few years of rapport with. Sometimes we're fighting against all of the negative experiences they've internalized in their life mixed with thousands of years of survival instincts that have been hard-wired into their genetic code. Sometimes those reflexes can make it work in our favor. Sometimes it will work against us.

I'm mentioning this strategy of interrupting with questions here because it shows you another way the OODA Loop can be used in an escalation. When we see how much some of our students are dealing with at home, how systemic and entrenched the disadvantages they face are, it can be overwhelming. What difference can I make if they are living in a terrible neighborhood, in a horrible home life with absent, uncaring parents, and a host of other challenges? When I feel overwhelmed, I find it helpful to break the war down into little battles. Then, I try to win each of those battles using the strategies I know have worked for me in real-life fights. **I would always rather interrupt those little fights than wage full mini-battles.** So, when I have a student confiding in me who just can't find hope or the will to continue, I try to interrupt their expectations one pattern at a time:

- Rather than focus on how far behind they are in a given class, let's focus on doing the best we can on this next assignment.
- Rather than focus on how little support they're getting at home, let's just focus on what we can learn by doing this alone.
- Rather than focus on what we don't have or can't do, let's just focus on just one thing that we can do right now.

Just like dealing with compulsive behavior, distraction is one of the most powerful tools we can have. If we interrupt patterns, we can more easily lay the groundwork for new habits. For me, the OODA Loop is about more than just beating an aggressor. Sometimes, it's about intercepting my expectations and self-doubt and staying mission-oriented so that I can complete my own loop and make my decisions into action.

DHARMA

Before I go any further, I want to briefly address an underlying element of everything in this book that can easily be overlooked. I want to discuss our fundamental motivation. I have worked in a lot of different school environments. The reality is that like any other organization, company, police agency, or military structure, schools have people in them who are passionate about their job as well as those who have given up. In every organization, some employees feel overworked and under-appreciated, ignored and underpaid. The most exceptional who thrive despite these challenges find a way to stay connected to the higher value motives that inspire them. They do a great job because they are motivated by their students and their love of teaching. Many however lose touch with this inspiration and then the burden of the job becomes terrible for them.

One common phenomenon I see in schools is that teachers begin to pigeonhole certain kids with specific labels. Sometimes it's observational like, *"This one is a tough case. She's problematic. He has rage issues"*. Other times they are far more judgemental like *"She's a lost cause"*. We're all human. We've all made value judgements like this. We've all been worn down and frustrated and felt like we weren't making a difference. Maybe we felt underappreciated and our effort seemed wasted. While this is human nature, when we get in a highly emotional state, we have two simple choices:

- **Keep emotional distance** from the subject, or
- **Try to use the opportunity to reconnect** with the student.

I've seen both. I've seen interventionists who enter with an attitude of anger, dominance, and resentment. They operate as if they were somehow superior to the subject. They have no interest in de-escalating the scenario. They just expect it to stop immediately simply through the power of their authority. This usually ends up badly. Often, I encounter staff who are extremely discontented. They are angry at the establishment, at the administration, with many of their colleagues, and with the students. Invariably, the teachers who complain the most loudly and frequently are the same people who are complained *about* by the remainder of the staff and the students the most regularly. In security fields, it's widely known that when the job becomes tedious, it's time to quit. When we no longer feel the motivation to be alert and attentive, we get hurt or killed and endanger our teammates or clients. If an individual lacks the self-awareness to realize it's time to go, their team will usually remind them. In teaching, however, because the risks are less immediate, there is no such incentive and some staff members linger far longer than they should. Not only do they do a poor job and make the lives of their colleagues and students miserable, but they also create negative habits for themselves and rob themselves of their true potential.

In Buddhism, there is a wonderful word that refers to one's true nature; It's Dharma. The Dharma of a teacher is to teach, to share, to inspire, and to help grow. When we take a job as an educator and don't apply ourselves fully, we don't fulfill our duty to the universe. **If a great teacher has the power to imprint change on eternity, a bad one has the power to injure it.** When we give ourselves to our task full, only good things result. If we are not meant for that task, we will realize it far more fully and far more quickly. In doing so we can move on to something that better suits our skills and passions. I need to mention this at this point because de-escalating a violent encounter is hard enough in the best of circumstances. If you are emotionally under-equipped to connect and should not be teaching to begin with, you're just making your job harder and putting your safety and the lives of your students at risk. It's imperative we honestly reflect on this and reconnect with our passion.

> "Until one is committed, there is hesitancy, the chance to draw back. Concerning all acts of initiative (and creation), there is one elementary truth, the ignorance of which kills countless ideas and splendid plans: that the moment one definitely commits oneself, then Providence moves too. All sorts of things occur to help one that would never otherwise have occurred. A whole stream of events issues from the decision, raising in one's favor all manner of unforeseen incidents and meetings and material assistance, which no man could have dreamed would have come his way. Whatever you can do, or dream you can do, begin it. Boldness has genius, power, and magic in it. Begin it now."
> —***William Hutchison Murray***—

EMPATHY

The reason I wanted to discuss Dharma and purpose now is that we're about to talk about *empathy.* **Empathy is the ability to feel what another is feeling.** It's a huge component of non-violent intervention and it's very hard to achieve authentic empathy if you're burnt out and you've given up. Empathy's natural opponents are apathy and ego. It's so easy to let stress accumulate. That can lead to resentment, under-appreciation, and even a feeling of self-pity and victimization. All of these inhibit our ability to stay authentically in the moment and sever our connection to the joy and gratitude that we deserve to experience.

Phrases that help convey empathy include:

- *"I understand."*
- *"I hear you."*
- *"It sounds like you're having a rough day."*
- *"You look like you need a hand."*

Or the phrases can be more involved like:

- *"Listen, this is not the way to resolve this. Let me help you find a better solution to this."*
- *"It sounds like you're handling a lot of stress right now. How long have you been feeling like this?"*

Empathy comes from a place of feeling. It's not about memorizing a simple phrase or two. It's about opening yourself up and trying to build a rapport with your student who is suffering and about to make a decision they will later regret. Empathy can start with you signaling that you see their anger, that you feel their pain, but then it should continue with questioning. You want to get the aggressor talking and keep them talking. This will help to keep them in a cognitive state while allowing you to find out more about what is motivating their outburst. It also keeps them venting. Preferably, we would like to use open-ended questions that cannot be simply answered by *yes* or *no*. Things like:

> *"What exactly are you feeling right now?"* or
> *"Can you tell me what happened to make you feel so angry?"*

If the subject still doesn't become verbal, then you can try injecting a closed question to make it easier for them to start talking. Something like:

"Did someone do something specific to make you this angry?"
Then you can use a *"yes"* answer to lead you toward more information:
"Can you tell me what happened?"

You can also try an assumptive question like:

"Trevor, it seems like you're pretty mad. Are you feeling angry about something?" and you could add something as simple as a triple nod to try to encourage agreement. This could lead to phrases like: *"I will help you, but I need to know more information. Can you please tell me exactly what happened?"*

Remember earlier when we discussed Alpha and Beta commands, I said it's unrealistic to expect to always only use Alpha commands. Sometimes, there are moments of quiet calm in an encounter where you get the subject's attention and you can see they are processing what you are saying. If you are trying to get them talking, people often use more qualifiers like:

"Do you think you could tell me what happened?" rather than,
"Tell me what happened?"

Earlier, we discussed the importance of Alpha commands. We noted that qualifiers weaken the strength of our commands. In the de-escalation phase of an interaction, however, qualifiers are often quite natural and well-tolerated. Some experts also consider cordiality and politeness to be a form of qualifiers. I disagree. I believe you can be polite while maintaining assertiveness. There are times when a simple *"please"* or *"thank you"* fits perfectly with a strong command and rather than weaken your authority, they can greatly increase your empathy.

Also, remember that someone may be non-verbal for a long time. You might give commands or ask questions and not get a response. They may not escalate or engage. If they give you signs that they are listening, they can still be in a cognitive state. It can take a while for their brain states to switch from a more primal state to a communicative one. Some of your students have also been raised in environments where they are either not allowed to express themselves or else no one listens to them. Both of these can lead to someone who favors long periods of silence and who will be reluctant to talk. The bottom line is that if you can get them thinking and listening, you are interrupting their OODA Loop and delaying their escalation. Keep asking questions, then pause and let the questions sink in. Give them some breathing room. Avoid having multiple people involved in talking and shouting orders. Like we saw earlier with Mike Malpass' example with the boy who had placed a knife against his neck, in the beginning, there were too many officers barking orders at him. When Mike took over and became the sole communicator, he was able to redirect the dynamic. By starting from a place of empathy, asking questions to get them talking and not interrupting, you can begin moving down the path of non-violent resolution.

EXERCISE #22:

Take a moment to think about how you would express empathy.

Write down three questions in your own words that show that you are concerned about your subject and that you are listening and want to know more:

1. _____
2. _____
3. _____

RECAP

A key aspect of empathizing with someone is to show them that you care, that you are listening, and to align yourself with them rather than appearing in opposition to them. One great tool to bolster your empathy is to **recap** what your aggressor is saying. It can include phrases like:

"So basically, what you're saying is..."
"If I understand you correctly, this is what happened..."

These are great phrases that can help you clarify what the other person is saying. Unfortunately, they can also be abused by debaters to trap people. Consider this debate between Fox News' Tucker Carlson and an immigration advocate. When the advocate said:

"When the United States interferes in these other countries (because of) a demand for their drugs, or invades a sovereign land like Iraq or interferes in the civil wars of Central America, that causes people to flee",
Carlson retorts *"So you hate America is what you're saying."*

This is a common debate tactic. It can make you seem impressive. It can fluster your opponent and in effect disrupt their OODA Loop. It can trap them in corners and paint them in an unflattering light. While this may work in a television debate where your opponent is unlikely to stab you, if you start trapping and frustrating the subject in a violent encounter, you risk fueling their emotion and encouraging them to escalate to violence. Debate tactics are rarely good for de-escalation.

By comparison, if you are sincerely listening to what the subject is saying, the subject is more likely to trust you and to express their needs. You might ask prompt questions like:

- *"Can you tell me more about that?"*
- *"Can you give me an example of what happened?"*
- *"How did that make you feel?"*

You want to keep them talking as long as possible. You NEVER want to interrupt them. You want them to return from the brink of emotion and move back towards a more cognitive state. Then consider if the exact same questions were asked but instead of it being quick and condescending, it was concerned and looking for clarity:

> *"So, are you saying x, y, z? Would that sound accurate? Is that basically what happened?"*

Now the difference is you are not trying to win an argument, but instead trying to bring clarity and facts to an emotional situation. The rule of recapping in an aggression encounter, therefore, is that you **do not proceed until the subject is satisfied with your recap**. If they correct you or disagree with your recap, listen to them fully. By expressing the argument fully and recapping it without malice, you can begin to move away from it. For example:

> *"Ok, there's obviously a lot that happened. We can sort out the details later. Right now, we just need to continue with the lesson..."* or
> *"...We can discuss this together after class, alright?"*

If the subject is delusional and what they are saying is completely impossible, **DO NOT argue with the delusion**. If they are experiencing a psychological breakdown, you do not want to trigger it. If in their emotional state they have exaggerated themselves into a ridiculous position, you do not want to embarrass them further and risk triggering them.

Ultimately, if the subject becomes more cognitive, you want to defer them, either to a later time, or a safer location. Sometimes, if things are escalating quickly, you may even need to relocate the argument immediately to another location as we will see next.

THE AUDIENCE EFFECT:

Audiences can sometimes cause an aggressive situation to escalate. Think of the textbook example of two kids in the schoolyard in an argument. A crowd gathers to watch. Someone begins to chant: *"Fight, fight, fight"*. As a bouncer, it was very difficult to keep people from moving towards de-escalation when spectators were screaming *"Knock his head off"*. Every classroom is a natural audience. Every hallway and schoolyard has the potential to become a gladiator arena. With social media, a simple comment posted online during recess can snowball into a frenzy of hype during class time and by the end of the next period, it can be a full-fledged outrage. To effectively manage escalations at school, we need to have some capacity to control crowds. The good news is that every second you spend in your classroom, you are cultivating the skills you will need.

The audience effect is a likely explanation for why the majority of adolescent violence not only occurs at school but actually occurs within the classroom itself.[77] Tightly connected to this is the phenomenon of *herd mentality*, sometimes called mob mentality, wherein an individual or small group of people inform the actions of a larger group. This is usually how riots start—a small group of individuals with bad intentions motivates the larger group to act badly.

A secondary danger of audiences is that sometimes they can create their own momentum and violence can erupt from the spectators. There are numerous sub-theories at play, including:

- **Contagion Theory**-which is the degree of influence the collective has on an individual's emotions[78];
- **Convergence Theory**-which stipulates that the behavior of a crowd is created by like-minded individuals being attracted to one another to form a group[79];
- **Emergent-Norm Theory**-which argues that like-minded individuals are attracted to gather together and that anonymity provided by the crowd leads to a reduction of individual inhibition.[80]

No matter what the exact mechanisms are that affect crowds and audiences, every teacher has experienced the feeling of "*losing the group*", whether it be their collective focus during a lesson, an overall feeling of the group sharing a similar energy level on a given day, or even the feeling that disobedience is slowly spreading like wildfire. In the case of aggression in the classroom, if you are unable to control it within the confines of the class, one of the most effective tactical measures to take is to immediately isolate the parties involved by ordering them into the corridor.

- **This will immediately deprive the hostile students of the motivation** that an audience can bring and can help de-escalation efforts. Controlling the spread of a fire begins with cutting off the fuel supply.
- **It will give the aggressive students a face-saver** and the privacy to concede, back down, speak openly and accept mediation more readily. It's very hard to back down if you are in front of a chanting audience.
- **It will protect the remainder of your class.** If your first responsibility is to your personal safety, it is followed closely by the reasonable expectation that you will show a duty of care to the remainder of your students. Even if you are mandated to

---

[77] Travis J. (dir.), "Violence among middle school and high school students: Analysis and implications for prevention", *National Institute of Justice*, October 1997
[78] Le Bon, G., "The Crowd: a Study of the Popular Mind", Penguin Books, NY, 1977
[79] Kerr, C., "Industrialism and Industrial Man", Oxford University Press, NY 1964.
[80] Turner, R.H., and Killian, L.M., "Collective Behavior, 2nd Ed." Prentice-Hall, Englewood Cliffs, NJ, 1972.

never intervene in a fight, you do still have a responsibility to the innocent students who are simply next to the danger when it erupts.
- **It reminds the remainder of the students of the consequence of poor behavior** and can intercept lurking members of the *"mob"* who are on an escalation trajectory before they pass the point of no return.
- **It allows you the opportunity to get backup.** You can immediately send one of your students to the front desk to request the vice-principal, security, etc.

STORY FROM THE FIELD:

Earlier, I introduced veteran bodyguard Luc Cantara. He served 31 years with the Royal Canadian Mounted Police, with 23 of those served in personal protection where he guarded some of the most elite diplomats and heads of state on the planet. Luc noted:

"The real key to protection is prevention. If you are stuck in reaction, then you've missed something. If you're in a school and you see two students starting an argument, intercept them immediately. Look at their interaction. There will always be one who is more aggressive. You need to be aware of this. Separate the violent ones immediately. Now instead of dealing with 32 students, you have to deal with 2. If you have the possibility to call for help, get backup right away. Use your commands. Keep your distance. Then you are in a better position to bring the situation down."

Luc went on to recount a particular incident from his career. He was part of a protection detail for Israeli prime minister Benjamin Netanyahu who was set to speak at Concordia University in Montreal.

"I went to do a dry-run two hours before. They had already had a code red situation so we were on high alert. The problem is that when we got there, there were already a lot of protestors. They could tell we were part of the security team and they started to surround us aggressively. The first thing I did was identify myself as a member of the RCMP and they started to retreat. I told them, 'I will let you know we're not coming back with him.' If they knew the client wasn't returning, maybe some of them would leave. The problem was that there was a more extreme group in the crowd that was trying to get onto the second floor to cause problems. They were trying to incite the crowd to violence. We only had two people up on the second floor and they would be overwhelmed easily. They had bomb-sniffing dogs onsite and I asked if they were also trained to attack. The handler said they were, so I took one of the dogs and went into the stairwell. When that group saw me moving there, they separated from the rest of the crowd. They were trying to lead people to go up with them. I was able to just hold them back with the dog long enough for my team to leave. Once everyone was gone, they backed down. It's always better to deal with smaller groups so if you have them separated, you can have more effect. The same applies in a classroom."

Separating the mob is the most effective antidote for mob mentality. Research has shown that blanket lectures that attempt to teach student groups social skills, like *"social citizenship"* and *"anti-bullying lectures"* are the least effective intervention strategies possible.[81] I believe the reason for this is again herd mentality. You're going to have such a hard time reaching those students who are in the most need because they can hide in the group. Some students will try to be invisible. Others will hide their need by loudly resisting, making jokes, and acting out to derail the efforts. All of this prevents the message from sinking in. By comparison, it's far more effective to address students in smaller groups, or one-on-one. Even in a larger group, if I have students who are acting up, I will try to get the group onto a task for a few minutes. During that time, I'll walk around and make a point of connecting with the more resistant students. I may compliment them and appeal to their ego:

"I know this may be a bit boring for you. You're obviously a very bright student, but you carry a lot of influence in the class. I would appreciate it if you could help me out. I think the other students can really benefit from your experiences."

The private message can also be stricter. You could take the student into the hallways and say:

"Listen, I need to get through the class material. The last thing either of us needs is for this to turn into a disciplinary issue, but right now you're on the verge. I know you're just trying to get a laugh, but I need the group to focus now. You need to raise your hand if you want to speak. Can you promise me that? I welcome your contributions but the comments need to be relevant and constructive. Can you do that?"

Another strategy is to appoint peers as leaders. Research shows that implementing peer leaders will increase the students' ability to make choices and to direct the curriculum. A democratic, collaborative effort is a great way to break up mob mentality. When individual students are given more responsibility, they will in effect help direct and regulate the group's behavior from the inside.

If counseling is to be provided, it's similarly more effective to provide it on an individual basis or in smaller groups. If you have a resource person on staff who can address the problematic students privately, this is a fantastic advantage that can massively improve the school climate. Moreover, if you can strengthen your rapport directly with those students, research has shown that individual attention through the form of student-teacher relationships also has a huge role in reducing the rate of violence in schools.[82]

---

[81] Mills J.A., "Mob mentality and classroom management: meeting student needs and building self-regulation skills", https://www.researchgate.net/publication/44389675, 2010

[82] Hopson L.M., Lee E., "Mitigating the effect of family poverty on academic and behavioral outcomes: the role of school climate in middle and high school", *Child. Youth Serv. Rev. 33, 2221-2229.* Doi: 10.1016.j.childyouth.2011.07.006, 2011.

ACTIVE SHOOTER

The 16-year-old male student entered the class and stabbed his teacher twice. He then brandished the knife at his classmates and screamed before leaving the class.

The school shooter admits: *"I wasn't wanted by anyone".*

The gunman realizes: *"I guess at first I just wanted the gun to show off."*

The killer's letter says: *"Now people will hear what I have to say."*

Sometimes, the greatest power an audience can have is its absence. Just as surely as a group can motivate an individual to act, the absence of group recognition and the yearning for approval can be even more dangerous.

Seemingly every week, the nightly news assaults us with stories about school shootings, stabbings, and other acts of violence. The prospect of a disgruntled person entering our school, office, place of worship or crowded public space and blindly attacking innocent people touches a powerful nerve in our fear centers. It completely encapsulates the senselessness of violence. It highlights the lacking of our social systems to recognize and integrate the disenfranchised, to correctly treat and support mental illness and a host of other issues. Although the United States is the clear leader in school shootings, acts of violence in schools worldwide have many educators fearing this possibility.[83] While American gun culture is often presented as the main culprit for their disproportionate volume of gun violence in schools, other less common variations remain a disturbing possibility worldwide:

- In 2009 a 24-year-old man in Belgium dressed as the Joker entered a nursery armed with a knife and the intent to kill all 18 children. He was stopped by a 54-year-old daycare worker who fought him off but died in the process.
- In 2021 in Brazil an 18-year-old man attacked employees and children under the age of 2 with a machete.
- In 2010, a farmer in Shandong Province, China, entered a nursery armed with a hammer and began attacking children under the age of 6.
- As I write this, a teen stabbed his teacher twice in front of his class here in Montreal. It was reportedly his favorite teacher.

At the outset of this book, we discussed the idea that our *duty of care* is interpreted by many schools to mean we should seek minimal to no physical intervention in the case of

---

[83] School Shootings by Country 2022 (worldpopulationreview.com)

school violence to avoid legal consequences. To date, we have been focusing on violence within the school amongst students.

- Would your reflexes change if the attack came from the outside? What if the attacker were an adult stranger rather than a fellow student?
- In the majority of nursery attacks, workers attempt to intervene. They usually receive among the worst injuries. What would you do in this situation?
- Regardless of what age group you normally work with, would you be more likely to intervene if the victims were babies or toddlers? Are you less likely to intervene if the students are older? Statistically, regardless of policy, educators are more likely to put themselves in harm's way if their students are younger.
- What degree of force would you be willing to employ to stop a gunman? Would it change if they had a knife or hammer?

I strongly recommend you deeply consider these scenarios and write them down in a journal. As you continue to implement some of the strategies in this book, it can be helpful to come back to them from time to time to see if your perspectives have changed. In the end, what matters is that you know what your motives, triggers, and limits are. **We cannot afford to wait until we are in the midst of a crisis to explore our limits.** We can't wait until we are staring down the barrel of a gunmen's weapon to contemplate our willingness to intervene or harm. We need to prepare now. Efficient planning depends on knowing our principles.

Within the domain of active shooter training (of course, the assailant could just as well be armed with a knife or hammer), the most common training structure currently taught in schools is known as the *Run-Hide-Fight* model. As the name states, it promotes that the priority should be to escape. When escape is not possible, the focus should be to hide and barricade yourself in the safest possible place. Finally, should hiding fail and you become confronted by the gunmen, only then should you fight back.

The value of this training is heavily debated. On one end of the spectrum, concerned parents and administrators argue that exposing students to these scenarios can be traumatic and cause more harm than good. This is a normal fear that we experience anytime we are forced to confront something uncomfortable and we'll get into this shortly. On the opposite end of the spectrum, tactical critics insist that the training doesn't go far enough. They stress that it generally lacks the realism and is too passive in its prioritization of running and hiding.

I will begin by saying that I have lived in both worlds: I have battled the soul-draining-uphill-frozen-molasses-drip-movement of administrative roadblocks. I have pleaded the case for the basic existence of what I teach against concerns for public perception, litigiousness, budget restraints, defunding, and related obstacles. I deeply know how difficult it can be to create institution-wide change. I was also bred in the tactical world, so

I have experience with violence that the average person does not. I know the consequences of failing to prepare. Ignorance is not a strategy; it's negligence. Pacifism is a choice contingent on the ability to defend yourself. Refusing to take precautions is simply irresponsible. As Thucydides said:

> *"The society that separates its scholars from its warriors will have its thinking done by cowards and its fighting by fools."*

Beyond the debate between administrators and tacticians, I consider myself an educator first. My goal is to improve the readiness of whoever I teach, period. While I am always researching and refining my approach, I also recognize that sometimes we must teach within certain limitations. Like most school teachers, I am often required to teach existing curriculums, which I may not necessarily agree with. My first goal is to deliver that material as effectively as I can no matter what the constraints may be. Many of my colleagues in the tactical world bemoan the *"naivete"* of the layperson and bark at the heavens denouncing the ignorance of the uninitiated. While I understand the frustration, I prefer to dedicate my energy to staying goal-oriented and using my time to deliver as much information as I can. We were all newbies at some point. We would still be there without the teachers we've had.

I also understand the concern of administrators, teachers, and parents, who fear exposing our youth to these harsh realities. They are realities nonetheless. School violence happens. Increasingly, professionals are referring to "*active shooter*" situations, as "*active killer*" situations, to illustrate exactly the shift in mindset that is required. We are talking about the possibility of someone entering into a place of learning, a place that should be sacred and safe, and violating one of our greatest freedoms. This *should* be disturbing. The truth is, some degree of exposure is necessary to prepare for the stress of a crisis. That being said, **training shouldn't be trauma**. I will show you shortly that there are safe and responsible ways to teach virtually any topic through games and unconventional exercises. Others argue that tactics like fighting back become unrealistic for elementary-age children. I understand their concern. Responses definitely need to be modified to the capacities of your student body, but as I hope to show, they do not negate the value of Active Shooter training. Rather they speak to the **need new innovations in how it is taught**. Let's look at the basics of the most accepted response model.

RUN:

Statistically, the strategy that consistently has the highest number of survivors is to run. The very first step to running is to *"act as if"*. If you hear something that could potentially be a gunshot or screams, commotion or other signs of crisis, mobilize your students immediately. It's not enough to remind students to leave their personal belongings behind, **they must be trained to do so**, both by rehearsing the practice and by you modeling that behavior. I've seen teachers telling their students to leave their belongings as they scramble to collect their own belongings. This sends the wrong message. Model your instructions.

Most active shooter training approaches the act of running like a fire drill. I would submit a few additional considerations. Teachers may be yelling or blowing whistles. Students are talking and absent-minded. The intention you bring to any rehearsal matters. Consider the following:

1. **Train your students to stay quiet.** Instruct every student to shut off their phone and to keep their eyes on you for visual signals. I've seen so many active shooter drills and fire drills done where everyone is laughing and talking. Silence is of the utmost importance.
    - First, it ensures that the teachers can **communicate** with maximum efficiency.
    - Second, it will **help you navigate** your school. In an active shooter scenario, it can be difficult enough to identify the source of the gunfire. Panic, combined with echoes in the corridors can lead to false reports of locations and even of multiple gunmen. Train your students to remain quiet so you can hear where the threat may be coming from and modify your escape route if necessary.
    - Third, it **avoids drawing undo attention to you**. The intruder may not always be making noise. They could be just around the next corner. By staying quiet, you avoid needlessly drawing attention to yourself and the students. Practice using hand signals to instruct your group and see if you can evacuate in silence. While there are a host of established tactical symbols, it doesn't need to be anything fancy. Holding an open hand up for stopping, waving a hand forward to signal "*go*", or holding a finger to the lips for silence is likely all that you will need in most cases.
2. **Stay in formation**. Train your students to create a tactical chain, with each student placing their hand on the shoulder of the person in front of them. This will help focus students on the task of staying connected. As you evacuate the school, speed will vary. Ideally, you will slow down to peek around corners before pushing past them as we'll see in a moment. That means there *will* be natural slowdowns. By having your hand on the person in front of you, it's easier to avoid bunching up and colliding with one another by accident. Even if you temporarily lose contact with your classmate's shoulder, by having your hand up and out in front of you, you are establishing a protective Fence. Under conditions of extreme stress, feeling connected to your team will also bring a sense of greater security and help mitigate freezing and related acute stress reactions. In a few more sections we will be discussing the role of touch and contact in helping students stay in the moment to overcome freezing with fear.

3. **Teach your students to stay low.** Squatting down slightly will help control the pace of your students, improve their balance and make them harder to target. Drills should include an emphasis on quietly but quickly creeping, in tactical circles what is commonly termed *"Ghost Walking".* Rather than loudly bouncing and falling with each step, strive for 50 percent of the motion coming from pushing off the back foot and 50 percent coming from pulling with the front leg. The head should try to maintain a constant and even height. As soldiers and SWAT teams are taught, *a balanced body supports a balanced mind.* Combined with shoulder contact with the person in front of you, Ghost Walking can get your class moving like a well-oiled machine, bringing a collective focus to the task at hand.

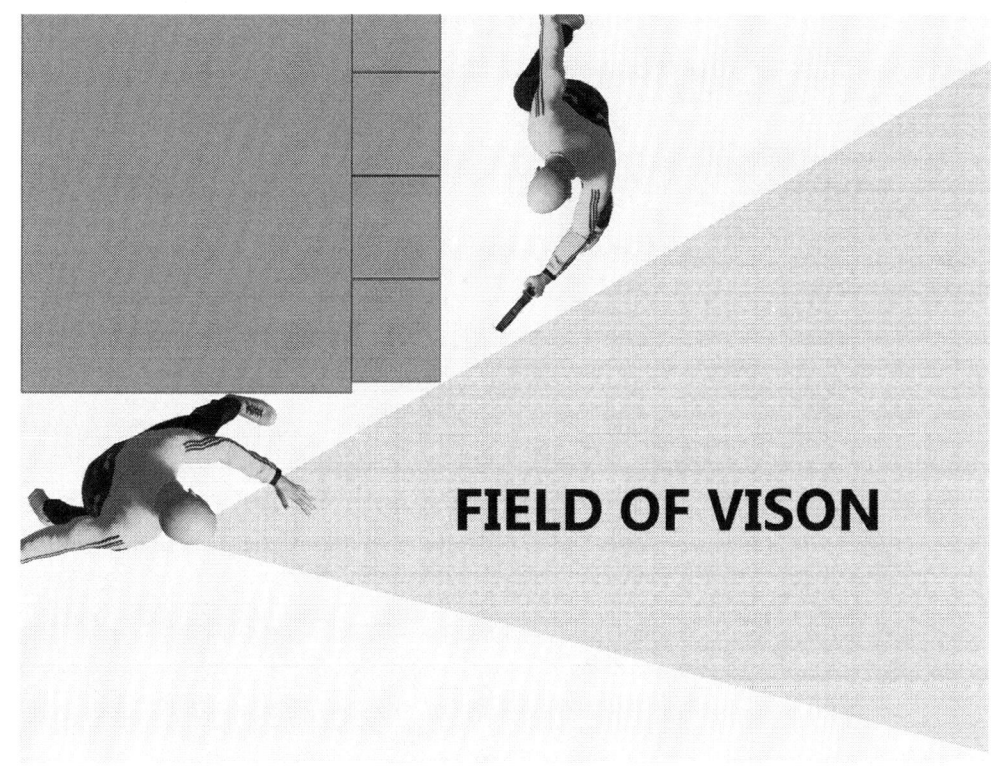

FIELD OF VISON

"Hugging the wall may limit your field of vision and place you at greater risk from bullets that 'ride' the wall."

FIELD OF VISON

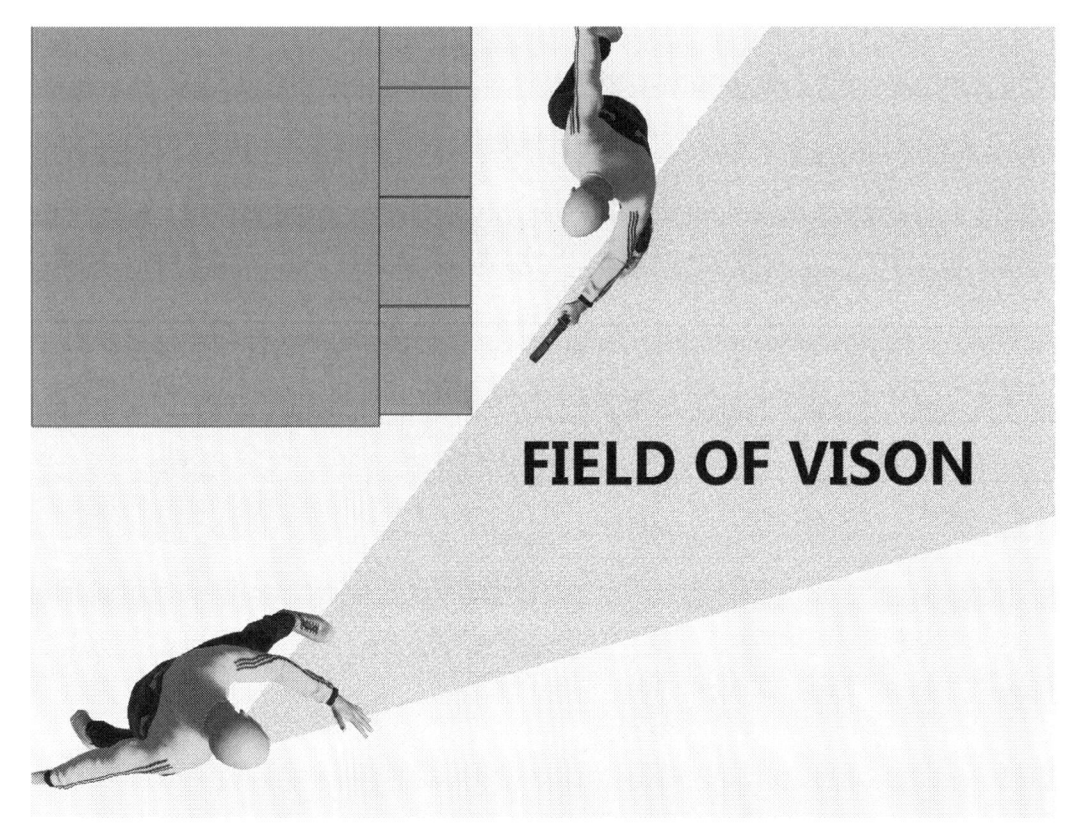

"Turning your corners wider will help you see more."

4. **Teach your students *where* to walk.** When you are in the open space of a corridor, avoid walking down the middle of the hallway as this makes you the easiest possible target. Obstructions can provide either **cover** or **concealment.** *Cover* can potentially block or weaken an attack while *concealment* only obscures visibility. A classroom door may not be thick enough to block a bullet but it can make it harder to see you and delay an attacker from shooting their way in. If your walls are made of brick and cinder blocks, they can provide some degree of protection from bullets. If they are made of drywall, they are only likely to provide concealment. In either case, avoid hugging walls. While bullets will normally ricochet at an angle equal to their approach on harder surfaces, different materials can cause bullets to ride the wall, rebounding and following the surface. For this reason, we never want to crowd and stick to walls. Instead, be within easy reach of the wall. I use the term *"tracing"* the wall, to imply that we go around the wall but stay close enough to touch it. Touching walls can give you a greater sense of comfort and balance and can make it harder to see from a distance around corners. As you approach a corner, the teacher should signal the students to stop. The teacher should then move further away from the wall to gain a wider field of vision as they peek around the corner. By turning a corner more widely, you will be able to see your potential aggressor sooner and more easily while exposing less of your own body.

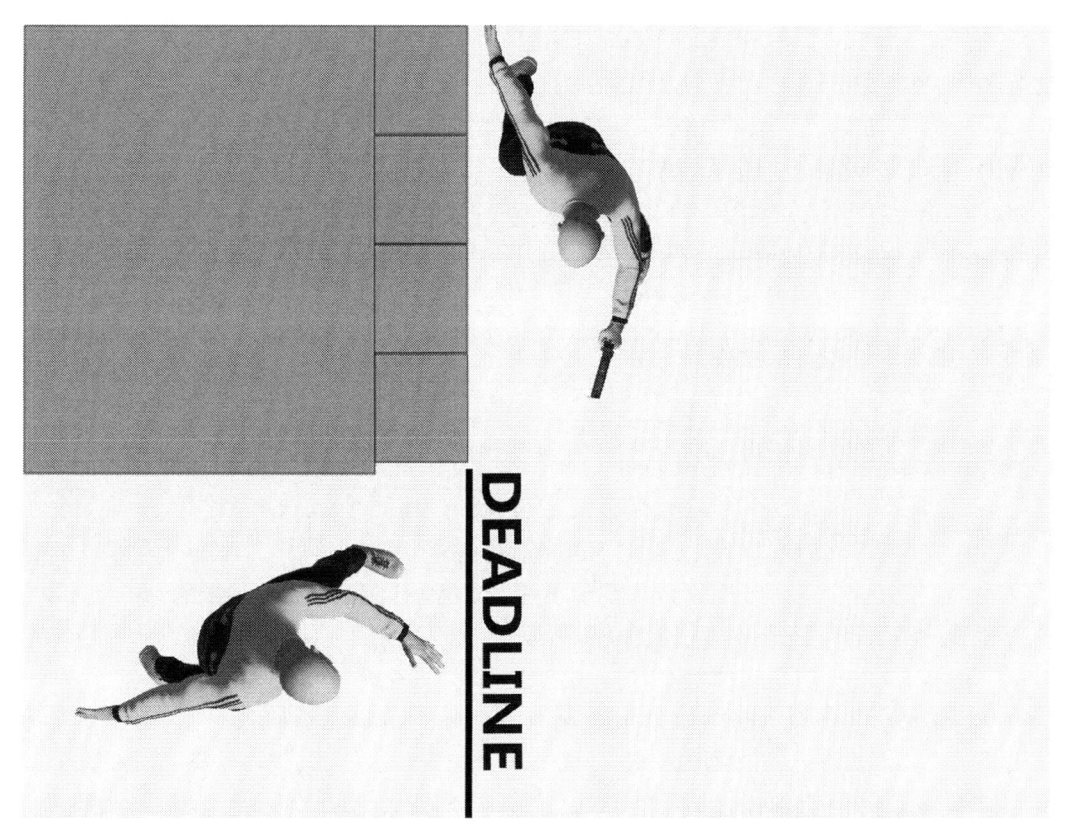

"Carefully approach every wall's deadline and "peek" before you proceed."

5. **Every corner has a *"deadline"*** that represents the imaginary continuation of the adjacent wall. As you approach the *"deadline"*, peak first to make sure the corner is safe then press forward. In stairwells, hug the walls. Stay away from the center of the stairwell as this increases your visibility. A stairwell is like a vertical corner. By staying closer to the wall, you will be more hidden from easy view down the center of the well. Remember:
   - **Trace walls and wells.**
   - **Turn corners widely** by peeking and then pushing forward, moving briskly and smoothly once the decision to move has been made.

Effective tactical movement takes practice. That's why I believe this type of movement should be used in **every** emergency drill. Fire drills for example are a simple way to create safe, non-threatening opportunities for training. Also, by training consistency you cultivate a single emergency response and less confusion. We don't have time to train one response for fires and another for active shooters. **Safe movement should be safe in every situation.**

One of the cases commonly cited as an argument *against r*unning in favor of always locking down is the 2010 shooting at Sullivan Central High in Blountville, Tennessee. In this particular case, the gunman pulled the fire alarms to lure the students into the hallway where he then opened fire. While immediately going into lockdown may arguably have saved more lives:

- This type of trap is statistically rare.
- In the overall sampling of school shootings as a whole, running still remains statistically preferable in most cases.
- The students in Tennessee were not shot because they ran. Moreover, we don't know that they wouldn't have been shot had they hidden or if they would have had time to barricade. They were potentially shot because of *how* they ran. Approaching all emergencies with increased tactical awareness could massively mitigate the dangers of Sullivan Central-style tactics. By maintaining quiet order and peeking around every corner to inspect before pushing forward past the *"deadline"*, students and employees would be in a better position to avoid traps. Even very young children learn how to test touch door knobs during fire drills to feel if it is hot before opening a door. In exactly the same way, staff and students could be trained to *"peak before pushing"* around corners to determine whether to run or hide.

Typically, *Run, Hide, Fight* strategies are taught sequentially, placing priority on more passive skills. Many tactical experts feel this is a mistake and that priority should be placed on aggressive action. Having taught in the school system for decades, I understand that staff demographics vary enormously. Many teachers may lack the physical capacity and confidence to fight back. I think it unrealistic to impose tactical norms on minimally trained civilians. For most teachers, the thought of a school attack is an affront to their mental security and it's far easier to refuse the responsibility and not think about it. Sadly, this leaves us woefully unprepared.

I will therefore say three things:

1. **We are all worth protecting.** We all have a right to live. While it is always tactically prudent to avoid confronting violence when it can be avoided if the moment comes when you have the choice to certainly die on your knees or to try to fight back, what would you do? Moreover, what could you do realistically to be as feral and vicious as necessary regardless of your age or physical capacity?
2. **Look around your staff** and you will certainly notice that not all members will be equally up to the task. Some will face greater physical challenges. Some will face even larger psychological ones. Where do you think you fit in within this spectrum? Were I on your staff, I would assume a role near the top for mental and physical preparedness. I know that I would carry a larger responsibility to support my team. I expect it and I accept it. Where do you fall in the preparedness spectrum with your staff? What do you consider your responsibility to be?
3. **Always be ready to fight.** Although I am using the commonly accepted *Run, Hide, Fight* model, I believe the very first step is to accept reality and **prepare yourself to fight**

back at any moment. Whether you are running or hiding, use every second that you have to arm your mindset immediately. When I run, I am seeking to evade detection but I stalk aggressively. I expect to be ambushed at any point. I will do everything in my power to avoid a conflict but I am always readying myself more with every step. When I hide, I am immediately barricading myself in if I can. Then, I am arming myself with anything at my disposal as we will see. Run from the enemy if you can, but don't run from your responsibility. Hide from the attacker if you are able, but don't hide from reality. If you are under attack, **do everything you can to make yourself the hardest target that you can be**. Fight with everything that you have at the moment.

EXERCISE #23:

Tactical awareness begins with you. The next time you're finishing up your day and you have a relatively empty hallway at your disposal, practice slowly walking your halls with a little more tactical awareness. Think about tracing the walls in the open corridors, then take your corners widely. Slow down to peek before pushing. Practice tracing the walls in your stairwells to see how it helps you stay hidden longer. Elite military will practice hundreds of dry-runs, often in exact replicas of their target location, before deploying. You have the opportunity to do the same every day in your school.

As you approach doorways, stay low and below any windows to remain hidden. Practice slowly and quietly opening the door to peek before pushing through. With a little practice, you can make these essential tactics a comfortable habit. If you're too embarrassed to act this out in your school, see if you can hide your actions, making them look normal and natural in your everyday motions. Find no excuse not to train yourself.

HIDE:

Hiding, or what is commonly termed *"locking down"*, is our second priority. When you are unable to safely flee, it is best to stay securely in your classroom.

- **Turn off your phones.** Make sure that all students have shut off their phones or placed them on silent. Call 911 yourself if you are able.
- **Turn off any lights or machinery** that might attract the intruder to your location.

"Outward swinging doors can be impeded by wrapping the 'swing arm' with a belt or extension cord."

- **Barricade the door.** If the door can be locked from the inside, lock it immediately. Place obstacles to obscure windows, block the swing of inward opening doors or fill the entrance with the heaviest objects possible. Depending on the height, chairs can sometimes be tilted to serve as ramparts, or else commercial bars can be purchased which serve the identical purpose or can be placed across the door to prevent them from opening. In the case of outward opening doors or if larger objects are not available or easily moved, you can wedge objects under the doors with your hands and then kick them into place. Rubber door stops, open books, or folded paper can make it very difficult for your door to be opened fully. Commercial door jammers can also be purchased. Alternatively, you can tether the doorknob to heavy objects with rope or extension cords. In the case of doors with swing arms, extension cords or belts can be wound around the arm to impede their opening. Officer Mike Malpass notes that when tested, short lengths of decommissioned fire hose slipped perfectly over swing arms and blocked the door from opening. As a

class exercise, you can experiment with building simple blockades to test each of their effectiveness.
- **Escape** if safely possible by a window or secondary exit. Begin ushering the students out one at a time, instructing them to stay low, together and to move towards the pre-established safe location.

The shooting at Virginia Tech in 2007 is a good argument for the power of barricading. The gunman killed 32 teachers and students. Consider these variables:

- In room 211, the teacher saw the shooter in the hallway, moved back to the classroom, and began to barricade the door with lightweight desks. The gunman pushed through the barricade killing an Air Force cadet who attempted to rush him, and opened fire, shooting everyone in the classroom. He even shot students who were attempting to play dead and those who were already dead, killing approximately two-thirds of the students. The barricade failed.
- In room 205, students attempted to barricade the door with a large teacher's desk. The gunman fired through the door and hit one student. He could not gain access to the room and no students were killed.
- In room 207, no defensive action was taken initially. The students began barricading too late as the gunman was opening fire. 85 percent of the people were shot and 38 percent of those in the classroom died.
- In room 204, they barricaded the door. The barricade held while the majority of the students escaped. 36 percent of the occupants were shot and 14 percent of those in the classroom were killed.
- Room 205 successfully denied the shooter access to the room. The shooter fired through the door, but no one was hit or killed.[84]

We learn a few important lessons here:

1. When the barricades held, injuries and death were low to none.
2. Barricades were most successful when the subjects *"acted as if"* the threat was real and took action immediately.
3. When barricades failed, the gunman continued to attack successfully. Therefore, even if you think your barricade will hold, be prepared to fight immediately if it fails.

---

[84] Blair J.P., et al., "Active shooter events and response", *CRC Press Taylor & Francis Group*, 2013 1

FIGHT BACK:

Now although the common mandate is to avoid engaging the intruder, when possible, our first goal is to accept responsibility for our survival. If you absolutely cannot run and your barricades have failed, then your only remaining options are to fight back or else to submit to the attacker's whims. The likelihood of verbal de-escalation being an option in cases like these is almost non-existent. Fighting back definitely carries a high risk, but the alternative is to volunteer for severe injury or death. **Fight back immediately and ferociously.** Active killers, with whatever tool they use, are generally indiscriminate. They will usually shoot you regardless of whether or not you are passive and cowering or even playing dead. A few keys to fighting back:

- **Keep it absolutely simple.**
- **Be the leader.** Equip all of your students with items to throw. Small books, metal water bottles, and staplers are small, heavy, and easily thrown. If they can have multiple items to throw in succession, even better.
- **Have your students flank the wall** along the entry point, behind the swing of the door to keep them out of sight as long as possible. Force the gunman to enter the room in order to get a clear line of sight on them.
- **Have the students closest to the door squat down** so they can throw objects from a lower perspective and to allow students behind them to throw over their heads more easily. The moment the gunman is visible, pelt him with as many objects as possible to make it harder to aim.
- **Charge the gunman,** prioritizing hugging and hanging on the gun arm and driving forward. When fighting a gun, **always push** to off-balance the attacker. Avoid the instinct to pull as this will cause the weapon's line of fire to move toward you. Push, drive and pin the subject into the wall or else follow him to the ground.
- If you have larger secondary school-age students in your class, having them pile on, particularly around the legs is extremely effective.
- As disturbing as it may be to consider, if you have large, more physically capable students, have them arm themselves with heavy blunt objects to strike, scissors to stab, flag poles to use as spears, or anything else that can be used as a hand-to-hand weapon.
- You can use fire extinguishers to fog and create concealment, or smash and hammer with the cylinder.
- Look around your classroom or office and see what else can be used in your favor.
- I've trained this approach in live scenarios with high school students and office workers. Distracting the gunman with thrown objects and swarming them with forward pressure can be an extremely effective tactic with a strong chance of overwhelming the attacker. The most important thing is that you do whatever it takes to survive. We never want to be a victim. We want to be the most resistant, hard-to-kill target possible.

THE TEACHER AS GUARDIAN

At the outset of this book, I identified apathy as one of our greatest opponents.
Thoughts like: *"That's not my job"* and *"That's not my problem"* are poisonous.
The duty of a teacher is to hope for a better tomorrow. To try, despite the odds. To inspire.

In interviewing many long-time friends for the various *"Stories From the Field"* you'll find throughout this book, I was inspired by their various approaches and diverse interpretations. Yet, as different as each individual was, I was struck by their overwhelming sense of transcendent affirmativeness. In law enforcement and military circles, it is quite common to have a creed. The idea had been bouncing around my brain as I wrote this book. Then, I fell upon a graduate thesis by John A. Whitney IV from the Naval Postgraduate School in Monterey, California. In it, he noted that there were many similarities between soldiers, law enforcement, and teachers.

> *"Both serve with a level of pride and dedication unique to their professions. Both commit to the service of others. Moreover, both find themselves directly responsible for the safety of themselves and those they protect."*[85]

Whitney suggested a Teacher's Creed which he adapted from the United States Department of the Army's *"Warrior Ethos: Soldier's Creed"* that encapsulates the proud acceptance of our roles not just as inspirations, but of protectors. Whitney inspired me to write my own creed which I'll share with you now:

> *"I am a Teacher.*
> *I am committed to my students and their community.*
> *I pledge to always continue learning and growing and to share my passion with my students.*
> *I dedicate myself to my profession and seek to inspire my students with my example.*
> *I am the guardian of my students. It is my duty to protect them.*
> *I will never quit.*
> *I am a Teacher."*

---

[85] Whitney, J.A. IV, "Defensive tactics and tactical decision-making for elementary school teachers and staff", *Naval Postgraduate School, Monterey, California*, 2017

I believe teaching is a noble and indispensable profession. I am proud to be a teacher. I hope that all of my fellow educators would have their own creed that conveys their passion. Reciting a creed has a powerful effect. It reminds us what matters most when negativity would otherwise threaten to seep into the well water of our spirit.

EXERCISE #24:

What would your personal creed look like? What do you feel is the most important part of your vocation? What unique strengths do you bring to your students? In your best version of yourself, what would you hope to represent in their lives?

Take a sheet of paper and write down a quick draft of what your creed might look like. Then, try to read it out loud. If you've never tried writing an affirmation, it can feel a bit silly at first, but that's just because you're not yet used to that level of positivity. With a little practice, this can become second nature. When you've finished your creed, fold that paper up and keep it in the back of this book. It might be interesting to come back to it occasionally or to revisit it when you're done reading to see if there is anything you might want to add. Creeds and affirmations are great ways of getting external support from within when you can't otherwise find it.

SAFE GAMES FOR A SAFE SCHOOL

Earlier, we saw that one criticism of Active Shooter training is that the training can be too traumatic for students. The difficulty is that we can't be inoculated against a virus without some exposure to it. In the same way, we can't overcome fear without experiencing some amount of it. Although so-called *"exposure therapy"* is a deeply proven and established clinical protocol, our innate desire to avoid anything unpleasant often leaves it grossly underused.[86] [87] [88] This reluctance is even higher with children and adolescents, although research confirms that the approach is completely safe and **bears minimal risk when correctly implemented**.[89]

How then can we balance responsible stress inoculation and appropriacy for the various age groups? It begins with introducing the training to the participants before they encounter it. Teachers need to be warned well in advance when a drill will occur so they can prepare their students. There is no value in surprising everyone to see how they will react. This is only likely to imprint a sense of learned helplessness and plant the seeds for future panic.

Let's take something as simple as a fire drill. Let's say you have an autistic student who you know has extreme auditory sensitivity. A fire alarm is likely to send them into a complete panic that will spiral downward and jeopardize the safety of the entire class in an actual crisis. As a teacher, by knowing the drill is coming well in advance, you have the benefit of introducing it repeatedly to the class in advance. You could perform a few dry runs beforehand, perhaps starting with the student you are concerned with alone. Then you could have a colleague lead the remainder of the class out while you and the student observe the drill. Observing the drill will help the student see how the other students are performing. It models successful behavior and reassures them that there is nothing to worry about. Just being allowed to experience the drill as an observer can help them begin replacing potential fear with familiarity.

You could progress to having the student experience an alarm on your phone. You could allow the student to control the alarm, turning it on or off, or the volume up and down to show them they are in control and there is nothing to fear. Some schools are

---

[86] Sars D., van Minnen A., "On the use of exposure therapy in the treatment of anxiety disorders: a survey among cognitive behavioral therapists in the Netherlands", *BMC Psychol.*, 2015; 3(1): 26, Aug 5 2015.

[87] Freiheit SR, Vye C, Swan R, Cady M., "Cognitive-behavioral therapy for anxiety: Is Fissemination working?", *Behavior Therapist.***27**(2):25–32, 2004.

[88] Becker CB, Zayfert C, Anderson E., "A survey of psychologists' attitudes towards and utilization of exposure therapy for PTSD", *Behavior Research and Therapy*, **42**(3):277–292. doi: 10.1016/S0005-7967(03)00138, 2004.

[89] Gola J. et al, "Ethical consideration in exposure therapy with children", *Cogn Behav Pract.*, May 1, 2017.

even equipped with silent alarms that simply flash rather than ringing. They could also experience the alarm while wearing headphones. Depending on the student's capacity, they could even be given the freedom to pull the headphones slightly off of their head to hear the full alarm and then to replace them to control the volume. Ultimately, on the day of the drill, the student could be given an advance warning and allowed to wear headphones. The remainder of the class would be equally trained to be sensitive to the student's needs. Buddy systems could be introduced to further help.

Following any type of drill, you must debrief the students. Congratulate them for what they did well and set objectives for improvement in areas that were lacking. Decompression exercises like stretching and deep breathing are also great to remove the stress of the training. A colleague of mine even created a chart showing all of the training increments that would be used, ending in the actual drill so the student was conditioned to understand that the training would end. He noted that he had an autistic student who was prone to fixating on routine. Having the experience on a chart provided a clear visual indicator that the experience was over, otherwise, he said the student would be prone to expect the drilling to continue every day.

Every student will have different specific needs and it can involve extra work that we might never have needed or experienced when we were in school, but consider the options: you have the capacity to plant a traumatic trigger in the student for the remainder of their life that could directly endanger their lives in a crisis or you could teach them how to resolve something that would otherwise be extremely traumatic through a few extra steps. By taking those few precautions, you can teach a life-saving coping skill that is very likely to be needed. You can simultaneously sensitize and educate the remainder of your class and school as a whole to the very present needs of others in their society. When you consider the enormity of this achievement, the few extra steps are actually remarkably small and inexpensive.

I give this example to illustrate that everything has the potential to be traumatic or the promise to be educational, life-saving, and life-affirming. Our obligation as a teacher is to show every student where potential anxiety pitfalls may lie and prepare them for it. We are not trying to make them stressed and fail. **We are trying to guide them to success.** Don't try to surprise them with the training. This won't better prepare them. Rather it will risk imprinting a sense of learned helplessness. Moreover, training must also be followed by a debrief, where students can share their experiences. This is absolutely essential to ensure that the training is correctly integrated.

I always tell my students: **the key to learning is play**. Even a tiger in the wild will teach its young through play. Even though the tiger cubs are learning urgent survival skills, they do not mangle their offspring or harm them with vicious training. They play. Here are just a few ways you can integrate play throughout the school curriculum to enhance tactical awareness:

"Integrate effective tactical movement in drills and games, like staying low and maintaining contact with the person in front of you."

- **Integrate improved tactical movement patterns in regular fire drills.** As I noted earlier, fire drills are common and widely accepted. While many argue that active shooter drills are traumatic, they rarely argue that fire drills are. In reality, getting burned alive is also a rather gruesome possibility. Yet because of perception and how the drill is handled, fire drills are seen as mundane. They aren't generally regarded as too traumatic to be beneficial. These same, widely accepted fire drills can easily be modified to include positive tactical attributes like absolute silence, effective tactical movement like placing a hand on the shoulder of the person in front of you, and the use of simple hand gestures like *"stop"* and *"go"* to keep them orderly and optimally efficient. This not only improves your fire drill but also lays the groundwork for an active shooter situation and provides them with sound tactical skills for any situation they may experience in the future. The work can be kept playful but efficient.
- **Create a school-wide policy of rounding your corners widely to avoid collisions.** Teach your students how to walk more effectively around corners in their day-to-day life. Having every teacher dedicate a few minutes to teaching the importance of the skill, a few general announcements, and even a few posters near the various corners of your school can massively increase awareness and change habits. This gets them ready for more serious situations while keeping them safer during regular movement.
- **Always employ effective tactical movement.** If you are going to take a class outside for any reason, why not use the opportunity to teach them how to do it safely?
- **If you are taking them outside for a Phys. Ed. class, turn it into circuit training.** Exaggerate the low squat walk. Stop to do push-ups in the hall (like taking cover),

perform chair squats against the wall (like hiding), and take tactical breathing breaks. Beyond being a great workout, you will be laying a subconscious foundation for a tactical escape without them realizing it.

- **In science class, teach the 6 simple machines** (lever, ramp, wedge, pulley, wheel & axle, screw). Then have a class competition to see who can create the best door barricades in the class. For example, if objects are too heavy to move, levers like broom handles or flag poles can be used to tip them open to block doorways, or belts or extension cords can be used to tie door handles to heavy objects. Folded paper can be wedged under door cracks to delay and impede opening. If the door has an automatic door closer, wrap a belt or extension cord around the hydraulic hinge arm to prevent it from opening. If the door can be locked from the inside, lock it.
- **In Phys. Ed. class, play a game of dodgeball using obstacles** like folded gym mats or foam plyo boxes to teach students how to employ cover.
- **In Art class, give a lesson on vantage points** and take the students throughout the school to draw various perspectives and angles in corridors and doorways as a great way to reinforce line-of-sight.
- **In science class, use laser pointers in the corridors to emphasize the line of site and visibility,** and teach refraction, reflection, etc. Please make sure laser pointers are permitted in your school and under no circumstances should lasers ever be pointed directly at a student.
- **Halloween is a great time to conceal survival games.** Even the CDC and Homeland security have used wargames that involve zombie outbreaks as a way to train their staff.
- **Provide first aid training that includes enriched topics** like how to drag an injured individual to cover (which could be necessary during natural disasters or fires as well) or show them how to shield a fallen colleague from debris or even a stampede of panicked individuals.

There is no limit to how imaginative you can get here. Over the years, I have consistently trained students as young as 6 years old, for serious topics including active shooters and abduction. I always use fun games that conceal the immediately frightening elements of those possibilities while nonetheless providing strong tactical skills and some exposure to the stresses involved.

ACUTE STRESS RESPONSE

Since we have been talking about the debate over trauma from Active Shooter training and related exposure, I will take this time to talk about two forms of stress responses: *Acute Stress Reaction* which happens during or immediately after a stressful event, and *Post Traumatic Stress Disorder* which can develop any time after a traumatic event. We will begin with Acute Stress Reaction (ASR).

In tactical circles, stress responses are often represented by a color-coded chart:

- **Condition White** refers to a state of complete relaxation like when you're peacefully sleeping.
- **Condition Yellow** refers to regular everyday stimulation, like walking through your neighborhood.
- **Condition Orange** occurs when we have targeted awareness. Our attention is drawn to something. This could be as simple as a dog barking, a light flashing, or even the feeling that someone is watching you.
- **Condition Red** means we are fully primed. We are in a state of high performance, fully focused, and ready to respond. We may feel the effects of adrenaline, like a dry mouth, gurgling stomach, sweating or light shaking, but the stress chemicals are giving us more than they are taking away, making us stronger, more resistant to pain and more energetic.
- **Condition Black** is when have become overwhelmed. The stress is too much. Our emotional brain centers have completely hijacked the thinking part of our brain. We may be panicking ineffectively, crying, lost in rage, acting erratically, or simply frozen.

Acute Stress Reactions can rob us of the increased performance advantages of a Condition Red state and shift us into a dangerous state of Condition Black. This can occur at a critical moment when there is simply no time to waste. If we are trying to run in the wake of an active shooter and one of our friends or colleagues begins to freeze, we may feel the reflex to simply scream at them or even slap them to get their attention back and to force them into function. This usually fails. The emotional centers of the brain are already hijacked. Adding more stress to them by screaming, shaking, and slapping the subject will usually just make things worse. The opposing reflex to gently coax or reassure the person out of their state is also likely to fail for the same reason. Soft, logical messages will generally lack the impact to penetrate the emotional veil. So, what is the best way to get the cognitive brain back in control?

The U.S. military has recently developed a protocol for Acute Stress Response, inspired by a model used by the Israeli military. It's known by the acronym **iCOVER**. It stands for:

1. Identify
2. Connect
3. Offer
4. Verify
5. Establish
6. Request [90]

Let's take a look at how this works.

IDENTIFY:

The first step is to identify that the subject is having a stress response. Making a simple statement like:

> *"John, you just froze on me. You're in shock."*

We will likely reiterate this a few times to help get their attention.

CONNECT:

Connecting is about getting the subject to focus their attention on you. There is a natural reflex in these conditions to shake or slap the subject *"back into awareness"* but although the intention is good, remember that adding stress to an already overwhelmed individual is not likely to help.

Instead, establish firm physical contact with the subject. Grab them by the shoulders and turn them to face you. Put yourself in their line of site and maintain strong eye contact. Try to occupy their attention and focus.

---

[90] Adler A. B., Start A.R., Milham L., Allard Y.S., Riddle D., Townsend L., Svetlitzky V., "Rapid response to acute stress reaction: Pilot test for iCOVER training for military units", *Psychological Trauma: Theory, Research, Practice and Policy*, Vol.12, No. 4, 431-435, 2020.

OFFER:

Third, offer your commitment.

"I'm gonna get you through this. It's ok. I've got you."

VERIFY:

The next component is to verify their cognitive brain is coming back online. We do this by verifying simple facts:

- *"John, tell me your last name. John, what is your last name?"*, or
- *"John, can you tell me where we are right now? What part of the school are we in?"* or
- *"I need you to squeeze my shoulder to tell me that you are hearing me. John, can you squeeze my shoulder? John, squeeze my shoulder if you hear me."*

Again, you want to use a loud, clear, firm tone and reiterate the question. Maintaining physical connection and eye contact to keep them focused on you. This is a great place for Alpha Commands. Be clear, simple, and ask for *"do"* actions.

ESTABLISH:

Once you've acquired some basic responses, you need to bring them back up to speed by establishing the order of events. These will help get the subject back in the moment.

"We have a shooter in the school. We're in the cafeteria."

REQUEST:

The final step is to request action.

"We need to keep moving. We need to get the kids to safety. I need you to get up and keep moving with us until we get outside and across the street. Are you able to move? I need your help to get the kids across the street. Can you help me get the kids across the street?"

The iCOVER protocol or similar approaches are simple yet extremely powerful for mitigating the effects of Acute Stress Reactions. In application, if you merge a few of the steps together, or forget one, the fundamental effectiveness of the approach remains intact.

- Tell them what's happening.
- Touch them to help bring them back to the present.
- Ask them simple questions to get their cognitive brain back online.
- Give them a task by focusing on the next step.

The goal is to get the thinking part of their brain to take the steering wheel back from their emotional brain. That starts with you as the interventionist. If you become emotional, you'll keep them emotional.

When taken as a whole, the sequence is very quick:

"John, you just froze. It's ok. I'm squeezing your shoulder. Can you feel that? Nod your head if you can feel that…

Good. John, I've got you. Everything is going to be ok. Do you know where you are? Can you tell me what part of the school we're in?"

"Good. Look, I think there is someone in the school with a gun. We need to get out of the hallway, ok? We need to get to the street. Repeat it back to me. What do we need to do?"

"I need you to get up now. The kids need your help. Are you able to get up with me?"

"Ok, keep the kids all together. Let's get everyone out of here now."

EXERCISE #25:

Visualize going through different scenarios so you can make these words your own. It's not about necessarily memorizing the exact steps, although the acronym can be a helpful study guide. By connecting from a place of logic and action you are more likely to bring the subject back into a functioning cognitive state and to get out of danger more efficiently. The more you practice this visualization and previous exercises, the more you will develop your capacity to stay calm and cognitive in the face of danger.

POST-TRAUMATIC STRESS

Exposure to any event can leave us emotionally and psychologically affected. When we encounter stress that completely exceeds our powers of processing and understanding, something that violates our expectations, those effects can be powerful and lasting, to a point of permanence if not treated. Symptoms can include insomnia, agitation, anxiety, anger, substance abuse, compulsive behavior, and a host of other problems. This is what is termed *Post Traumatic Stress Disorder* (PTSD).

I've suffered from PTSD for a good part of my life from exposure to violence. I tried a lot of different things to resolve it but ultimately, the only way I was able to process it was to come to terms with the harsh reality that there are some terrible things in the world. The truth is, many of our childhood myths flat-out lied to us. Good people do not always get rewarded. Bad people don't always get punished. Often, they don't even feel guilt. The world is not generally safe. My PTSD was an explosively sudden loss of innocence and my suffering came from trying to cling to my previous naivete after my illusion had been shattered.

Sometimes, especially when I'm teaching teens, I tell them I've traveled a lot, that I've seen a lot and some of those things were terrible. I tell them that when people hear some of the places I've been or the things I've experienced, they have a tendency to assume that everywhere else is somehow more dangerous and that here at home we are so safe. The reality is, there are good people *everywhere* in the world—even in those places that we think are scary. There are also some very bad people in the world—and that includes right here. On an optimistic day, I feel like most people are fundamentally good and that there is only a small sliver of people out there that are truly malevolent. On less optimistic days I feel like there may perhaps be more evildoers and certainly many apathetic individuals who just let the evil flourish. Either way, the solution remains the same; the good people everywhere must fight the good fight.

Edmund Burke said:

> ***"The only thing necessary for evil to exist is for good men to do nothing."***

I would submit, this is also the only thing necessary for our trauma to linger as well. We just have to do nothing and it will never leave. When we do nothing, we give trauma free reign over our consciousness. This leads us to feel bitter, eventually resentful, and ultimately distances us further from society. This can lead to slow self-destruction, intentional self-harm, and harmful behaviors toward those around us. This is what creates active shooters to begin with.

Evil does exist. Viciousness does exist. It exists everywhere, including in us. We can either try to ignore this and in our denial become prey to it or we can be confident caregivers who choose to actively fight against it despite the odds. I have used and agree with the common habits for coping with and treating PTSD. These include:

- **Speaking with peers** you trust, therapists and experts. This is essential. If you don't do well in therapy, then find a comrade, call a helpline, or connect with an old friend. If you don't have any, keep a journal. If that makes you uncomfortable, destroy every page after you've written it.
- **Avoiding alcohol** and drugs. You think they will help in the short run but they will make it much worse and keep you in self-pity and resentment. I can't tell you how many times someone told me: I know drinking is bad but I'm totally in control of it.
- **Exercising**, particularly stretching and deep breathing. It doesn't need to be complicated but it must be a routine.
- **Getting out into nature**. Nothing reconnects you with the world like nature. I also find animal companionship a huge part of this. My cats have been the greatest sources of nonjudgmental love ever.
- **Feeling gratitude**. Do something every day to feel grateful. If you don't remember *what* you are fighting for, it's very tough to maintain *why* you are fighting. Rick Fields said that a warrior exists for a purpose beyond themselves, like thorns, protecting a rose.
- **Becoming mindful of the moment.** PTSD keeps us trapped in the past. To combat this, pick any one sense and exaggerate it. For example: take a moment to touch something as if for the first time, and to mindfully feel its texture, to study it, and to appreciate it. Take a drink of water or a bite of food and fully savor it. Feel the full texture and body of flavor. Hold it in your mouth. Swallow it slowly. Feel it go down. Take a moment to truly listen to your environment. Hear all of the subtle sounds that you were previously neglecting. Let the sounds soak into you. Any mindful concentration on the sense of the present will help pull you from the past and back into the moment.
- **Building a support system**. In more extreme cases, finding people we can trust can be extremely difficult. There are experts out there however and they can help us build the right support system—seek them out. As difficult as it may be at first, this can help give you your life back.
- Above all else, recognize that you are a part of nature, no better or worse or different. Realize that **this too shall pass**.

STORY FROM THE FIELD:

Earlier, I introduced you to my friend Pete Jensen, PhD., whose credentials are longer than the Bayeaux Tapestry. In addition to having served as the Human Performance Program Chief at the U.S. Special Operations Command, Pete has also served as the Director and Associate Professor at the U.S. Military Academy Center for Enhanced Performance at West Point. There, he oversaw extensive research on human performance, including the effects of experiencing and witnessing hand-to-hand combat. Pete noted:

> *"Observing student-on-student violence can be a particularly distressing experience. Seeing and hearing – in close proximity – the injuries and physical harm of another person can elicit vicariously aroused distress.[91] We need to accept this. That is, stress, anguish, fear, distress, disgust, fear, nausea, horror –all the emotions and physiological experiences that can arise from being up close to the physical harm of others."*
>
> *"Additionally, David Livingston Smith, philosopher and author of The Most Dangerous Animal: Human Nature and the Origins of War, theorizes that the mirror neurons of the human brain can foster a neurological empathy for the experiences of other humans in our presence. With respect to violence, this can mean that a teacher observing violence can form an empathetic connection with those involved with violence and begin to experience the emotions of those involved, especially the overall distress that comes with physical violence."*

The very first step in coping with Post Traumatic Stress is recognizing and accepting that exposure to violence can create these responses. It is perfectly normal. It can happen to anyone and it can be overcome by anyone.

---

[91] Bandura A., "Moral disengagement in the perpetration of inhumanities", *Personality and social psychology review"*, *3*(3), 193-209, 1999.

INTEGRATING SPECIAL NEEDS

Integrating students with special needs is an enormous topic. Research in this domain advances rapidly and government mandates and guidelines can change just as quickly. It's a topic filled with subtle nuances that every teacher should delve more deeply into. A deep treatment far exceeds the scope of this book but the ineffective integration of a student can be an additional source of violence in schools and a huge source of stress for teachers and staff, so I will briefly address a few key points to show that many of the strategies we've seen so far in this book still apply.

- As many as 14 percent of all public-school students in the U.S. were considered to have special needs in 2019-2020.[92] In Europe, most countries average around 10 percent.[93] This means that in an average-sized class, teachers can be expected to have a number of students with special needs.
- Students in special education made disproportionately more threats and more severe threats than their peers in general education. Students classified as emotionally disturbed (ED) exhibited the highest threat rates.[94] Generally, this is due to a lack of integration and inclusion and its effect on poor self-image which in turn leads to a gradual escalation towards violence.
- Students with intellectual disabilities reported the lowest rates of violence and students with hearing disabilities reported the highest.[95]
- A lack of integration also leads to higher rates of violence *towards* students with special needs as well.[96]

Teaching a student with special needs can be extremely challenging. Even specialists in the field reported higher levels of fatigue. Research in 2020 showed that as many as 40% of special needs teachers burn out within their first five years.[97] It's not surprising therefore

---

[92] *Students With Special Needs*, National Centers for Education Statistics, 2020.
[93] "Learning disabilities affect up to 10 percent of children", *University College London,* ScienceDaily. 2013.
[94] Kaplan SG, Cornell DG, "Threats of Violence by Students in Special Education", *Behavioral Disorders*, 31(1):107-119. doi:10.1177/019874290503100102, 2005.
[95] Girli A., "An examination of the relationships between the social skill levels, self concepts and aggressive behavior of students with special needs in the process of inclusion education", Cukurova University Faculty of Education Journal, Volume 42, Issue 2, 23-38, 08.03.2014, 2013.
[96] *Canadian Press*, Canadians with disabilities twice as likely to be victims of violence: StatsCan - National | Globalnews.ca, 2018.
[97] Herman K. C., Reinke, W. M., & Eddy C. L., "Advances in understanding and intervening in teacher stress and coping: The Coping-Competence-Context Theory", Journal of School Psychology, 78, 69–74. https://doi.org/10.1016/j.jsp.2020.01.001, 2020.

that general population teachers, who often lack the basic strategies to cope, experience even more difficulty with integration.

Studies have shown that most general population teachers were resistant to accept empirical evidence when considering how to teach special needs students. Instead, they were more prone to rely on their assumptions or else the advice of their colleagues. More interestingly, this tendency happened regardless of teaching experience, with novices and veterans reacting the same way.[98] Resistance to change has been widely documented in educational settings. Usually, change is perceived as a threat to the teacher's independence.[99] Consulting outside experts and resource specialists, or receiving direct coaching is often regarded as a loss of autonomy and in many cases even as an insult to the teacher's skill level. The reality is, no one has all the answers. There is no greater quality in a teacher than the ability to admit when we don't know something and then to take the necessary steps to learn more about it. Sadly, when ego and emotions get in the way, it can be very hard to see and accept this.

---

[98] Murik J. et al, "Reported Strategies for Responding to the Aggressive and Extremely Disruptive Behavior of Students Who Have Special Needs", *Australasian Journal of Special Education*, Cambridge University Press, 2016.

[99] Musanti S.I. and Pence, L., "Collaboration and teacher development: unpacking resistance, constructing knowledge, and navigating identities", *Teacher Education Quarterly*, 37 (1), 73–89, 2010.

STORY FROM THE FIELD:

J.D. is a special needs research consultant who specializes in elementary education who notes, *"Everyone learns differently but ultimately, everyone wants to be included. Integration is key. Everyone who is responsible for integrating a child with special needs has to be involved in the process. Everyone needs to have the right training and they have to communicate with each other. We start with a plan but we will need to adapt the plan as we go. It's true, some teachers are very resistant to trying new things. They say they're open to integrating a new student and they may try a few new ideas but if it disrupts the way they've always done things, they often resist."*

"Some years are more intense than others, but there are always new challenges. If a child joins your school late in the year and they haven't just moved to the area, then there's usually a problem. Often this is someone who has already been failed by another school and they are looking for a better environment. The first step is to find the 'why'. You may not always have the luxury of inheriting a complete file with the child. The parents may not even want to admit they have a problem. So often, the first indication you will have is an incident in the school setting. You need to find out why it happened. What happened before? Where was the trigger? Then you need to look for solutions to avoid that behavior from triggering again."

"For example, we had one student who was kindergarten age who would just get up in class and run out. This presents a huge challenge for a classroom teacher. How do you balance managing your class and then run after this child? The boy would immediately run into a bathroom or into a closet. It quickly became apparent he was trying to isolate himself." After they interviewed the parents. *It turned out that at home, whenever he was feeling overwhelmed, he would lock himself in the bathroom and shut off the lights.* *"He wouldn't hurt himself. It was obvious he was self-soothing but the parents hadn't mentioned this because they assumed this was only happening at home."* Without understanding the behavior, the teachers were mistaking this as misbehavior and trying to control it. Once they understood the trigger, they equipped the boy with a private space in the classroom where he could go to isolate himself. They filled it with objects he could play with and squish in the dark and this allowed him to isolate himself when he was feeling overwhelmed and quickly regain control. Not only would this resolve his running issue, but it was also teaching him how to control his feelings independently.

"The key to understanding behavior is to ask questions. Talk to the parents. Communicate with staff. You need to ask a lot of questions because parents may be resistant to admitting things and they may not be seeing behavior patterns. Then once you determine what the triggers are, try to replace that behavior with something that is less disruptive in the short run. This will give you time to teach the child different strategies. The important thing is that whatever you make available to that child should be available to everyone. If it can help one student, it can help everyone. If one of your students is fidgeting and it's disturbing the group, you can stick small Velcro pads under his desk so he can quietly reach under there and play

with it to calm himself down. But if you put it under one desk, put it under every desk because it can benefit other students and you need to normalize it."

Many skills are transcendent and will help all of your students equally. For example, introducing breathing techniques in your class is an amazing self-care skill that can benefit everyone—including the teacher. Taking *"breathing breaks"* during the day is a quick and easy way to reset the group and establish a positive routine in your class.

If you're fortunate enough to have a special needs resource person on staff, it's important that you work together. Rather than seeing them as a threat to your autonomy, realize that they are not only there to help you, but that you can each learn from each other. Resource specialists are under a tremendous amount of stress:

- They're responsible for meeting with students, assessing their needs, and creating an Individual Education Plan.
- They are required to maintain detailed files, incident reports and regular reassessments, and behavior analyses on every child they follow.
- They are often required to meet with parents much more regularly than most teachers do.

We quickly see that they share very similar responsibilities with the teachers they support. Now imagine adding the stress of needing to adapt to every single classroom environment, every subject being taught, differing protocols, discipline styles, routines, and even technology platforms. They are in effect co-teaching with every member of staff.[100] It's not surprising that most special needs teachers report higher levels of role conflict, more confusion, and ambiguity in their responsibilities while feeling less support than most teachers.[101]

The two key takeaways I would like you to leave this chapter with are:

- **We have seen the incredible power of *empathy* in de-escalating conflict and connecting with students**. The same applies to interacting with your colleagues as well. Try reframing your perception of resource staff and students with special needs. They are opportunities to see familiar things in a new light.
- **Teaching is a journey and learning is a habit. Neither are final destinations.** We owe it to ourselves and our students to be excited by and open to the process of learning. Embracing the opportunity as a challenge rather than fighting it, is a single decision we alone have the power to make. Embracing learning can completely affect our joy, and success and provide the fulfillment we feel.

---

[100] Eastwood A., "Strategies to Overcome Special Education Teacher Burnout", *Minnesota State University Moorhead RED: a Repository of Digital Collections,* 2020.
[101] Brittle B., "Coping strategies and burnout in staff working with students with special educational needs and disabilities", *Teaching and Teacher Education,* 87, 102937–. https://doi.org/10.1016/j.tate.2019.102937, 2020.

INHALING GRATITUDE

Throughout this book, we've touched on the importance of breathing. The truth is, there is a ton of material available on breathing. Some of it is contradictory. Some of it is quite complex. The good news, as I've noted earlier, is that it's much less important *how* you breath and much more important *that* you breathe. It seems likely that different people respond differently to different exercises. I will share with you some of the simplest breath exercises that have worked for me. Just have fun with them. If you don't enjoy them, ignore them.

EXERCISE #26:

Simply becoming aware of your breath is the first step. At first, we would like to breathe in and out slowly by the nose. This is how we should naturally breathe in a resting state. Although our mouth is much bigger than our nose, we should be much more comfortable breathing entirely through the nose. Your nose is a miraculous filter. It controls the temperature of the air, moisturizes it, and filters out dirt and allergens. Our sense of smell can help warn us of dangers like rancid food. Reconnecting with nasal breathing helps create a powerful union with our natural healthy state. It also provides us with an easy measurement of that state. If we are too sick or stressed to easily inhale by our nose and must adopt mouth breathing to assist, this is an important reminder that our body is out of balance. The next time you find yourself hyper-ventilating or short of breath, or particularly congested, try slowing down and challenge yourself to breathe by the nose.

I try to take a few minutes every day just to celebrate the sacredness of breathing. I just breathe mindfully and feel grateful for this simple life-giving act. Try it out. Appreciate your breath for all that it's doing, all the quiet, thankless chemical processes, carrying oxygen and life to every recess of your body. Mindful breathing should be this simple. Breathe and be thankful. This is literally enough to completely change your mind and body. This simple act:

- Promotes autonomic changes increasing changes in heart rate (Heart Rate Variability and Respiratory Sinus Arrhythmia) which creates additional changes in the Central Nervous System[102]

---

[102] Cooper HE, Parkes MJ, Clutton-Brock TH, "*CO2-dependent components of sinus arrhythmia from the start of breath holding in humans*". Am J Physiol Heart Circ Physiol. 2003 Aug;285(2):H841-8. doi: 10.1152/ajpheart.01101.2002. Epub 2003 May 1. PMID: 12730051.

- It increases *"cognitive activity"* in cortical and subcortical portions of your brain[103]
- It increases comfort, relaxation, pleasantness, vigor and alertness
- It conditions you to have stronger emotional control and reduces symptoms of aggression, anxiety, depression, anger, and confusion.[104]

EXERCISE #27:

One of the most life-changing breath techniques I have ever learned is called **Square Breathing.** The concept is simple:

We tend to think of breathing as having two parts; inhaling and exhaling. In square breathing, we divide the breath into four parts:

1. Inhaling
2. Holding full
3. Exhaling
4. Holding empty

For this exercise, we are going to start by trying to allocate equal importance to all four steps, so:

- Inhale by the nose for roughly 3 seconds.
- Hold the breath comfortably without adding pressure to our face and neck for roughly 3 seconds.
- Exhale from the mouth like we have a slow seeping leak for roughly 3 seconds.
- Hold empty by just closing our throat—we don't want to add stress to the face—again for roughly 3 seconds.

You would like to do this for 3 cycles (around 36 seconds total), so you have a chance to become comfortable with the pace and allow it to become automatic. This is a go-to baseline breath check that I do every day. It warms up my body and brain and gives me an idea of where my stress levels are on a given day. After a minute or two, you can play with stretching the breath, performing 4-4-4-4 and so on, but go up slowly. Never jump up more than one count per cycle, so that your body has a chance to adjust.

---

[103] Heck Detlef H. et al, *"Breathing as a fundamental rhythm of brain function"*, Frontiers in Neural Circuits, Vol. 10., DOI=10.3389/fncir.2016.00115, 2017.
[104] Zaccaro A. et al, "How breath-control can change your life: A systematic review on psycho-physiological correlates of slow breathing", *Front Hum Neuroscience, 12: 353,* 2018.

Over time you may find that you can go longer on certain parts of the breath and shorter on others and you may discover you like 4-8-4-2 or some other specific pattern. Discover what "shape" works best for you.

EXERCISE #28:

In the last exercise, we started with a simple 3-count square and then customized the rhythm to our liking. In this exercise, I will give you a specific count that has been clinically tested.

We'll be using a triangular breath:

- Inhale for approximately 4 seconds
- Hold your lungs full without strain for 7 seconds
- Then exhale through the mouth with a slow seeping breath for roughly 8 seconds

Make sure not to bloat the face or add strain to the process. When exhaling, think of a slow seeping exhale rather than trying to push the air out. This will help you last the full 8 seconds. Sometimes, not pausing after the exhale for at least a second can be tough. A slight controlled pause is normal and fine however eventually, you can focus on a more elastic breath that feels like once you've reached the end of your exhale, you'll "bounce" right into your inhale.

This specific breath pattern was found to have the best balance between:

- Safety
- Tolerance by the subject
- Adherence and consistency

Performing 30 cycles per day, one study found that adults 50-75 years of age improved blood pressure, endothelial function, and arterial stiffness. It was found to provide greater benefits than taking a 30-minute walk every day and was on par with some blood pressure medications.[105] Breath resistance training has also been found beneficial for sufferers of chronic heart disease, asthma, and bronchitis. Even in completely healthy individuals, inspiratory resistance training was found to decrease breath fatigue and improve recuperation.[106]

---

[105] Craighead D.H. et al, "Time-efficient inspiratory muscle strength training lowers blood pressure and improves endothelial function, NO bioavailability and oxidative stress in midlife/older adults with above-normal blood pressure", *Journal of American Heart Association*, 2021.

[106] Romer L.M., McConnell A.K., Jones D.A., "Inspiratory muscle fatigue in trained cyclists: effects on inspiratory muscle training", *School of Sport and Exercise Science, The University of Birmingham*, 2002.

It's interesting to note that while some studies on breath-holding and resistance training show clear results, other studies have been conducted that show no change. This likely points to a greater need for greater personalization, customizing breath exercises to the end purpose of the user.[107] Variations should be tested and measured in frequency, and load resistance. Training should be periodized with variations to trigger greater adaptation. Adjustments should be made for size and capacity (do you have smaller airways, greater lung capacity, etc.). Healthier individuals seeking larger gains need larger challenges which may include concurrent training, such as using resistance breathing while performing other exercises like cycling.

All of this shows how important it is to *"make your own shape"*. In the square breath exercise I introduced earlier, I said once you've experienced the 3-3-3-3 square, stretch it and adapt it and find your own shape. The same is true of every exercise. Starting with established tested shapes like 4-7-8 breaths is a great starting point, but remember that you the individual matter most. You are the greatest expert on *you* that exists. Listen to your body and push respectfully. Learn to train your intuition, your self-worth, and your limit setting at the same time as your breath capacity.

Breath training is an incredible way to train active coping skills and a bridge to deeper bodily control. While most of the time, we breathe automatically without conscious involvement, when we choose to direct our attention to our breath, our conscious control can allow us to unlock a variety of health benefits.[108] Breath control allows us to affect our heart rate, circulation, and even our overall immunity. Likewise, when we intentionally disrupt our breath through deprivation or resistance training, we mimic the effects of stress and train ourselves to cope with these irregularities more effectively. Over time, this can help us view potential stressors as challenges to be overcome rather than as threats and losses.

---

[107] Shay R.J. et al, "Time to move beyond a 'one-size fits all' approach to inspiratory muscle training", *Front. Physiol.*, January 2022.

[108] André C., "Proper breathing brings better health", *Scientific America*, January 15, 2019.

BUILDING OUR CONFIDENCE

"It's so easy to laugh
It's so easy to hate
It takes strength to be gentle and kind."
-Morrissey-

In the coming sections, I will be giving a brief introduction to some principles of physical intervention. Although our greatest focus should always be on prevention, violent incidents can still occur. Moreover, as I've already noted, I recognize that our individual schools or boards may have differing perspectives on intervention that range from: "*never do it*" to "*you must stop it*". We will discuss this in more detail shortly, but before we even open this pandora's box, I want to address the basic idea of confidence because if we're lacking too much in this department, we may be volunteering for defeat before we even leave the gate.

We begin by thinking:

- How am I supposed to make a difference?
- Even if I read this book, even if I think of these concepts and learn to detect, avoid and diffuse danger before it erupts, how am I ever going to realistically have the skills to stop two students from physically fighting?

In reality, these concerns are our greatest strength. **A healthy understanding of our limits is far more powerful than a delusional overestimation of our capacities.** We will all have different abilities and I will take this into consideration as you will see, but first, I want to address how we can grow our confidence.

STORY FROM THE FIELD:

"Jormungand the Serpent"

To find our way to greater confidence, I'm going to take you back to Norse mythology. Jormungand (pronounced "*YOUR-mun-gand;*"), or the "*Great Beast*", was a giant snake believed to live in the oceans around Midgard (the visible world of humans). He was so long that his body enveloped the entire world. That's pretty long, but Jormungand was still shorter than my friend Pete Jensen's resume. We've met Pete twice already in this book. He is among the most impressive human beings I know, so I've had to deliver his resume in installments. Here comes the next part:

Pete is an alumnus of the U.S. Naval Academy and an honor graduate of the U.S. Army Special Forces Sniper Course. He served as an officer in the Navy and Army, leading combat missions in Iraq and Afghanistan, and served on planning staffs for strategic engagements throughout the Middle East. He retired as an Army Special Forces Lieutenant Colonel after 22 years of service. Pete also has a master's degree in organizational and social psychology from Columbia University and a PhD in kinesiology from the University of Tennessee in Knoxville. He is a Certified Mental Performance Consultant by the Association for Applied Sport Psychology. He's also a certified yoga teacher, a black belt in Aikido, and an instructor in the Russian martial art of Combat Systema.

Pete has been a compass for my brain for over a decade, sending me literature and research, educating my ignorance, motivating my training, and genuinely reassuring me that there is a lot of hope in the world and I am indebted to him for all of this. There's nothing quite like getting a book with 300 sticky notes attached, highlighting passages he thought I'd be interested in, to force me to up my research game. In keeping with his history of blitzing me with knowledge, he has generously contributed repeated interviews to me for this book as you've seen.

Pete notes that once violence begins in a classroom/school setting, the teacher is entering into a very uncommon event. They are unlikely to have much training or experience with this. The daunting task of changing your approach to communication, discipline and student interaction may be overwhelming. He shares this story to give us a realistic look at the challenges anyone faces when preparing for the unknown:

> *"When I was interviewing soldiers about their experiences of fighting enemy soldiers in hand-to-hand combat during such conflicts as Iraq, Afghanistan, and Vietnam, there was one US Army Special Forces soldier who told me an interesting story about training. This soldier was extremely competent in fighting and hand-to-hand combat, being an experienced BJJ black belt and MMA fighter when he wasn't busy deploying overseas to fight in close combat battles. This soldier served as an instructor for more junior soldiers who were in training to enter Special Forces. As an instructor, one of the classes he taught these junior soldiers, usually in a 100-person group, was hand-to-hand combat. He always started his first class with the same thought experiment that went something like this":*

> *"He would ask the group of students to raise their hand if they had ever been in a school fight or bar brawl or some other "fist fight." Nearly all of the students would raise their hands. The instructor would say, "Good. That's a good start. Having one experience of violence means you have some idea of what to expect." Then the instructor would ask the students to think about all of the fights they had experienced and try to calculate the total amount of time all those fights added up to. At this point, he got some quizzical looks and head-scratching but he could see most of the students trying to figure out how much total time they had spent in all their fights. Then the instructor asked, how many of you have been in 5 minutes worth of fighting? A lot of hands from the first group of "experienced fighters" raised their hands. "How about 10 minutes?" Fewer hands went up. "How about 30 minutes?" A couple of hands went up hesitantly. "How about a few hours worth of fighting another person where you were truly trying to hurt or kill the other person?"*

No one would raise their hands.

> *"Let's get this straight: none of you have more than an hour of time actually fighting another person in a situation where you can really get hurt or killed. There are very few things in life that we have such little experience in. Think about driving. You all have hundreds, probably thousands of hours driving*

in all sorts of situations. You are experts. Many of you already have a lot of hours, many dozens or hundreds, shooting your weapons at a variety of targets in a variety of situations. You are really good already – or you wouldn't be a candidate for Special Forces. But, when it comes to putting your hands on someone to inflict life-threatening physical violence you are all babes in the woods. I am going to instruct you on hand-to-hand combat, you are going to get some skills, and I am going to make it as tough as possible, but it will never be a full substitute or replicate a real fight. Keep that in mind during your training and just how dangerous a hand-to-hand fight can be."

One of the most renowned researchers on stress, Richard Lazarus, believed that a stressor that caused a person to believe their life was in danger is the most stressful and threatening thing a person can experience. Figuring out what to do and then taking effective action can be really difficult under this kind of extreme stress. For example, in a study where people were interviewed after they witnessed a life-threatening disaster (Leach, 2004), only 10% to 15% of those interviewed described themselves as remaining relatively calm and responding effectively (e.g., able to take needed emergency actions). The remaining people interviewed said that they either *"froze"* (i.e., responded with *"bewilderment"* and/or inaction) or they acted in behaviors that were counterproductive (e.g., screaming, uncontrollable weeping, etc.).

Although this may sound discouraging at first, Pete notes that this is a life-saving realization:

"If a teacher has a realistic sense of the fragility of their ability to manage violence, then they can emphasize training that can best weather the storm of stress and difficulties that can be present during a violent encounter."

This opens the floor to the debate of how to train teachers. It is widely known that the more effectively training replicates the stress of the end encounter you are training for, the more beneficial it is likely to be. Rather than using plastic, brightly colored guns for Active Shooter training, or rubber knives, it is more stressful to use gas-powered training pistols that create noise and replicate the firing actions of a real gun or a dull steel or aluminum knife. Added problems can include:

- Using appropriately aged actors—having youth acting as the offenders rather than adults,
- Having some degree of physical interaction and contact with staff members who may be completely unaccustomed to physicality,
- The legal concerns this can raise.

Pete emphasizes:

"Replicating the stress, demands, physicality, and emotion of a violent encounter is difficult – maybe impossible – to recreate in a practice setting. What we know about how people best prepare for difficult or stressful situations is that we need to replicate as much as possible the experience, the tasks, demands, and challenges of the intended performance environment (criterion environment). That is a very tough problem for facing violence in a classroom. One way to make some progress towards preparing for such a demanding situation is through a training protocol called Stress Exposure Training (SET)."[109]

"SET is multifaceted but the aspect that is most applicable for teachers is the first part titled: **Information Provision**. *Information Provision is a deliberate, structured effort to provide a person with details about what demands, stressors, thoughts, emotions, and physiological experiences might be expected and encountered in a difficult performance setting. For example, information provision for soldiers in training to provide medical care to a fellow soldier while under enemy fire might include an in-depth discussion where an instructor describes all the tasks that have to occur when providing medical support, the stress of being injured by enemy weapons fire but also the stress of a fellow soldier being injured and seeing explicit wounds on another person, all of which might cause fear, anger, panic, and bodily experiences of sweat, shaky hands, rapid/shallow breathing. Soldiers who are informed about these experiences of combat and helped to understand that these are normal reactions to a terrible situation can be better prepared when they face such realities in combat. This type of training can minimize the novelty of a stressor, which – as noted by Richard Lazarus – can be an extreme source of stress within a dangerous setting."*

"Information management helped sailors perform better in simulated naval combat and information provision was a critical part of the U.S. Army's efforts to improve close combat performance in soldiers. For teachers, information provision can take the form of teachers who have experienced violence talking in-depth about their personal experiences and sharing the stress, demands, emotions, thoughts, and physical aspects that can occur."

"In dealing with any violence, whether it is the violence between students or teacher-directed violence, a teacher's personal self-confidence in their ability to manage the situation is a critical psychological performance aspect to consider. Confidence, also known in psychological literature as **self-efficacy**,

---
[109] Driskell J.E. et al, "Stress exposure training: An event-based approach", *CRC Press*, 2008.

is a person's belief in their ability to successfully accomplish a specific task. There is an immense amount of scientific literature showing the importance of confidence in performing well on a task. Although similar literature around confidence and teacher performance in successfully managing violence is still quite limited, there is enough research to encourage teachers to build their confidence in dealing with violence."[110]

So how do we improve a teacher's confidence?

"Based on what we know about confidence/self-efficacy, there are a number of ways we can sustain and even enhance our confidence for any situation. Keeping in mind that a strong confidence is related to strong performance in nearly every setting:

1. **Regulate emotions.** *High, out-of-control emotions can decrease confidence. Trying to stay as calm as possible during violence can help your confidence. How we respond to everyday stressors lays the groundwork for how we will handle ultimate stress. If we lose our cool and linger on negative emotions throughout our day, we will be more prone to be overwhelmed by larger stressors.*
2. **Regulate physiology.** *"Fight or flight" activation, nerves, butterflies, "adrenaline," "bubble guts" – all these terms reflect the heightened physical activation that can occur during extreme stress. High levels of physiological activation can decrease confidence. Aiming to relax some of the normal activation that comes with the high stress of physical violence can help your confidence.*
3. **Encouraging, positive self-talk.** *That inner voice we have that makes up our thoughts throughout our conscious mind can have an impact on our confidence. During stressful situations, negative, counterproductive thoughts can enter a person's mind and undermine confidence. Having a range of more positive and performance related self-talk can help a person keep their confidence strong during a difficult performance setting."*

Beyond the preparation for violence, Pete notes that an effective aftermath debriefing is also essential:

"In the aftermath of a violent encounter, whether student-on-student or student-on-teacher, recent research shows that many teachers report a negative affect.[111] *This can include a teacher blaming themselves for the students' violent actions against one another (or against the teacher)."*

---

[110] Fischer S. M., John N., & Bilz, L., "Teachers' Self-efficacy in preventing and intervening in school bullying: A systematic review. *International Journal of Bullying Prevention*, 3(3), 196-212.), 2021.
[111] Anderman E. M. et al, "Teachers' reactions to experiences of violence: An attributional analysis", *Social psychology of education*, 21(3), 621-653, 2018.

Instead, a teacher will be more successful if they aim for a *"growth mindset"* that views violent experiences and any beliefs around failure as a way to grow. This encourages them to build new strategies, become more competent for future violent encounters, and more importantly have lessons they can pass on to other teachers so that they are better prepared.

This doesn't only apply to violence. It applies to anything that we are looking to grow our confidence in:

- **Take responsibility for your emotions.** Get cognitive and try to stay calm. Think of how many times you get sidelined, wound up and ultimately burnt out by letting your emotions get the better of you. Remember, out of control emotions slowly erode your confidence.
- **Take control of your physiology.** Heightened physical activation doesn't only happen in violent encounters. It happens any time you get over stressed, so learning to relax some of the normal activation that occurs goes a long way to increasing your confidence.
- **Keep the self-talk positive.** We will encounter more than enough naysayers in this world. Don't be one of them. Remind yourself constantly why you're doing this and what the end goal is. Stay on task. You have what you need to do this. You just need to stay goal-oriented.

PHYSICAL INTERVENTION

Crack out the Olivia Newton-John headbands; it's time to get physical. For those too young to understand that reference, it's time for a YouTube break. The entirety of this book has been written with the knowledge that many of us work in environments where any form of physical intervention is discouraged, if not completely forbidden. Other readers may work in a school with metal detectors at the front door, security guards in the hallways, and where the debate to arm teachers rages on. Many of you may not even clearly know what your freedoms and responsibilities are with regards to your potential use of force.

Your first responsibility is to find out from your administration exactly what you are expected and permitted to do in the case of violence. Generally speaking, teachers have a *"duty of care"* to provide reasonable and necessary care for all of their students. Many parts of the world have some form of Good Samaritan law. In the United States, starting in 1959, courts began to provide protection to individuals who embody Luke 10:29-37, stating that *"no person who in good faith renders emergency care at the scene of the emergency, shall be liable for any civil damages as a result of any acts or omissions by such person in rendering the emergency care."* In Canada, the law is virtually identical. There are exceptions. Whereas the Good Samaritan Law generally applies to protecting people who intervene, it generally does not oblige you to act. Vermont, Minnesota, and Rhode Island are the exceptions in the U.S. where there is a duty to provide assistance where reasonable. In Canada, the province of Quebec where I live is unique in Canada in that it imposes a duty on everyone to help a person in danger. Failing to do so can result in liability.

Even within these regions, schools can be the exception to the rule. Schools have their own sets of restrictions. Many have guidelines that say:

> *"A teacher, vice-principal, principal, or any other employee of a school, shall not be subject to criminal prosecution or criminal penalties, during the performance of their duties, for exerting physical control over a pupil that a parent would be legally privileged to exercise but which in no event shall exceed the amount of physical control reasonably necessary to maintain order, protect property, or protect the health and safety of pupils."*

Or similarly:

> *"An amount of force that is reasonable and necessary for a person employed by or engaged in a public school to quell a disturbance threatening physical*

injury to persons or damage to property, for purposes of self-defense or to obtain possession of weapons or other dangerous objects within the control of the pupil, is not and shall not be construed to be corporal punishment within the meaning and intent of the law."

In Canada, although education falls under Provincial control, the Federal criminal code states:

"Every schoolteacher, parent or person standing in the place of a parent is justified in using force by way of correction toward a pupil or child, as the case may be, who is under his care, if the force does not exceed what is reasonable under the circumstances."

In most legal parlance, the key terms to focus on are *reasonable* and *necessary.* Simply put, **reasonable** means that if you put many people in the same situation, most would do the same thing given the same information. Your actions were justifiable and logical. **Necessary** means that you only did what was required to stop the level of threat that you perceived. Naturally, this is open to interpretation. In most parts of the world, however, there is no consequence if you do nothing. The fear of litigation and liability often leads schools to request that teachers do just that. If a child gets injured, teachers are often asked to wait for a medical professional to arrive because they are afraid of making things worse. I've actually worked at a school where first aid and CPR training was abandoned for teachers because knowing what you're supposed to do and making a mistake was seen as being more liable than not knowing and doing nothing. It's not surprising that these same schools forbid teachers from breaking up fights.

So before internalizing this chapter please ensure that you clearly know what *your* school expects of you. Ask your administrators and google your district's laws so that you have a clear answer. Secondly, please note that regardless of these laws as I've said repeatedly, preparation and avoidance are the vast majority of the solution. Even in those cases and situations where you *may* be permitted to intervene, doesn't mean you *must* intervene. Any time we can avoid physically intervening, we should.

FLANKING

The first physical principle we will look at is flanking. We already know that distance is our friend and that any time we are unable to maintain distance, we need to make sure that our Fences are up. What if we are required to intervene? How should we approach a violent situation?

*"Whenever possible, maintain distance and
take a moment to scan the environment."*

First, as we approach from a distance, we should do everything we can to **collect as much information as possible** before taking any action. We would always prefer to maintain as much distance as possible and to keep some form of barrier between us and the threat when possible. If you see an escalation occurring but the threat is not imminent, take a moment to look around and see how many people appear to be involved. If you have the time, it's always a good idea to change your vantage point. During high-stress situations, our body can experience **tunnel vision,** which is a natural narrowing of our field of vision. Tunnel vision evolved to increase our focus but sometimes can cause us to fixate and overlook important details. Changing your vantage point can help fight the natural limitations of tunnel vision.

Pay attention to your hearing as well. Just like our field of vision can narrow under stress, so too can our hearing. Actively paying attention to the sounds in your environment can help overcome auditory exclusion. It can also help you to take an extra breath, to slow things down a little, and keep your cognitive mind engaged. **Try to never run blindly into a situation.** Remember, the best way to avoid the negative effects of stress is to control your stress to begin with. Sometimes however there may be no time and you *may* need to rush into a situation faster than you would have otherwise liked to.

• •

EXERCISE #29:

As I said earlier, **we can't wait until we're at knifepoint to consider what we'd be willing to do to protect our lives and our students.** In the same way, we can't wait until we are so stressed that we're experiencing tunnel vision and auditory exclusion to try increasing our awareness. That's like waiting till the day of the race to try running for the first time. We need to practice taking *"awareness breaks"*, moments to actively pay attention to our senses in our everyday lives. Of course, this can include while driving, walking, shopping, etc., but since the focus of this book is school safety, the very best place you can practice applying these skills is in the classroom and the corridors of your school.

Take a moment, wherever you are, to just let your eyes relax. See what attracts your field of vision. When you look at things, pay extra attention to them to deeply see them. Pay attention to what noises and sounds you hear. You'll be amazed at what sights and sounds your body reflexively filters out to allow us to function more easily.

Once you've performed your scan, it may be time to approach. If you must get closer, always try to stay outside of arm's reach. Try to identify the key parties who are involved. Sometimes it can be difficult to determine where a particular group begins and ends within a crowd. Any spectator can be a potential threat, but usually, you will see primary actors who are instigating the event. As a teacher, you will often have prior knowledge of the parties involved. You may know their names, their history, and even factors that might likely be involved in the escalation. If you don't know the students by name, the students may know *you* or at the very least, because you are an adult in a school setting, they will likely assume you are an authority figure. This may lend you some degree of control simply by virtue of your presence. Try to make yourself visible as you approach. Call out or make noise like clapping your hands or blowing a whistle to redirect attention toward you. This simple act can help trigger a more cognitive state in the subjects by reminding them that they are not alone and that there are consequences to their actions. Upon realizing there is an authority figure, subjects may begin to deflate and the crowd may thin out but of course, this is not always the case. Anything that can redirect the attention of the parties involved toward you, can help you assert control, bring cognition back into the dynamic, and slow things down.

Order everyone to step back. *"Everyone take 3 steps back now! Step back!"* is a simple and clear instruction that can motivate spectators and lesser motivated participants to step back. Avoid general statements like the cliché *"Nothing to see here. Move along."* Clear, specific, *"do"* commands are best.

If you are able to identify a student nearby that you trust, you can send them immediately to get back up, whether it be security, the vice-principle, or a specific teacher. If you have a walkie-talkie or cell phone, you can contact them yourself, but practice using your device from a safe distance, while maintaining complete awareness of your surroundings. The more backup you can get, the better. It's entirely fine to be loud and open in your request as this can further remind the parties involved about the consequences at stake. Everyone benefits from backup. **Do everything you can to bring more attention to your situation and more authority figures to the scene.**

If you are unable to divert attention onto you or if the students continue to escalate and are on the verge of violence or in the act of violence, you must decide whether or not you are going to intervene physically. If you are **not** permitted or willing to physically intervene, then the most you can do is:

1. Stay in a tactically safe position;
2. Ensure that backup has been requested and;
3. Continue to attempt to control the situation. Keep yourself safe and control the onlookers, ordering the crowd to disperse. Alternate between general commands that address the whole group and directed commands aimed at individuals. Move and collect any objects that can be used as weapons or amplify harm—scissors on desks, chairs, tables, etc.

Realize that some students may comply quickly and others may be slow or refuse completely. Expect this to happen. By starting with general commands like *"everyone get back to class"* you treat everyone equally and show due diligence but by adding direct commands like *"Paul. You and Mark please go back to class"* you connect with individual students that you may know better and add individual identity to the crowd. This can infiltrate the mob mentality. **Anything that reduces the crowd decreases the risks.** Moreover, the fact that you attempt to control the crowd shows due diligence and a reasonable effort to protect everyone involved.

FILMING

Do not be distracted by students filming. This is a controversial topic. We live in an era of social media and real-time documentation. Many schools disallow cell phones or at the very least the filming of other students. As such, many institutions prescribe controlling the filming of escalations first. I get the intent but tactically speaking, it's misdirected energy. Imagine two boys are squaring off to fight with knives. There is a group of boys around them, watching and smoking. Smoking is not allowed in the school. Would your priority be saying: *"Hey guys, put those cigarettes out"?* Of course not. Every escalation contains potential risk. Even if knives are not present, risks are. Do not let anything distract you from stopping the escalation and controlling those risks. Even if phones are banned, you can expect some to come out during a crisis. It has become second nature for people to film. Don't let this distract you from the safety of your subjects.

Consider the challenges that the police face every day. In the domain of law enforcement, it has become common practice for citizens to record the police during arrests and it is generally within their right to do so providing they are not impeding the police action or placing anyone at greater risk. Many officers feel natural resentment towards this type of citizen interference and become antagonistic. This can range from them ordering civilians not to film, getting into arguments with bystanders, counter-filming using their own cameras, or even playing copyrighted music with their own phones to limit the redistribution of the video online afterward with the original audio—yes, all of these things have really happened. While all of these actions may be understandable emotional reactions, they are tactically terrible and only serve to weaken awareness. Moreover, I've yet to see a video of a police officer arguing with a civilian over their right to film where the cop is viewed in a positive light by the public. Arguing just weakens their command presence. If you're not doing anything wrong, who cares if it's being filmed?

As teachers, we need to learn from this precedence. Stay focused on the safety of the students involved. While it's normal to feel added pressure from the presence of phones, remember that if you are responding with respect and care for student safety, the presence of video documentation should help you. Many schools do have strict anti-phone policies. Most have existing policies on the public distribution of video or images without the consent of the subjects involved. Therefore, after the fact, should students publicly disseminate footage or photos of the incident, actions do need to be taken to avoid sensationalizing the event or contributing to the victimization of those involved. Within the context of the immediate incident, however, avoid getting sidetracked by arguing with students who are filming. Stay focused on keeping everyone safe first. Focus instead on getting bystanders to a safe distance and containing the hostile subjects if possible.

For a moment we'll skip the fight itself. Perhaps it fizzles before erupting. Maybe you play a part in defusing it. Maybe it explodes. Either way, after the fact, you have to sift through the guilty parties and spectators. At that point we need to interview everyone potentially involved. Ask simple questions and listen. In emotional situations, students may compete to tell their side of the story. Maintain control but be judicious. In less severe cases, the interviews can occur at the scene. Allow one student to talk for a moment, then stop them. Then, allow the other party an opportunity to offer their perspective. Alternate equally between parties. It's extremely important to take the reports one at a time and to assert strong control over the flow of information. Getting the students to talk can help keep them cognitive and avoid further escalation. Be careful to keep control over the dialogue. Do not allow screaming, insults or swearing. Make them take turns. If you lose control of the dialogue, the students could potentially escalate. In more serious situations, you will not be able to interview them in the primary scene of the aggression. Separate students. Interview them individually in private.

If the parties remain quiet and refuse to talk, solicit information from the onlookers. Maintain the same control that we mentioned above. Often, spectators will speak more openly since they may feel like they have less risk or penalty for being honest. Just avoid questioning them in front of the subjects as this can trigger fears of repercussions. When subjects see witnesses getting taken aside privately for questions it may also trigger them to begin telling their side of the story.

SHIELDING

The moment a violent encounter is within reach of you, the potential for you to be inadvertently or intentionally hit is significant. The next element of intervention we'll be looking at is how to protect ourselves.

"Shielding"

One of the difficulties with blocking or parrying force with force is that it presupposes a degree of timing, conditioning, and mass necessary to stop an incoming hit. A far more reliable defense is to simply shield our heads and to move *with* the force. By shielding our heads, we are protecting our brain, the computer that controls our body. If our brain gets injured, chances are the fight is over. Moreover, most violence is sudden and quick. Fights rarely last long. Our first goal is to survive that first eruption of 15-20 seconds. If we are unable to maintain and control distance, we want to use our arms to make a protective helmet around our head. Shielding helps to brace our head to reduce the amount that our brain gets shaken, thereby reducing the risk of a knockout. It also functionalizes our primal grasp response. Rather than clutching desperately at the incoming threat, which is what our untrained reflexes want to do, shielding directs our grasp response toward our heads.

This functionalizes our flinch, in effect keeping our hands busy by grabbing our heads. Shielding also encourages movement. When we reach for a strike we expose our heads, off balance our body, and trigger the reflex to brace our feet and stay dangerously stationary. By comparison, if we pull our arms in and grab our head, our body is more compact and mobile. If you imagine a professional boxer at close range, they will always turtle up in a ball and move with the incoming force rather than reaching for it and trying to stop or block it.

EXERCISE #30:

One of the most important aspects of shielding is learning how to transition from our Fence (with our palms facing outward and away from our heads), to a shield (with our palms turned towards our bodies and touching our heads). Standing powerfully, practice maintaining your Fence, and then train yourself to turn your hands inward and grab your head. Ideally, I like to plunge slightly, bending my legs and dropping into my shield to add extra strength to my stance and to increase the chances of evading the strike. I also would prefer to grab my head near the top or back of the skull rather than keeping my hands near my face. This will help protect the vulnerable bones of the hands and will offer the much harder points of my elbows or the ramps of my forearms towards my opponent's strikes.

For an added challenge you can perform this drill facing a wall. Fence, keeping your hands just out of reach of the wall. Then shield, leaning into the wall to test the strength of your shield.

RAMPING

"Try to avoid situating yourself directly between two aggressors."

"Instead, enter from a diagonal flank, staying arm's distance from the closer attacker and as far as possible from the second aggressor."

If the decision has been made to physically intervene, avoid positioning yourself directly in the middle of the parties involved. Imagine for a moment that two students were arguing in the cafeteria. Interventionists will often instinctively insert themselves directly between the aggressors. This happens reflexively because it subconsciously gives you the feeling that you are at the best vantage point to see both parties equally. Unfortunately, it's the worst possible position to be in since you are at the ideal range to be powerfully hit by both parties involved. Standing directly in the middle also makes it harder for you to predict which direction an attack will come from since you're equally close to both attackers. Instead, you should always approach closer to one person. By doing this, you will gain a few advantages:

1. One of the parties involved will be less able to see you and there is a chance this can create a distraction and cause them to turn to better see you. This can help break the rhythm of the escalation and temporarily divert focus onto you.
2. By approaching closer to one party, you will tend to enter from the rear diagonal angle, which is usually a blind spot for the closer subject. This places them at a disadvantage. If they don't turn as described in point one, they are more vulnerable to being surprised by your approach which gives you the element of surprise against one aggressor should you need to intervene.
3. By approaching one party more closely, you naturally become farther away from the second party. This gives you a better vantage point and more reaction time. I would rather have an advantage against one of the parties than no advantage against either.
4. If I do decide to physically intervene, I will always push and displace the closer aggressor. Try to avoid getting too close to the nearer subject. I still would like to maintain arm's distance, which will give me more reaction time. If I decide to intervene, then I will compress that space fully and push into the subject's personal space, to smother and overwhelm their capacities.

"Avoid the temptation to collide with the aggressor's force directly."

If you must insert yourself physically into a fight, avoid getting entangled in a wrestling match. Reflexively, most individuals will turn to face their closest subject. Tactically, this is extremely dangerous since this involves turning your back to the other parties involved, which cripples your awareness. It also tempts us to resist with brute force, pushing directly against the subject. Directly opposing force with force requires the most mass, the most muscular force, and is the most likely to trigger resistance and get you hurt. Instead, we should seek to maintain awareness of everyone involved while trying to **displace** one subject, moving them out of direct alignment with the other aggressor rather than pushing them back.

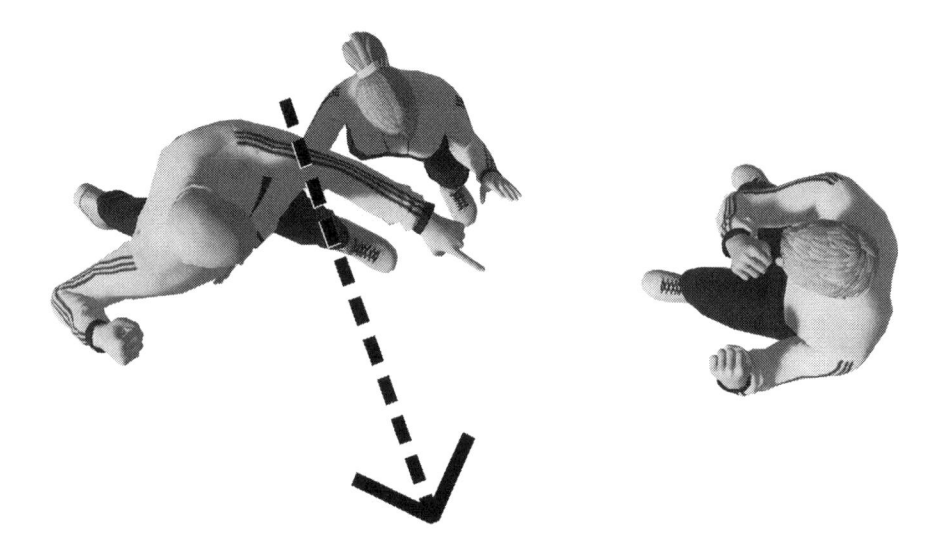

"When attempting to separate two aggressors, prioritize 'ramping' the subject away by diverting their forward pressure on a diagonal path."

The best way to understand this is to visualize a rushing river. If you ever have to cross a raging river, you cannot simply enforce your will and go directly across the river. Ignoring the current will get you hurt. Fighting the current head-on will deplete your energy and risk sucking you under or causing you to lose your footing. Instead, if you must cross a river, you want to merge your desire to cross with the direction of the current. Rather than trying to impose a straight path across, you will effectively move on a diagonal *with* the current. The same is true of breaking up fights. Rather than entering into a direct wrestling match with one of the parties, extend one arm out in front of the subject. Ideally, be careful not to push into the face or throat. You can angle your arm as required to try to push across the subject's shoulder axis instead. Rather than attempting to push the subject directly backward, think of walking in front of them, pushing the subject diagonally to the side using the mass of your hip and shoulder. **Try to be a ramp that diverts their force rather than a wall that stops it.** Even if the aggressor has significant mass and is pushing powerfully, this is the most efficient way to redirect them. This is the exact same way that a bodyguard moves a subject out of harm's way. Ramping will maximize your force and move the subject out of the direct path of the second aggressor with the least amount of energy.

Of course, there are no guarantees. If the aggressors are significantly larger or stronger or if you are particularly frail, it may not work and you should seriously consider your reality before ever attempting to insert yourself into violence. Moreover, you can get hit and hurt at this range and the risks involved can never be underestimated. Always consider soliciting help instead of engaging directly in the aggression. If you *are* attempting this, however, I am assuming you've decided that the risk is necessary or that there simply is no better alternative. I've used this tactic to redirect aggressors, separate scuffles, and cut through violent crowds in security work more times than I can count. It allows you to redirect significant force and mass with the least amount of energy while maintaining your balance. Moreover, because you will effectively be placing your side towards the subject that you are ramping, you will be able to maintain awareness of both parties to stay on top of incoming threats. Remember, more distance permits more reaction time, so in that interval where you're close to both aggressors, there is a high degree of danger. Your goal is to ramp one subject away from the other to increase the distance between them and to create a safe distance to encourage de-escalation. Remember, this is a ramp. **This is science, not magic. It will maximize your power not imbue you with something you don't have.**

While ramping, it's important to also use loud, strong Alpha commands to order the other party back.

"*Step back John! Step back!*" or

"*Get your back on the wall now!*"

Of course, if a second interventionist is available to ramp the other aggressor away, this is even better. Once you've separated the quarreling students, you may need to hold the subject you've moved at bay to prevent them from re-inserting themselves. The "*harness*", which we will cover next, is ideal for this. If at any point you feel like you are losing the struggle, abandon the effort and move yourself to a safe distance if you can. Remember, your safety and the safety of innocent bystanders are always your priority.

EXERCISE #31:

One great way to train the muscular coordination you will need for ramping is to place your arm outstretched against a wall. Practice pushing strongly into the wall while walking along it. This can be done at a regular pace, walking as you would normally, or with a slower and more measured slide step, advancing with your front foot, then sliding your rear foot in, stepping and sliding in a low wide base like an Olympic fencer as you might against a very vigorous aggressor.

THE HARNESS

Ramping can fail. Aggressors can be too powerful or dynamic and manage to break through your ramp, effectively leaving you behind them. In other cases, while approaching from the rear diagonal flank, you may decide the intensity is too severe to attempt ramping but you may still feel that intervention is required. In both of these scenarios, if you must attempt to cinch a student to remove them from behind, there are a few essential guidelines I recommend that you:

1. **Avoid grabbing the head.** Any manipulation of the head, while extremely effective in a life-and-death fight, is inappropriate for the responsible restraint of a student. It risks causing significant injury to the subject's neck and spine. In fact, in a restraint setting, we will make every effort to *protect* the subject's head from impact and to cradle it during any takedown as we'll see shortly.
2. **Avoid any impact on the throat.** While some incidental contact may occur with the neck, we must minimize the amount of intentional, malicious force that we apply to it. Any direct pressure to the trachea can cause lasting injury or death. Arterial pressure to both sides of the neck is more controllable and predictable, but any pressure against the arteries can still injure the spine, brain, and the arteries themselves. There has been a massive shift away from the use of vascular restraint holds in law enforcement in recent decades. Personally, I am a believer that chokeholds are safe when correctly and sufficiently taught and I am at odds with popular opinion. I have used vascular restraint often in real encounters and even more in training. Injuries are minor and rare. The effectiveness so far outweighs the risk and I believe they are an indispensable restraint tool. Nevertheless, many medical experts caution against any form of oxygen deprivation to the brain. There is some evidence that arterial chokes may damage the arteries, potentially carrying the risk of tearing the artery wall.[112] Fears of brain damage due to oxygen deprivation (Chronic Traumatic Encephalopathy) are much less well established.[113] Despite the sparse research, recent instances involving the misapplication of carotid restraint by law enforcement have tainted public opinion regarding these

---

[112] Demartini Z Jr, Rodrigues Freire M, Lages RO, et al. "Internal Carotid Artery Dissection in Brazilian Jiu-Jitsu", *Journal of Cerebrovasc Endovasc Neurosurg*. 2017;19(2):111-116. doi:10.7461/jcen.2017.19.2.111

[113] Stellpflug S.J., "No Established Link between Repeated Transient Chokes and Chronic Traumatic Encephalopathy Related Effects. Comment on Lim, L.J.H. et al. Dangers of Mixed Martial Arts in the Development of Chronic Traumatic Encephalopathy", *Int. J. Environ. Res. Public Health 2019, 16, 254. International journal of environmental research and public health*, 16(6), 1059. https://doi.org/10.3390/ijerph16061059, 2019.

holds. Any attempt to choke, whether intentionally or accidentally is likely to be regarded as excessive in the current climate. So, while our arms may inadvertently contact the neck, it should never be our intent to apply pressure there and every effort should be made to minimize the risk.

3. Tactics and techniques that try to control a violent subject using small joint manipulations and pressure points are very difficult. While such strategies feature heavily in traditional martial arts like Jujitsu it must be remembered that they were devised for defense against opponents who were typically armed with long weapons like swords and spears. In fighting these weapons, it is very difficult to enter even to the range of someone's hands, therefore many of the traditional controls and disarms occur against the small joints. Moreover, the added leverage provided by the weapon and the fixation it triggers in the wielder could arguably allow for the more probable control of a subject by the arm. Many modern law enforcement curriculums were developed from these traditional concepts. They trustingly adopted techniques without adapting them to modern considerations. The result has been a high degree of failure in real-world applications. Moreover, classical training usually assumes much more dedication and investment of time than most police academies can allocate. Through my decades of experience both in Jujitsu and in working as a security professional, I can confidently suggest that you prioritize working against the trunk of the subject rather than the limbs. **Trunk control is easier to acquire under stress because it is larger, less mobile than the limbs, and can be manipulated using gross motor skills.** Controlling the trunk will better allow you to minimize the risks to the subject should you need to take them down.

4. Similar exploration and testing have consistently shown that it is far less dangerous and more efficient to direct your energy towards **sitting an opponent down**, taking them towards their rear, rather than driving them forward and pushing them onto their front. Again, in traditional Jujitsu, driving an armed samurai face-first onto the ground was a hugely effective choice. If you broke their arm on the way down, smashed their face into the ground, or crushed their rib cage, so much the better. Within the modern context of responsible power, especially in a school setting, forward pressure is less ideal—it makes it harder for the interventionist and easier for the subject to resist the intervention. It's easier for the subject to bend forward from the waist than it is to arch backward. It's easier for the subject to reach forward with the free arm to stop a takedown than it is to reach backward. It's easier and faster for the subject to step forward than to step backwards. The end result is that it's simply easier for the subject to resist forward pressure. More potential for resistance means more force is usually required and more injuries typically occur both in training and real-world application. Instead, every effort should be made to pull an opponent backward in an attempt to sit them down. This

will capitalize on their relatively lower degree of mobility and adaptability toward the rear, **working with the more natural reflex and capacity to sit, rather than against the less efficient capacity and willingness to engage the ground face first**. It will also better allow you to protect the subject's head.

Building upon these four principles, the baseline technique I am advocating, is what I term the *Harness*.

• •

EXERCISE #32:

"The Harness"

To perform the Harness, approach your opponent from a rear angle, slipping one arm over the subject's far shoulder and the other arm under their close armpit.

Ideally, you will clasp your hands together as if you were clapping to applaud. Try to place your hands in the crease of your subject's nearest shoulder joint. Try to avoid placing the clasped hands over the subject's chest as this can compress the chest and interfere with breathing.

"The Open Harness"

If you are unable to reach your hands together, you may cup their shoulders with *"short hooks"*. When cupping the shoulders, the grip is weaker and can more easily slip off. It's important to keep your forearms and elbows tight against the subject's torso. Do not flare them away from the subject's torso as this will weaken your grip further. This so-called "open harness" provides less control than a closed grip, but sometimes, due to size differences or positioning it is necessary to use.

"To break their balance, step forward between the subject's legs with your lead leg and briskly disrupt their hips with your own hip."

To disrupt a subject's balance, step forward briskly with your lead leg, taking a deep step through the space between the subject's legs. Your goal should be to bump the subject's hips forward using your own hip. By moving their center of mass past the base of their feet, you will temporarily disrupt their balance. This step must be explosive. It should land deeply in front of the subject. The moment it arrives, it should rebound off of the ground and retract fully behind the subject, as far as you can comfortably step. This will create an opening for them to sit down. If you simply step forward and stay there, the subject will in effect collapse onto your thigh and remain supported by your leg.

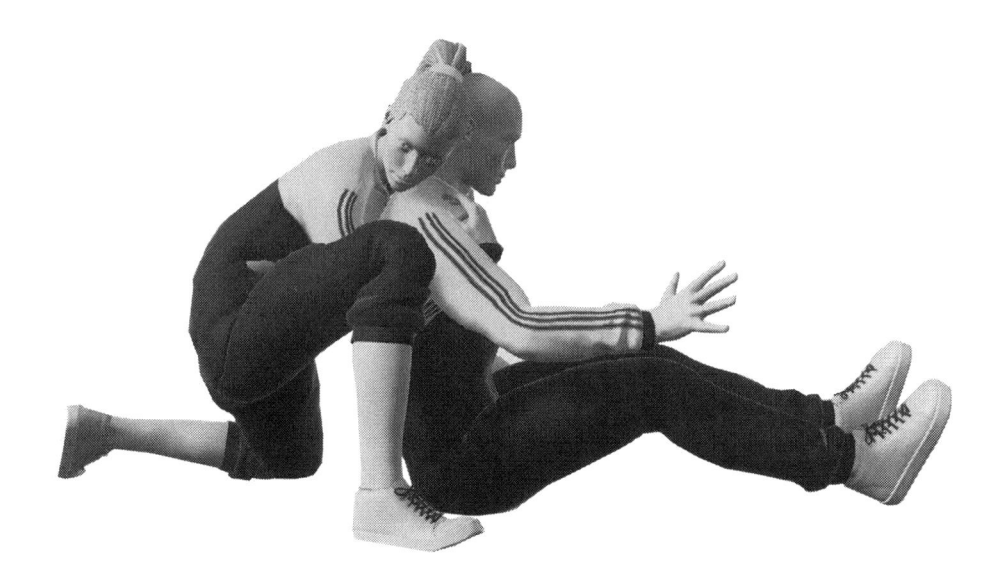

"Prioritize sitting the subject safely on the ground rather than driving them forward onto their face and stomach."

When sitting the subject on the ground, lower their hips first. Be sure to squat from your legs. Do not bend from your back. Stay tightly stuck to your subject's back, turning your face to one side to protect it from impact. To practice your stability, you can stand in your stance alone. Step all the way forward with your rear leg, touch the ground with your foot and bounce back to your starting position. Once this becomes comfortable, try to step back while squatting, like you are performing a lunge, lowering your knee close to the ground, but protecting it from impact. If you can't perform a forward and reverse lunge alone, the presence of a resistant partner won't make it any easier.

Once the subject has been seated on the ground:

- You may opt to maintain control through the harness and engage in verbal de-escalation
- You may be required to release the subject in order to intervene on other subjects;

SIDE VIEW **AERIAL VIEW**

"If you require more control or lose your balance, prioritize moving onto your back or side and hooking your feet around their hips to further control their movement."

- You may even be required to pull a subject into a deeper control position, laying them down on their side or even wrapping your own legs around their body as we'll see shortly. Every effort should be made to avoid placing a subject on their front, which can impede breathing and cause complications

EXERCISE #33:

Sometimes we may lose our balance during the struggle. Other times we may successfully sit the subject down, but their continued resistance will require us to enhance our control position. We must make every effort to avoid landing on top of the student or placing them on their stomach as this can make it difficult for them to breathe (known as *"positional asphyxia"*). Instead, when possible, the interventionist should seek to align themselves on their back or side, keeping the student in front of them. To further limit the mobility of the subject on the ground, your legs can be wrapped around their waist and your heels can be *"hooked"* over their hips or thighs. Controlling the hips is essential to maintaining some degree of control until the student has either de-escalated or else backup has arrived. Avoid scissoring the waist as this can impede breathing.

At one of the schools where I teach, a member of staff intercepted a student who, in a state of extreme distress, was attempting to jump from the upper landing of a stairwell. Using a harness, she pulled the student back onto the safe side of the railing and onto the ground where she used leg hooks to further limit his movement. The student eventually was calmed down and brought to the administration for further questioning and care. Although the harness and hooks can look a bit odd when you first encounter them, they allow you to maximize the power of your entire body to best control a subject and minimize the risk of injury and escalation.

MEETINGS, COMMUNICATION & PRE-ESCALATION

Aggression does not always manifest as two students fist-fighting in the hallway. Most of the time, it's far more subtle. Often, it proceeds through phases, growing and intensifying if it's not correctly handled. It's important to understand how to intercept these emotional escalations rather than wait until they're physically erupting in your face.

One simple strategy is to defer an escalation. If you can safely delay an agitated person and speak with them at a later date, that may be enough to give them time to cool down and you more time to prepare a simple strategy. If the escalation is occurring through an email or phone call, it's always best to meet in person to avoid miscommunication.

- When meeting in person, it is essential that you keep your emotions out of it. Although you might be boiling on the inside, try to stay calm and remain objective.
- Give the complainant time to vent and listen to what they want to say. As we saw in our treatment of verbal de-escalation, we must do our best to empathize, avoid introducing negative words or concepts and try to recap the subject's key points. Remember, you haven't effectively summarized their points until they agree with your recap.

    "So, if I understand you correctly, basically what you're saying is..." and then wait for a confirmation. If you don't get an agreement, then ask for clarification, listen, and re-summarize.

- Remember, every encounter should have an *"A"* plan and a *"B"* plan, meaning you should have a clear primary objective and if that isn't working, an immediate secondary objective. For example, if a parent is complaining that you are a terrible teacher and unfairly treating their child, beyond listening to their complaints and allowing them to vent and be heard, your primary goal might be to express that their child is rarely completing their homework. If the parent refuses to listen, your secondary objective might be to introduce a protocol for helping to remedy this, like having the parent sign the student's agenda every night or making sure they log in to the student portal every night to see what homework is expected to be done for the following day. Through a simple strategy, you can entertain complaints, better understand the subject, and allow them to vent, but ensure that you ultimately bring the focus back to the main objective.
- Tightly connected to having a plan is the idea of having a time limit. I am a firm believer that good fences make good neighbors and limits keep things from running

too far off track. Let them know in your correspondence that the meeting will be a specific length and set an alarm to remind you when the session is done. Something as simple as a phone alarm ringing can massively help you wrap things up. When the alarm goes off, hit snooze so it will ring again in 5 or 10 minutes, and continue to emphasize the limits of your availability. Alarms are a simple way to help assert your limits.

If you are nervous about meeting with the parent or student, bring backup. It's always a good policy to have an objective witness to help keep things civil, to offer you a different perspective after the fact, and to be there to help ensure your physical safety should things escalate. If you can't have back-up, you can record the meeting, with their consent (or without depending on the laws in your district and guidelines in your school).

After the meeting, it's important to record the event in three ways:

1. First, send a **thank you email** to the parent or student summarizing the points of the meeting and the follow-up actions.
2. Second, keep a **personal log book** wherein you can add personal details for your private reference. This is an important way for you to process what happened. This is also where you can honestly evaluate your successes and your failures and give yourself short and mid-term goals for improvement.
3. Finally, **report it to your admin**. This can include resource persons, guidance counselors, principals, and recording it in any centralized registry that you might have. It is imperative that this be in writing—as the Romans used to say: "*Verba volant, scripta manent*"—spoken words fly away, written words remain.

Most teachers have been the victim of some form of aggression. While it is usually from the students themselves, it can also come from parents. Recognizing this probability is the first step in preparation. I must be clear here: **while violence may be probable it is never acceptable**. Every incident of aggression matters. No detail is insignificant. You should always log it somewhere. Too often we dismiss incidents as being unimportant or we think that it's already over and we'd rather not think about it anymore. The reality is that we never know what role it will play in establishing a larger overall pattern. Every incident matters. Good tactical decision-making relies on awareness and information. Take a minute to document any incidents at the end of your day. Report them when your intuition tells you to. You matter and no one has a right to disrespect, challenge or threaten you.

CREATING CHANGE

"Teachers are more than any other class the guardians of civilization."
-Bertrand Russell-

Violence never truly happens *"all of a sudden"*. It always has a cause and usually more than one. It can grow slowly, building, bubbling, until it invariably explodes. Many of the security professionals I've interviewed for this book have intentionally or inadvertently emphasized the importance of detection and avoidance. Each of them has survived hard-learned lessons that show that **long after the ego, raw physicality, and bravado of youth fail, the maturity of early detection and prevention remains the only true solution to violence.**

Throughout North America, violence against teachers remains at disturbingly high levels. Teachers who perceive that their safety is in danger will tend to have higher absenteeism, which in turn erodes classroom continuity and accountability and worsens relationships with students.[114] In addition, the added stress has been shown to decrease overall effectiveness in the classroom, creating a detachment from responsibilities and often burnout.[115] [116] In fact, student behavior along with school safety are the leading reasons for teachers quitting.[117]

So, what can we do to intercept violence at its roots? How can we weed out aggression before it can fester? Many schools turn to punitive, reactive discipline. Research is increasingly showing that this is not truly a solution. Strict punishment comes too late in the cycle of violence and does little to correct the underlying causes. While it can feel successful (and let's admit it, it can feel satisfying) it's ultimately based on fear. **Strict punishments do not teach students how to improve.** Rather, they teach students to be fearful, they model punitive responses to be imitated, and ultimately, they contribute to a negative school environment.[118] This can include increases in vandalism and violent

---

[114] Payne A. A., Gottfredson D. C., Gottfredson G. D., "Schools as communities: the relationships among communal school organization, student bonding, and school disorder", *Criminology* 41, 749–778. doi: 10.1111/j.1745-9125.2003.tb01003.x, 2013

[115] Ingersoll R.M., "The teacher shortage: a case of wrong diagnosis and wrong prescription", *NASSP Bull.* 86, 16-31. Dpi:10.1177/019263640208663101, 2002.

[116] Wang, M. T., and Degol, J. L., "School climate: a review of the construct, measurement, and impact on student outcomes", *Educ. Psychol. Rev.* 28, 315–352. doi: 10.1007/s10648-015-9319-1, 2016.

[117] Marinell W. H., Coca, V. M., "Who stays and who leaves?" *Findings from a Three-Part Study of Teacher Turnover in NYC Middle Schools*, Online Submission, 2013.

[118] Sidnman M., "Coercion and its fallout", *Authors Cooperative*, 1989.

behavior.[119] Often, administrators on this path then get pushed to a point where they feel *"zero tolerance"* policies are the only solution remaining. I understand the desperation that leads to these measures and I'm not questioning the authentically good intentions behind them. Tactically speaking, however, these policies are dead-ends. They only end up depriving administrators of the flexibility to use their experience to make value judgments. Zero tolerance really means zero options, zero places for insight, zero places for your experience, zero communication, and zero trust. One-size-fits-all approaches to behavior correction, ultimately harm teacher-student relationships. Similarly, surveillance cameras, metal detectors, and security guards are of debatable value. Some research even suggests that they do more to promote the perception that the environment is unsafe than they do to actually discourage violence.[120] Ultimately, zero-tolerance policies signal that the administration is frustrated and out of ideas.

Of course, if your school is on the verge of decay, I understand why these measures are implemented to act as a levy against the rushing flood waters. They should be viewed as temporary however and at most a delay to give you the time to implement true change.

A healthy school, by comparison, should be adaptive and inclusive. It should:

- Teach students to be **respectful and kind** by modeling that behavior
- **Encourage** positive behavior rather than threaten punitive and consequence-driven repercussions
- **Express clear rules and consequences** throughout all aspects of the school. Random, isolated school assemblies and lectures from professionals are among the least effective interventions. Measures must be **consistently modeled** at all levels of staff, from admin to lunch monitors.
- **Set high expectations.** As my first sensei used to say, the only way to grow is to make you stretch by reaching for something beyond your grasp. Students must be challenged by material that is age and skill-appropriate and it must be made relevant to their immediate lives and their futures.
- **Measure and evaluate efforts.** Students have to know where they stand and what needs improvement.
- **Make learning a habit for everyone.** Support training for all of your staff and provide opportunities for enrichment. You can't expect your students to be excited to learn if the teachers aren't.
- **Be democratic** and regularly encourage and integrate student involvement.
- **Maintain healthy lines of communication** through all five pillars of school life: Student, teacher, administration, parents, and community.

---

[119] Walker H.M., Ramsey E., Gresham F., "Antisocial behavior in school (2nd ed)", *Wadsworth Thomson Learning*, 2004.
[120] Kitsantas A., Ware H.W., Martinez-Arias B., "Students' perceptions of school safety: Effects of community, school environment, and substance use variables", *Journal of Early Adolescence*, p 413-430, 2004.

I would imagine that many of you may be thinking:

> *"But how am I going to do all that? I've tried. My school is so resistant to change. I can't do it alone"* or *"we have no budget."*

It all goes back to Laurence Gonzales and his first rule of survival: take responsibility for staying alive. Don't expect reinforcements. Don't wait to be rescued. Remember that the greatest poison for a teacher's mindset is thinking:

> *"It's not my problem. That's not my job."*

I agree. *That* is <u>not</u> your job. Your job actually involves so much more than that. We have the power to mold the future. Our job is to guide our students to their fullest state of being.

STORY FROM THE FIELD:

I didn't always want to be a martial artist or a teacher for that matter. When I was 5, early exposure to Frank Sinatra convinced me I was actually destined to be a crooner. I wanted desperately to be a lounge singer. The Elvis Comeback special in 1968 also played a big role in my consciousness and I deeply wanted a leather jumpsuit for much of my early life. I actually listed having a leather jumpsuit as a life goal in my scrapbook for that year but I had to settle for a Steve Austin red track suit. By the age of 7, I aspired to be a Pip backing up Gladys Knight. I knew I would have to drastically improve my dance choreography but I was down for the challenge. When I was 10, I got jumped by 4 older boys and badly beaten up. This led me to join the martial arts. I had no idea at the time that this would lead to a life-long journey. At the time, I only wanted to train long enough to be able to beat them all up.

By the time high school rolled around, I was still training in the martial arts but that was just part of my lingering vengeance mandate. Career-wise I was convinced I would either be an author or an artist. Then I met my Jujitsu sensei and he planted the seeds for everything that would follow. That one teacher changed my life. Without knowing it, he established my standard for martial training. After he moved away, I struggled to find a school that matched what he taught. Unable to find the environment I wanted, I was forced to create it, so I began teaching two friends in the park. That's when my teaching career started.

Soon, the approaching winter forced me to rent spaces at community centers and in church basements to continue my classes. I didn't have the certainty of having 32 students show up for me every day. I started with those two boys and worked my way up. I also wasn't making enough money from the school to cover rent so for the first 10 years I had to subsidize my school with my meager part-time student salary which meant I was paying to teach. The simple fact is that I couldn't do otherwise. The fact that students showed up always felt like a huge responsibility. They had planned their day, even their week, around being there. I had an obligation to give them the very best I could. I quickly learned to go well beyond just planning my lessons. I started researching, reading, studying, and training. That habit has never left me.

Flash forward 30 years and the global pandemic hit. COVID crippled most gyms. I was closed for 20 out of 24 months. It was brutal. Throughout that time, I had to hustle on a lot of outside contracts. Often, I was teaching self-defense in public schools. When I was there, I heard a lot of teachers complain about how underappreciated they were during COVID, how stressful it was to teach with the threat of the virus around, and how demanding it was to act as surrogate parents. It's true. It was a tough time to be a teacher. Many teachers got stuck providing even more regularity and structure for students who were lost and looking for reassurance. Many young people were spending far too much time on the internet and were left unsupervised. Many were feeling the stress and anxiety and financial burdens of their parents. A generation of youth suffered a two-year gap during a critical time in their development. Of course, everyone was affected. My friends working in the medical field and as first responders encountered constant fear and illness. They were often required to be proxy families for isolated victims who would otherwise be left to die alone. Many still suffer from PTSD as a result. Friends that owned bars and restaurants went bankrupt from prolonged closures, losing their life savings. It was brutal in many sectors.

As a gym owner, I was resentful that we were obliged to be closed while big box stores that had thousands of times more traffic than I did, were allowed to be open. I was envious of those school teachers complaining in the staff lounges because they had a fixed salary. I even had friends that got raises and *"stress pay"* for working from home where they lived comfortably. Some even admitted it was the best work experience they had ever had. Meanwhile, I had to sell possessions to cover rent. It started to eat away at my motivation. The only solution that worked was to start working out harder, and changing my routine. I built mannequins and homemade dummies since I couldn't have human partners. I reconnected with old friends online. I researched and read more than usual. More than anything though, I just focused on being thankful for my health and my loved ones. As people I knew started to die around me, gratitude kept me mentally healthy.

I have always taught from a place of gratitude. Gratitude brings passion and joy and excellence to life. COVID showed me again that gratitude was still the solution. It also showed me that it can be easy to forget and difficult to regain your bearings. I believe the real solution to violence begins with gratitude. If we are unable to be thankful for and motivated by what I consider to be the best job on earth, then I believe we have a duty to change professions. **Our students need role models.** They look to the adults in their lives for strong examples. Just one positive adult role model can change the future of one of their lives. You can be the anchor to a youth who would otherwise be adrift. If you are a teacher, this is a privilege to be grateful for.

TEACH THEM TO CARE

At the start of this book, I brought you back to my childhood, where I was schooled in the shadow of the principal's strap—that strip of leather discipline, soaked in the tears and terror sweat of past generations. Corporeal punishment is now largely illegal. In our modern society, it is at best a vestige of archaic quick-fix, reactive punishment. What behavior were we modeling by punishing a child for hitting someone by hitting them ourselves? What message did we think we were sending? Many of the practices that are still commonly accepted, however, like zero tolerance threats, police state cameras, metal detectors, and security guards, are not much more evolved logically speaking but they are still nevertheless widely accepted.

True change, just like true protection, must begin in prevention, not remain in reaction. Here are a few different ways we can begin building a healthier environment. Of course, you don't need to use any of them, but maybe something here will at least inspire your own ideas:

- Begin by welcoming everyone as they enter your room. This was one of the most powerful things I learned working the door at clubs. If I stood there like a gargoyle keeping watch, I was treated as something to be feared, deceived and often opposed. If instead I established rapport and welcomed them, I set a very different tone. So let your students know that you see them. Greet them warmly. Start to create a rapport the moment they walk in. You have the ability to begin changing their mood (and yours as well) from the second they walk in the door. You can also immediately tell who is not in a good mental space, and that can help you direct your awareness throughout your session. More than anything, this will change your mindset and help you get into character, get focused, and get connected to your inner gratitude.
- In everything that you do, model courtesy, respect, and kindness. Then, expect it in return. Be the way you want your students to be. **Act the way you want them to act.** If you want them to be kind and considerate, then choose your words carefully. I've encountered so many teachers that try to connect through casualness and modern language but who end up being sarcastic or condescending and who end up alienating and insulting students instead. If you wouldn't want to be spoken to and treated in this manner, then change it. If you act like a bully and run your class like a police state, you will create students that behave like prisoners.
- **Clearly establish your rules and routines.** You can start with one change at a time. Ultimately, its smooth operation should be systems-driven, not person-driven.

Create a habit of order. Say exactly what you expect the students to do, consistently model that behavior yourself, acknowledge when it is done correctly, and correct it immediately when it is not.
- There is value in rewards and a need for consequence, but be careful how it is done. I've always found that **student involvement creates lasting motivation and a stakeholder mindset.** It makes people care and want to be involved. Carrot-and-stick motivation only works in the short term and ultimately creates a need for greater and greater rewards or harsher and harsher punishments. As Alfie Kohn noted: **"Whenever you have a carrot and a stick, rest assured you always have a jackass in between."** The praise-or-punish model kills intrinsic motivation. Unconditional support by comparison teaches kids not only what you expect but also how you expect them to achieve it.
- **Create inclusion.** Students from minority ethnic and cultural groups can have an even harder time fitting in.[121] Find out about your students. Acknowledge their various cultures in your lessons and classroom décor. Model diversity and celebrate different holidays. Learn from them to set an example so they will in turn be willing to learn from you.

You can create a microcosm of these principles in each class:

- Start your class by greeting your students. This is relationship building 101. Get a sense of where the group is at emotionally:

    o Tell them what you expect for the session. Set the goals you expect for them and then expect those goals, showing them the few simple steps that are required to realistically get there.
    o Measure as you go. Let them know where the group's progress is at. As Ken Blanchard noted, *"if you can measure it, you can manage it."*
    o If specific students need one-on-one attention, check in with them to make sure they are on track. Some students are a struggle to keep motivated, but every time you check in you are modeling the routine and teaching them to self-assess.

---

[121] Holcomb-McCoy C., "Ethnic identity development in early adolescents: Implications and recommendations for middle school counselors", *Profession School Counseling, p120-127,* 2005.

IN 1-ON-1 CONFERENCES

If you're meeting with a student individually or in small groups:

1. Make sure you have the appropriate privacy and time to have a suitable conversation. It's always better to wait for the time or make the time than to rush a situation.
2. Take a breath and think about what your goal is for the meeting. Make sure you are in control of your emotions otherwise postpone it. Don't meet when mad.
3. Take a look at your student to see where they are at emotionally. Begin by asking a few questions to hear their side of things and to see what is going on in their life. Both of you want to be in a cognitive state to get the most out of the exchange.
4. When the incident involves more than one student, have each student express how the incident made them feel and have them explain what their motives were. Have them think about alternative behaviors and what they could have done differently.
5. Have the offending student make a sincere apology. Kathleen Murray, in her excellent book *"Teach Kindness First"* suggests having the offended student participate in deciding if punishment is necessary and if so, what a suitable punishment would be.[122]
6. Just listen. Everything goes back to the empathy skills we discussed earlier. Don't expect yourself to have all the solutions. The reality is you won't always be able to fix things. So many passionate teachers get burnt out because they get overwhelmed by all the things they can't change. Many others just avoid getting involved for the same reason—because it feels like it's just too much. You can't easily solve the problems of a student who has an abusive home, who suffers from neglect, and who has had a terrible upbringing, but you can listen and you can show them that you care. You can provide support and be someone they look forward to seeing. If there are resources that are available that you think might help, then by all means you can point them in the right direction. Returning to Kathleen Murray, remember that it takes a village. You're not alone.

Empathy is always the key. I was always an extremely nervous student in elementary and high school. I really only started to find my groove in my college years. This may be why I've had so much empathy for my students. I deeply remember the stress of my school years. Students of every age face their own unique challenges. Our elementary-age students are learning to be independent, away from the security of their parents, forming

---
[122] Murray K., "Teach kindness first", *self published*, 2017.

their first friendships and laying the foundation for their personality. Our adolescent students are dealing with the added stress of explosive physical development and huge hormonal shifts. Consider the research:

- Girls generally mature earlier than boys and those that develop earlier than normal are more likely to feel alienated from their classmates and will often develop a poorer self-image.
- By comparison, boys that develop sooner are more prone to becoming aggressive.
- Late developers in both genders generally get less attention from their peers and are more likely to focus on academics.[123]
- The remainder who are on par with the average, are volatile cocktails of hormones who wake up every day in a new body that they can't fully control or understand.

These are huge stressors. In every case, our students are looking to us as educators to get them through this. There is a direct correlation between a teacher's belief in a student and that student's ability to achieve.[124] We owe it to them to be there for them and we should be grateful for the incredible trust that has been placed in us.

The keys to weeding out the origins of violence are the same steps we need to take to become the best teachers we can be. Violence is not a separate problem. Violence is a potential that exists to some degree everywhere and which can easily begin to fester. Violence is a by-product of an unhealthy school. **It flourishes, in the shadow of apathy**. Let your passion and hope be the light that illuminates every corner of your classroom and every corridor of your school so that the seeds of violence can never grow the deep roots they crave.

As you begin to successfully implement strategies, consider returning to the Gambrill and Richey assertiveness survey that you did back in Exercise #4 in our chapter on Aggression vs Assertiveness. Revisit those questions, particularly the areas where you recognized you were weaker.

- Do you feel like you have more tools to strengthen those weaknesses?
- Do you feel you can continue to make improvements in these areas?

Having a few simple tools and the ability to measure where you're at is all it takes to make a massive change. Even making slight improvements in one of these areas can massively improve your power as a teacher.

---

[123] Susman E.J., Bogol A., "Puberty and psychological development", *Handbook of adolescent psychology (Lerner R. & Steinberg L. (Eds.),* p 15-44, 2004

[124] Bouchey H.A., Harter S., "Reflected appraisals, academic self-perceptions, and math/science performance during early adolescence", *Journal of Educational Psychology, 97, 673-686,* 2005.

CONCLUSION

"I believe everything we dream
Can come to pass through our union
We can turn the world around
We can turn the earth's revolution
We have the power."
-Patti Smith-

In 1974, Arleen Lorrance was a teacher drowning in despair and on the verge of burnout in a high school in Brooklyn, New York. Her school was underfunded and neglected and swarming with rats and roaches. Drug use was rampant and a good portion of her students simply didn't care. She describes a feeling many of us have felt at our lowest points:

"For seven years I served my sentence and marked off institutional time; I complained, cried, accepted hopelessness, put down the rest of the faculty for all the things they didn't do, and devoted all my energies to trying to change others and the system."

In 1968 she had a burnout. During a 6-month leave, she had a revelation. She couldn't give up. Something inside of her needed to go back.

"It came in on me loud and clear that I was the only one who could imprison (or release) me, that I was the only one I could do anything about changing. So, I let go of my anger and negativism and made a decision to simply be totally loving, open and vulnerable all the time."

Arleen returned with her new agenda but of course it's never that easy. Shortly thereafter, during an assembly for a school election, a racially charged fight broke out between two boys in the balcony.

"I jumped from my seat and rushed into the combat area. The hate being generated in that little circle was overwhelming. Some 40 students stood around egging them on, crying for blood. By the time I got there, one boy had already fled the area. I grabbed hold of the other's hand with all of my strength and love I could muster and said quietly: 'Please don't go; please sit down'. Our eyes locked for a moment and I could feel him hesitate. His eyes seemed to say,

> *"I don't want to go but I must". We both knew in that moment, the tragedy of his life, as it had been structured in this society."*

The boy pleaded to be released and ultimately, she let him go to pursue the fight. Later, when everyone returned to class, Arleen was deeply affected by the anger and the senseless cycle of violence. She felt helpless in her inability to stop it and she began to cry in front of her students. Her newfound hope, it would appear, had failed.

> *"At one point, I said to myself 'what's wrong with you? You're a professional. You're not suppose to behave this way'. Then I said 'thank god I'm human and can feel'. I became aware of the compassion and love etched on the faces of 20 students in their seats. I did not apologize for my feelings but rather felt good for having shared them. Then we discussed the tragedy of hate and the vulnerability of those who chose to love. We agreed that only through love could we achieve joyful co-existence."*
>
> *"In that classroom on that very day, 21 people formed a circle of love and set about the task of trying to find another way to communicate, a gentle way to reach those with whom we shared the earth. We were determined to find avenues of constructive change without chaos. In this earnest and unselfish atmosphere, the seekers, the teachers and the students dedicated to the principle that beautiful relationships can exist between all people if we consciously choose to make it so, came into being."*

Arleen then initiated what she termed *"The Love Project"*, a kindness-first initiative that began with volunteerism, through acts of kindness, donations, charity drives, food and music festivals. The students ate together, worked together, celebrated together. Students led and directed the initiative and slowly the old walls of separation began to erode. They raised funds, participated deeply in community outreach and even democratically participated in policy, banning smoking for teachers and students on campus. In making no excuses, by waiting for nothing and expecting nothing from others, they relied only on themselves for survival. Arleen notes: "*we encountered no objections and made it a reality*".[125]

Nearly 50 years later, Arleen's words ring as true as the day they were written. **We must be the change we want to see happen.** Incidentally, although that last line is often attributed to Gandhi, it was actually Arleen who first expressed this idea. The internet, as it often does, usually misattributes it. At the outset, I said that **your motive matters more than your method.** What I've shared here are simply my experiences and a glimpse into some of the research I've encountered. I believe there is an incredible amount of potential

---

[125] Kellough R.D., "Developing Priorities and a style: Selected readings in educator for teachers and parents (second edition), *California State University*, google books, 1974.

transference between the tactical world and the teaching world. Unfortunately, there is also a huge divide between those communities. Having straddled both of these domains for decades, I feel uniquely suited to help bridge that gap.

Violence *is* a persistent challenge in our world. It's deeply connected to our most primal survival reflexes. We wouldn't be here without it. When it's misplaced however, and it bleeds into the sacred halls of our learning institutions, these same ancient reflexes harm us and interrupt our opportunities for continued growth as a species. There is, however, tremendous hope. We live in a time of unmatched potential for sharing, learning and communicating. The call for greater inclusion has never been louder and the promise of integration has never been greater. We've seen that the most important part of the solution is prevention, not reaction, and there are many small, simple changes we can make that will massively benefit us not only in a crisis but in all of our daily interactions. The key is our mindset. Recognizing as Arleen did, that true change starts with us is nothing less than a superpower. **You are all that is required. Nothing more is needed.**

I began this book with a dedication thanking my teachers. I would like to end it by thanking you. By caring enough to read this book, you affirm the long and powerful tradition of all educators and I am honored to share the path with you as we collectively stride toward a better tomorrow.

BIBLIOGRAPHY

Adler A. B., Start A.R., Milham L., Allard Y.S., Riddle D., Townsend L., Svetlitzky V., "Rapid response to acute stress reaction: Pilot test for iCOVER training for military units", *Psychological Trauma: Theory, Research, Practice and Policy,* Vol.12, No. 4, 431-435, 2020.

Afkinich J.L., Klumpner S., "Violence Prevention Strategies and School Safety", *Journal of the Society for Social Work and Research* Volume 9, Number 4, 2018.

Anderman E. M. et al, "Teachers' reactions to experiences of violence: An attributional analysis", *Social psychology of education*, *21*(3), 621-653, 2018.

André C., "Proper breathing brings better health", *Scientific America*, January 15, 2019.

Bae R., "The effects of pausing on comprehensibility", *Iowa State University Dissertation,* 2015

Bambaeeroo F., Shokrpour N., "The impact of the teacher's non-verbal communication on the success of teaching", Adv Med Educ Prof., Apr; 5 (2): 51-59, 2017

Bambaeeroo F., Shokrpour N., "The impact of the teacher's non-verbal communication on the success of teaching", Adv Med Educ Prof., Apr; 5 (2): 51-59, 2017

Bandura A., "Moral disengagement in the perpetration of inhumanities", *Personality and social psychology review",* *3*(3), 193-209, 1999.

Becker CB, Zayfert C, Anderson E., "A survey of psychologists' attitudes towards and utilization of exposure therapy for PTSD", *Behavior Research and Therapy,* **42**(3):277–292. doi: 10.1016/S0005-7967(03)00138, 2004.

Becker W. C., "Consequences of different models of parental discipline", *Review of child development research* (Vol. 1, pp. 169–208). New York: Sage, 1964.

Berkowitz, L., "Whatever happened to the frustration-aggression hypothesis?", *American Behavioral Scientist,* 21, 691-708, 1978.

Bhatia M., Kumar A., Kumar N., Pandey R. M., Kochupillai V., "Electrophysiologic evaluation of Sudarshan Kriya: an EEG, BAER, P300 study", *Ind. J. Physiol. Pharmacol.* 47 157–163, 2003.

Bianco M, Ferri M., Fabiano C., Giorgiano F., Tavella S., et all, "Baseline simple and complex reaction times in female compared to male boxers", *Journal of Sports Medicine and Physical Fitness*, 51. 292-298, 2011.

Bishop S., Duncan J., Brett M., & Lawrence, A.D., "Prefrontal cortical function and anxiety: Controlling attention to threat-related stimuli", *Nature Neuroscience, 7, 184-188. doi:10.1038/nn1173B,* 2004

Blair J.P., et al., "Active shooter events and response", *CRC Press Taylor & Francis Group*, 2013 1

Bouchey H.A., Harter S., "Reflected appraisals, academic self-perceptions, and math/science performance during early adolescence", *Journal of Educational Psychology, 97, 673-686,* 2005.

Brittle B., "Coping strategies and burnout in staff working with students with special educational needs and disabilities", *Teaching and Teacher Education*, 87, 102937–. https://doi.org/10.1016/j.tate.2019.102937, 2020.

Buchanan T.W., Laures-Gore J.S., Duff M.C., "Acute stress reduces speech fluency", *Biological Psychology Volume 97, pages 60-66,* March 2014

Burgoon J., Birk T., "Nonverbal behaviors, persuasion and credibility", Human Communication Research, 17 (1): 140-169, 1990.

Canadian Press, Canadians with disabilities twice as likely to be victims of violence: StatsCan - National | Globalnews.ca, 2018.

Carssen B., de Ruiter C., van Dyck R., "Breathing retraining: A rational placebo?", *Clinical Psychology Review, Vol. 12, pp. 141-153,* 1992.

Causer, J., & Williams, A. M., "Improving anticipation and decision making in sport", *The Routledge handbook of sports performance analysis* (pp. 21-31). London: Routledge. 2013

Chang S.B. et al, "Effects of abdominal breathing on anxiety, blood pressure, peripheral skin temperature and saturation oxygen of pregnant women in preterm labor", *Korean J Women Health Nurs* 15 32–42. 10.4069/kjwhn.2009, 2009.

Christenson A., Buchanan J., Houlihan D., Wanzek M., Command Use and Compliance in Staff Communication with elderly Residents of Long-Term Care Facilities, Minnesota State University, https://doi.org/10.1016/j.beth.2010.07.001, 2011

Cooper HE, Parkes MJ, Clutton-Brock TH, "*CO2-dependent components of sinus arrhythmia from the start of breath holding in humans*". Am J Physiol Heart Circ Physiol. 2003 Aug;285(2):H841-8. doi: 10.1152/ajpheart.01101.2002. Epub 2003 May 1. PMID: 12730051.

Corbetta, M., & Shulman, G. L., "Control of goal-directed and stimulus-driven attention in the brain", *Nature Reviews Neuroscience*, 3(3), 201-215. 10.1038/nrn755, 2002.

Corbetta, M., Patel, G., & Shulman, G. L., "The reorienting system of the human brain: From environment to theory of mind", *Neuron, 58, 306-324. 10.1016/j.neuron*, 2008.

Cornell D.G., Mayer M. J., & Sulkowski, M. L., "History and future of school safety research", *School Psychology Review, 50*(2-3), 143–157, 2021.

Craighead D.H. et al, "Time-efficient inspiratory muscle strength training lowers blood pressure and improves endothelial function, NO bioavailability and oxidative stress in midlife/older adults with above-normal blood pressure", *Journal of American Heart Association*, 2021.

Crocket, Z., "What data on 3,000 murderers and 10,000 victims tell us about serial murderers", *https://www.vox.com/2016/12/2/13803158/serial-killers-victims-data,* Dec. 2016

de Shazer S: Keys to Solution in Brief Therapy. New York, WW Norton, 1985.

deGelder B., "Nonconscious emotions: New findings and perspectives on nonconscious facial expression recognition and its voice and whole-body contexts", Barret L.F., Niedenthal P.M., Winkleman P., (Eds), *Emotion and Consciousness*, p 123-149, 2005.

Demartini Z Jr, Rodrigues Freire M, Lages RO, et al. "Internal Carotid Artery Dissection in Brazilian Jiu-Jitsu", *Journal of Cerebrovasc Endovasc Neurosurg.* 2017;19(2):111-116. doi:10.7461/jcen.2017.19.2.111

Driskell J.E. et al, "Stress exposure training: An event-based approach", *CRC Press,* 2008.

Eastwood A., "Strategies to Overcome Special Education Teacher Burnout", *Minnesota State University Moorhead RED: a Repository of Digital Collections,* 2020.

Eddy, C. L. et al, "Does teacher emotional exhaustion and efficacy predict student discipline sanctions?" School Psychology Review, 49(3), 239–255. https://doi.org/10.1080/2372966X.2020.1733340, 2020.

Eftedal I., "What the immune system is up to while you're holding your breath", *NTNUhealth*, 21 December 2016.

Erickson MH: Further clinical techniques of hypnosis: utilization techniques. 1959. Am J Clin Hypn 51:341–362, 2009

Ericsson A.K., Charness N., "Expert performance: Its structure and acquisition", *"Science Watch,* 1994.

Ericsson K. A., Lehman A.C., "Expert and exceptional performance. Evidence of maximal adaptation to task constraints" *Annual Review of Psychology, 47, 273-305,* 1996.

Estami A., Ahmand R., Masoudi R., "The effectiveness of assertiveness training on the levels of stress, anxiety and depression of high school students", *Iranian Red Crescent Medical Journal*, Howsar Medical Institute, 2016

Ezake E., Ozougwu A., Okoli P., "An investigation on parenting styles and gender influencing assertiveness on undergraduates", *International Journal of Innovative Research and Advanced Studies,* University of Nigeria, Volume 7, Issue 6, June 2020

Felix E. D., You S., "Peer victimization within the ethnic context of high school", *Journal of Community Psychology, 39*(7), 860–875. https://doi.org/10.1002/jcop.20465, 2011.

Fischer S. M., John N., & Bilz, L., "Teachers' Self-efficacy in preventing and intervening in school bullying: A systematic review. *International Journal of Bullying Prevention, 3*(3), 196-212.), 2021.

Foulsham T., "Functions of a quiet and un-quiet eye in natural tasks – comment on Vickers", *Current Issues in Sport Science 1,* 2016

Francis R., "An examination into the effects of speech rate on perceived stress in monolingual and bilingual populations", University of Chester, Rachel_Francis[1].pdf (mmu.ac.uk), 2018

Freiheit SR, Vye C, Swan R, Cady M., "Cognitive-behavioral therapy for anxiety: Is Fissemination working?", *Behavior Therapist.27*(2):25–32, 2004.

Girli A., "An examination of the relationships between the social skill levels, self concepts and aggressive behavior of students with special needs in the process of inclusion education", Cukurova University Faculty of Education Journal, Volume 42, Issue 2, 23-38, 08.03.2014, 2013.

Girvan E. J., McIntosh K., & Santiago-Rosario, M. R., "Associations between community-level racial biases, office discipline referrals, and out-of-school suspensions", *School Psychology Review, 50*(2-3), 288–302, 2021.

Girvan E. J. et al, "The relative contribution of subjective office referrals to racial disproportionality in school discipline", *School Psychology Quarterly: The Official Journal of the Division of School Psychology, American Psychological Association, 32*(3), 392–404. https://doi.org/10.1037/spq0000178, 2017.

Gola J. et al, "Ethical consideration in exposure therapy with children", *Cogn Behav Pract.*, May 1, 2017.

Grayson B., Stein M., "Attracting assault: victim's non verbal cues", *Journal of Communication Volume 31: Issue 1, p 68-75,* Winter 1981

Heck Detlef H. et al, *"Breathing as a fundamental rhythm of brain function"*, Frontiers in Neural Circuits, Vol. 10., DOI=10.3389/fncir.2016.00115, 2017.

Hedarpour S., Dokaneifard F., Bahari S., "The impact of communication skills on the handicapped students' self esteem and the reduction in their shyness", *New Ideas in Educational Science,* 3 (4): 65-73, 2008

Helrich H., Weidenecher P., "Impact of Voice Pitch on Text Memory", *Swiss Journal of Pscyhology 70 85-93, 10. 1024/1421-0185,* 2011.

Herman K. C., Reinke, W. M., & Eddy C. L., "Advances in understanding and intervening in teacher stress and coping: The Coping-Competence-Context Theory", Journal of School Psychology, 78, 69–74. https://doi.org/10.1016/j.jsp.2020.01.001, 2020.

Holcomb-McCoy C., "Ethnic identity development in early adolescents: Implications and recommendations for middle school counselors", *Profession School Counseling, p120-127,* 2005.

Hopson L.M., Lee E., "Mitigating the effect of family poverty on academic and behavioral outcomes: the role of school climate in middle and high school", *Child. Youth Serv. Rev. 33, 2221-2229.* Doi: 10.1016.j.childyouth.2011.07.006, 2011.

Hristovski R., Davids K., Aranjo D., Button C., "How boxers decide to punch a target: Emergent behavior in nonlinear dynamical movement systems", *Journal of Sports Science and Medicine,* 2006.

Ingersoll R.M., "The teacher shortage: a case of wrong diagnosis and wrong prescription", *NASSP Bull. 86, 16-31. Dpi:10.1177/019263640208663101,* 2002.

Jacob S., Hartshorne T.S., "Ethics and the law for school psychologists (6th Ed.)", *Wiley,* 2007.

Kap S., Ashker S., Kapo A., "Winning and losing performance in boxing competition: a comparative study", *Journal of Physical Education and Sport,* May 2021.

Kaplan SG, Cornell DG, "Threats of Violence by Students in Special Education", *Behavioral Disorders,* 31(1):107-119. doi:10.1177/019874290503100102, 2005.

Kavnagh L. et al, "When it's an error to mirror: the surprising reputational costs of mimicry", *Association for Psychological Sciences,* 22(10) 1274–1276, 2011.

Kellough R.D., "Developing Priorities and a style: Selected readings in educator for teachers and parents (second edition), *California State University,* google books, 1974.

Kenneth Gibson J., "Stress p and verbal commands for law enforcement in high-stress situations", *Walden University,* 2021

Kerr, C., "Industrialism and Industrial Man", Oxford University Press, NY 1964.

Killian S., "Distributed practice and massed practice: What works best?", *Evidence Based Teaching,* August 9, 2019.

Kitsantas A., Ware H.W., Martinez-Arias B., "Students' perceptions of school safety: Effects of community, school environment, and substance use variables", *Journal of Early Adolescence,* p 413-430, 2004.

Komatsu H., "The neural mechanisms of perceptual filling-in", *Nature Reviews Neurosciences, 7 (3), 220-231,* 2006.

Kwon Y.H., Kwon J. W., Lee M.H., "Effectiveness of motor sequential learning according to practice schedules in healthy adults; distributed practice versus massed practice"

Laidlaw, K. E. W., Foulsham, T., Kuhn, G., and Kingstone, A. (2011). Potential social interactions are important to social attention. *Proc. Natl. Acad. Sci. USA* 108, 5548–5553. doi: 10.1073/pnas.1017022108

Land, M. F., Vision, eye movements, and natural behavior. *Visual Neuroscience,* 26, 51-62. 10.1017/S0952523808080899, 2009

Le Bon, G., "The Crowd: a Study of the Popular Mind", Penguin Books, NY, 1977

"Learning disabilities affect up to 10 percent of children", *University College London,* ScienceDaily. 2013.

Lee S., Kwon S., Ahn J., "The effect of modeling on self-efficacy and flow state of adolescent athletes through role models", Psychology, *14 June 2021,* https://doi.org/10.3389/fpsyg.2021.661557

Lust K., Wittbrodt J., "Hold your breath!", doi: 10.7554/eLife.12523, December 16, 2015.

Maloney M.E., Moore P., "From aggressive to assertive", *International journal of women's dermatology,* 6 (1), 46-49

Marinell W. H., Coca, V. M., "Who stays and who leaves?" *Findings from a Three-Part Study of Teacher Turnover in NYC Middle Schools,* Online Submission, 2013.

Mathews A., & Mackintosh B., "A cognitive model of selective processing in anxiety", Cognitive Therapy and Research, 22(6), 539–560. https://doi.org/10.1023/A:1018738019346, 1998

McPherson S.L. "Expert-novice differences in planning, strategies during collegiate singles tennis competition", *Journal of Sport and Exercise Psychology,* 22, 39-62

Meyer A.S., Wheeldon L., van der Meulen F., Konopka A., "Effects of speech rate and practice on the allocation of visual attention in multiple object naming", *Front. Psychol.,* https://doi.org/10.3389/fpsyg.2012.00039 *20 February 2012*

Milgram S., Bickman L., Berkowitz L., "Note on the drawing power of crowds of different size", *Journal of Personality and Social Psychology,* October, 1969

Mills J.A., "Mob mentality and classroom management: meeting student needs and building self-regulation skills", https://www.researchgate.net/publication/44389675, 2010

Morgenroth T, Ryan M.K., and Peters K., "The motivation theory of role modeling: how role models influence role aspirants' goals", *Rev. Gen. Psychol. 19, 465-483/ doi: 10/1037/gpr0000059,* 2015

Mori S., Ohtani Y., Imanaka K., "Reaction times and anticipatory skills of karate athletes", *Human Movement Science* 21, 213-230, 2020.

Munro H., Plumb, M.S., Wilson A.D., Williams J.H.G., Mon-Williams M., "The effect of distance on reaction time in aiming movements", *Expert Brain Research,* Nov, 183(2) 249-57, 2007

Murik J. et al, "Reported Strategies for Responding to the Aggressive and Extremely Disruptive Behavior of Students Who Have Special Needs", *Australasian Journal of Special Education,* Cambridge University Press, 2016.

Murray K., "Teach kindness first", *self published,* 2017.

Musanti S.I. and Pence, L., "Collaboration and teacher development: unpacking resistance, constructing knowledge, and navigating identities", *Teacher Education Quarterly,* 37 (1), 73–89, 2010.

Patterson G. R., "Coercive family process", Eugene, OR: Castalia, 1982.

Paulus M.P. et al, "Subjecting elite athletes to inspiratory breathing load reveals behavioral and neural signatures of optimal performers in extreme environments", https://doi.org/10.1371/journal.pone.0029394, January 19, 2012.

Payne A. A., Gottfredson D. C., Gottfredson G. D., "Schools as communities: the relationships among communal school organization, student bonding, and school disorder", *Criminology* 41, 749–778. doi: 10.1111/j.1745-9125.2003.tb01003.x, 2013

Pelphrey K.A., Viola R.J., and McCarthy G., "When strangers pass: processing of mutual and averted social gaze in the superior temporal sulcus", *Psychol. Sci. 15, 598-603. Doi: 10. 1111/j.0956-7976.2004.—726.x*, 2004

Pessoa L., Thomson E., Noe A., "Finding out about filling-in: A guide to perceptual completion for visual science and the philosophy of perception", *Behavior and Brain Sciences, 21 (6), 723-748*, 1998.

Peterson C.A., Reschley D.J., Starkweather-LundnA., "Training teachers to give effective commands: effects on student compliance, academic engagement, and academic responding", *Iowa State University Psychology Dissertation*, https://dr.lib.iastate.edu/handle/20.500.12876/6399

Radke-Yarrow M. R., Campbell J. D., & Burton R. V., "Child rearing: An inquiry into research and methods", San Francisco: Jossey Bass, 1968.

Romer L.M., McConnell A.K., Jones D.A., "Inspiratory muscle fatigue in trained cyclists: effects on inspiratory muscle training", *School of Sport and Exercise Science, The University of Birmingham*, 2002.

Sars D., van Minnen A., "On the use of exposure therapy in the treatment of anxiety disorders: a survey among cognitive behavioral therapists in the Netherlands", *BMC Psychol.*, 2015; 3(1): 26, Aug 5 2015.

Saslow L.R. et al, "Speaking under pressure: low linguistic complexity is linked to high physiological and emotional stress reactivity", Published online Dec. 20, 2013. Doi: 10.1111/psyp.12171

School Shootings by Country 2022 (worldpopulationreview.com)

Schwarzkopf N., Houlihan D., Kolb K., Lewinski W., Buchanan J., and Christenson A., "Command Types Used in Police Encounters", *Law Enforcement Executive Forum, 8 (2), 99-141.*, 2008

Shay R.J. et al, "Time to move beyond a 'one-size fits all' approach to inspiratory muscle training", *Front. Physiol.*, January 2022.

Sidnman M., "Coercion and its fallout", *Authors Cooperative*, 1989.

Sigler K., Burneett A., Child J.T., "A regional analysis of assertiveness", *Journal of Intercultural Communication Research 37 (2) 9-104*

Starkes, J.L., Allard F. (Eds.), "Cognitive issues in motor expertise", Amsterdam, North Holland, 1993

Stellpflug S.J., "No Established Link between Repeated Transient Chokes and Chronic Traumatic Encephalopathy Related Effects. Comment on Lim, L.J.H. et al. Dangers of Mixed Martial Arts in the Development of Chronic Traumatic Encephalopathy", *Int. J. Environ. Res. Public Health 2019, 16, 254. International journal of environmental research and public health*, 16(6), 1059. https://doi.org/10.3390/ijerph16061059, 2019.

Stromberg S.E., Russel M.E., Carlson C.R., "Diaphragmatic breathing and its effectiveness for the management of motion sickness", *Aerosp., Med. Hum. Perform.* 86 452-457, 2015.

Students With Special Needs, National Centers for Education Statistics, 2020.

Susman E.J., Bogol A., "Puberty and psychological development", *Handbook of adolescent psychology (Lerner R. & Steinberg L. (Eds.)*, p 15-44, 2004

Sutherland S., "When we read, we recognize words as pictures and hear them spoken aloud: Words are not encoded in the brain by their meaning but rather by simpler attributes such as sound and shape", *Scientific American*, July 1, 2015

Toldos Romero M., "Adolescents' Predictions of Aggressive Behavioral Patterns in Different Settings", *The Open Psychology Journal*, 4, (Suppl 1-M6) 55-63, 2011.

Travis J. (dir.), "Violence among middle school and high school students: Analysis and implications for prevention", *National Institute of Justice*, October 1997

Treleaven A.J., Yu D., "Training peripheral vision to read: Reducing crowding through an adaptive training method", *Vision Research Volume 171 pages 84-94*, June 2020

Turner, R.H., and Killian, L.M., "Collective Behavior, 2nd Ed." Prentice-Hall, Englewood Cliffs, NJ, 1972.

Urgesi C., Makris S., "Sport performance: Motor expertise and observational learning in sport", 2016.

Vickers J., "Origins and current issues in Quiet Eye research", *Current Issues in Sports Science 1*, 2016

Walker H.M., Ramsey E., Gresham F., "Antisocial behavior in school (2nd ed)", *Wadsworth Thomson Learning*, 2004.

Wang S.Z. et al, "Effect of slow abdominal breathing combined with biofeedback on blood pressure and heart rate variability in prehypertension", *J. Altern. Complement. Med.* 16 1039–1045. 10.1089/acm.2009.0577, 2010.

Wang, M. T., and Degol, J. L., "School climate: a review of the construct, measurement, and impact on student outcomes", *Educ. Psychol. Rev. 28, 315–352. doi: 10.1007/s10648-015-9319-1*, 2016.

Weatherholtz K., Campbell-Kibler K., Jaeger F.T., "Socially-mediated syntactic alignment", Language Variation and Change, 2014; 26(03): 387, 2014

Whitney, J.A. IV, "Defensive tactics and tactical decision-making for elementary school teachers and staff", *Naval Postgraduate School, Monterey, California*, 2017

Wilmore J., Costill D. "Physiology of sports and exercise", *Human Kinetics*, The University of Michigan, 1999

Wilson S.J., Lipsey M.W., "The effectiveness of school-based violence prevention programs for reducing disruptive and aggressive behavior", *Document No.: 211376 Date Received: Sept, U.S. Department of Justice Commissioned Paper*, 2005.

Wisecarver C., Tucker M., "Force science reactionary gap", *U.S. Department of Justice*, Septembe 2007.

Zaccaro A. et al, "How breath-control can change your life: A systematic review on psycho-physiological correlates of slow breathing", *Front Hum Neuroscience, 12: 353*, 2018.

ABOUT THE AUTHOR

Kevin Secours B.Ed. is a master martial artist and a world-renowned personal security expert. He has taught for some of the most elite security units around the world, consulted for the entertainment industry and works closely with schools and institutions for improving their readiness.

Made in the USA
Las Vegas, NV
27 May 2024